New Literacies
Changing Knowledge
and Classroom Learning

New Literacies
Changing Knowledge and Classroom Learning

COLIN LANKSHEAR and
MICHELE KNOBEL

Open University Press
Buckingham · Philadelphia

Open University Press
Celtic Court
22 Ballmoor
Buckingham
MK18 1XW

email: enquiries@openup.co.uk
world wide web: www.openup.co.uk

and
325 Chestnut Street
Philadelphia, PA 19106, USA

First Published 2003

A catalogue record of this book is available from the British Library.

ISBN 0 335 21066 X pb   0 335 21067 8 hb

Library of Congress Cataloging-in-Publication Data
Lankshear, Colin.
    New literacies: changing knowledge and classroom learning/Colin Lankshear and Michele Knobel.
        p. cm
    Includes bibliographical references (p.) and index.
    ISBN 0-335-21067-8 – ISBN 0-335-21066-X (pbk.)
        1. Literacy. I. Knobel, Michele II. Title.
LC149 .L27 2003
302.2'249–dc21   2002074950

Typeset by Type Study, Scarborough
Printed in Great Britain by St Edmundsbury Press, Bury St Edmunds, Suffolk

For JPG
colleague, compañero, friend

Contents

List of Figures and Tables

Foreword

A good book opens a window onto new vistas; an excellent one, on the other hand, pulls readers through the opening and beyond, inviting critical dialogue at every turn. *New Literacies* belongs in the excellent category. Colin Lankshear and Michele Knobel pull us into spaces beyond the proverbial school door and into different arenas peopled with everyday users of new literacies – the stuff that formal education (and traditional schooling in particular) is yet to welcome, let alone fully understand. Yet it is the promise and potential of just such an understanding that pulls at the curious reader and makes the journey through this book an efficacious and delightful one.

It would be difficult, if not impossible, to find two scholars better versed than Lankshear and Knobel in the interface between digital technologies and new literacies. The influence of their collective thinking, research, and writing continues to cross national borders, even continents. Through their ears, eyes, and uncanny sense of timing, we are treated to a first-hand, up-close look at the social practices that embed the new digital literacies. But I'd wager it is more than simply 'a look' that is at stake here; rather, through the authors' careful weaving of theory and research, we are offered numerous opportunities to consider how these practices position us, and, in turn, how we use them to position others.

Lest readers think that *New Literacies: Changing Knowledge and Class-room Learning* is aimed solely at educators and their interests, one need only skim the book's table of contents to correct this misconception. The authors' thoughtful and lively interpretations of such diverse topics as attention economics, eBay's regulating devices, and digital epistemologies provide a context for sharpening our understanding of the ways in which media and the Internet are affecting each of us personally, whatever our walk in life. Recognizing one's membership in this broader audience is but another way of acknowledging the profound impact that new information and communication technologies are having, and most likely will continue to have, on the literacy practices of young and old.

Some readers will view this book as a milestone in literacy education if for no other reason than because it steps to the front and offers rich (and heretofore largely ignored) historical insight into how we in the English-speaking world – teachers, administrators, researchers, parents, policy makers, the general public – have come to think about reading and writing as we do. Others will see *New Literacies* as representing a challenge to their belief that the world is as it always has been, considerably more technologized perhaps, but the same nonetheless. Still others will sense in the authors' writing a willingness to take risks here and there – to stick their necks out, so to speak – perhaps in the hope that doing so will help to loosen the stranglehold that current ideas about literacy education have on us and the students we teach. Presumably, we could learn much from listening to our students, which is the message Lankshear and Knobel seem to convey in their chapter on New Ways of Knowing: Learning at the Margins. Finally, there will be readers who, like myself, will finish this book firmly convinced that many of the literacies young people are successfully using outside school can be connected to what goes on within formal schooling, if only we are willing to give it a try.

Donna Alvermann
University of Georgia

Acknowledgements

This book builds on work we have done collaboratively with friends and colleagues, and that has otherwise been encouraged and supported in diverse ways by folk to whom we are indebted. We want to acknowledge their support and generosity here.

First, a great deal of what appears in these pages has been developed in collaboration with Chris Bigum and Leonie Rowan. We have worked increasingly closely with them since 1995. Where our work does not draw directly on collaborative activities undertaken with them, it nonetheless owes much to intellectual stimuli they have given us in conversations, seminars, and in each other's homes. We doubt we could ever amply repay the debt we owe them, but nonetheless want to acknowledge it and express our deep appreciation.

We have also drawn heavily on inspiration from other friends and colleagues with whom we have worked closely. In the case of this book we owe much to Michael Doneman and, as always, James Paul Gee. In their different ways they exemplify the critical, enquiring, progressive spirit that is always asking how to promote the greatest good from the resources we have available.

Donna Alvermann has played a very important role in helping us understand more clearly who we are trying to write for and why. She has supported our work in the most generous and unobtrusive ways, while at the same time continuing her own tireless and selfless work in the name of better education for all, and especially for those who have received less than their due share of social benefits from the systems within which they are constrained to live. Despite already having more than enough tasks to complete, Donna generously accepted our invitation to write a foreword for this book. We know what this kind of unsolicited added pressure involves, and treasure the collegiality woven into her text. We also thank her for encouraging us to think through the concept of the 'attention economy' in relation to new literacies. Chapter 5 builds on work we initially did at her invitation and which appears in her edited volume (Alvermann 2002).

Other colleagues have in various ways made valued contributions to producing this book. As with the people we have already named, they are entitled to enjoy anything in the following pages that may be of educational worth, but share no responsibility for the book's shortcomings. We want especially to thank Shirley Steinberg, Joe Kincheloe, Tom Lawler, Christina Davidson, Steve Thorne, Lynn Smith, Ilana Snyder, Michael Peters, Scott and Alex Balson, Robert Bleicher, Julia Corzo, Manuel Medina Carballo, Wakio Oyanagi, Peter St James, and Lucy, Ben, Jarrod, Kyle and Stuart from the Yanga Headlands study. Ilana Snyder invited us to contribute a chapter on eBay to her *Silicon Literacies* collection (Snyder 2002). Chapter 6 extends work we originally began writing about for Ilana's book, and we thank her for providing the incentive to explore a very interesting dimension of online practice.

As always, we appreciate greatly the support of Shona Mullen and our other colleagues at Open University Press. They are a wonderful team to work with, and we hope that our efforts in this book are enough to repay their continuing faith in our work.

Several of the chapters in this book build on earlier work that has been published in English and Spanish. We have benefited from the opportunities we have had to rehearse ideas in other places. Thanks are due here to the *Journal of Early Childhood Literacy*, *Desencuentros*, the *Journal of Literacy and Technology*, the *Journal of Philosophy of Education*, Blackwell, Consejo Mexicano de Investigación Educativa y la Universidad de Colima, University of Lapland Press, Open University Press, Peter Lang, Routledge-Falmer, and Palgrave Press.

During the period in which this book has been conceived and written we have enjoyed strong support from friends, colleagues, and institutions in

México and Australia. Without this our work during the past four years simply would not have been possible. We want to thank Adolfo Gómez Cortes, Silvia Mendoza Gáloz, Hilario Rodríguez, Angela Guzmán, Alicia de Alba, Edgar González Gaudiano, María Esther Aguirre, Marcela González Arenas, Rigoberto Morales Landa, el Consejo Nacional de Ciencia y Tecnología (México), el Posgrado en Pedagogía, la Coordinación de las Humanidades, and el Centro de Estudios sobre la Universidad of the National Autonomous University of México (UNAM), Language Australia, the Australian National Research Council, the School of Education in the University of Ballarat, the Faculty of Education and Creative Arts at the Central Queensland University, and the Department of Education at the University of California, Irvine. Finally, we wish to thank the following for permission to use material for which they hold copyright as follows. Adbusters Media Foundation for permission to use images from their website on the cover and in Chapter 2. David Bennahum for permission to use his meme logo on the cover and in Chapter 2. The Global Business Network for permission to use the map image from their website which appears in Chapter 2. Channel 4Learning for permission to reproduce an activity sheet image from their website, and which appears in Chapter 4. This image was produced by Sheila Fraser and designed by Lucy Mackenzie for SFTV on behalf of 4Learning.

PART 1

What's New?

CHAPTER 1

From 'Reading' to the 'New Literacy Studies'

Introduction

Literacy has become absolutely central to education policy, curriculum development, and our everyday thinking about educational practice. It is hard to credit that just two or three decades ago the term 'literacy' hardly featured in formal educational discourse. Instead, there was a long-established field of 'reading'. This was mainly grounded in psychology and associated with time-honoured methods of instruction for teaching new entrants into school how to decode printed text and, secondarily, how to encode text.

Prior to the 1970s, 'literacy' was used generally in relation to non-formal educational settings, and, in particular, in relation to adults who were deemed to be *illiterate*. 'Literacy' was the name given to programmes of non-formal instruction – not associated with formal educational institutions like schools – which were offered to illiterate adults to help them acquire basic abilities to read and write. At this time within Britain, North America, Australasia and similar countries, official statistics obtained for census measures and the like indicated almost zero levels of adult illiteracy.

Such adult literacy initiatives as existed in these countries were small-scale, largely voluntary endeavours involving adult literacy tutors working with individuals or small groups of learners. Indeed, within First World English-speaking societies, 'literacy teaching' named marginal spaces of non-formal education work intended to provide a 'second chance' for those whose illiteracy was often seen as directly associated with other debilitating or dysfunctional conditions and circumstances. These included 'conditions' like unemployment, imprisonment, drug abuse, teenage pregnancy, inferior physical and psychic health and so on.

The situation was different in the Third World of so-called 'developing countries'. In these countries relatively few people received any substantial formal education. Often as many as 80 per cent or more of the adult population was illiterate relative to popular measures of the day – such as lacking reading abilities roughly equivalent to second or third grade levels of primary school. During the 1950s, and again in the 1990s, it became fashionable among development theorists to associate a country's 'readiness' for 'economic take-off' with attainment of a certain level of adult literacy across the nation. For example, it was widely argued during the 1960s by development theorists that literacy of a large minority of males is a precondition for underdeveloped economies to make any significant transition to economic growth (Anderson 1965). A figure of at least 40 per cent of adult (especially male) literacy was seen as a threshold for economic development. This became a rationale for promoting adult literacy campaigns throughout many Third World countries in Africa, Asia, and Latin America as a strategic component of economic and social development policies. Illiteracy was seen as a major impediment to economic development, and literacy campaigns were prescribed as cost-effective measures for developing the minimal levels of 'manpower' needed to give a country a chance for economic take-off. These campaigns were usually undertaken as non-formal programmes aimed at adults – although children often participated – conducted outside the education *system* as such.

Whether we think in terms of First World settings or Third World settings, however, in no way was 'literacy' identified as a formal educational *ideal* prior to the 1970s. At most, within formal educational settings, reading and writing were seen as essential tools for learning to occur, and as vehicles for accessing and communicating meanings via printed texts. They were a *means* for learning, not an end – let alone *the* end. Functional mastery of reading and writing was effectively taken for granted as bottom line outcomes of classroom learning for all students other than those designated intellectually impaired or as having severe learning disabilities. And it is worth repeating that so far as curriculum and pedagogy within formal education were concerned, what was talked about, researched, debated and so on was not *literacy*, but *reading* and, to a lesser extent, *writing*.

This situation changed considerably during the 1970s in the US and, to varying degrees, in other Anglophone countries. All of a sudden a focus on 'literacy' was projected into the centre of the formal educational stage. A number of reasons have been linked to this change, three of which seem to us especially interesting.

One was the rise to prominence of Paulo Freire's work within the larger context of the radical education movement of the late 1960s and early 1970s (see Freire 1972, 1973; Freire and Macedo 1987). His work with peasant groups in Brazil and Chile provided an example of how literacy work could be central to radical approaches to education aimed at building critical social praxis. Freire's concept of literacy as 'reading the word and the world' involved much more than merely decoding and encoding print. Far from being the sole objective of literacy education, learning how to encode and decode alphabetic print was integrated into an expansive pedagogy in which groups of learners collaboratively pursued critical consciousness of their world via a reflexive or 'cyclical' process of reflection and action. Through their efforts to act on the world, and to analyse and understand the results of their action, people come to know the world better: more 'deeply' and 'critically'.

'Illiteracy', in the everyday sense, was seen as one consequence of unjust social processes and relations that had been created historically and become 'woven' (or as we might say today, 'hard wired') into the social structure. Because these unjust social arrangements had been created and were sustained through human activity, they could be changed by human action. Before such 'transformative cultural action' could occur, however, it was necessary to understand the nature and origins of social oppression. In Freire's pedagogy, learning to write and read words became a focus for adults in pursuing critical awareness of how oppressive practices and relations operated in everyday life. Words that were highly charged with meaning for them – words that expressed their fears, hopes, troubles and their dreams for a better life – provided the vocabulary by which they learned to write and read. These words were discussed intensively in order to explore how the world worked, and in the context of this discussion the written forms of these words, as well as other words that could be built out of their syllables and phonemes, were introduced. In the context of discussing and thinking about these words, participants learned what they 'looked like' as text, and how to write and read them.

Learning literally to read and write words was, then, an integral part of learning to understand how the world works socially and culturally to produce unequal opportunities and outcomes for different groups of people. Ultimately, this analysis was to provide participants with an informed starting point for undertaking what Freire calls 'cultural action on the world'. In undertaking cultural action, people act together in the light of their analysis of their own circumstances to challenge established social practices and relations that systematically benefit some individuals and groups at the expense of others – including themselves. The goal is to transform such practices and relations, as well as the ideologies that sustain them, into ones that are more socially, economically, culturally and politically just. Within Freire's kind of pedagogy, oppressed groups would analyse important aspects of their circumstances and undertake some kind of transforming action in the light of their analysis of their circumstances. Groups would undertake cultural action for change on the world in the light of their analysis of their circumstances. They would then analyse and evaluate the results of that action as a basis for taking their next step in cultural action. This *praxis* of reflection and action was the means for knowing the world more deeply and accurately, since it involved 'testing' it to see how it works in the light of concepts and theories developed collaboratively in discussion of experiences and beliefs. Freirean literacy education was, then, an integral component of a radical, politicized pedagogy purposefully designed to stimulate action for change.

A second factor in the development of 'literacy' as a widely used concept in education was the dramatic discovery – many called it an *invention* – of widespread illiteracy among adults in the US during the early 1970s. This alleged literacy *crisis* coincided with early awareness of profound structural change in the economy, as the US moved toward becoming a postindustrial society. Postindustrialism entailed far-reaching restructuring of the labour market and employment as well as deep changes in major organizations and institutions of daily life. Large numbers of people were seen as poorly prepared for these changes. The 'literacy crisis' quickly spread to other emerging postindustrial societies. Whether it was Britain, the US, Canada, Australia or New Zealand, much the same storyline emerged: schools were failing to ensure that all learners became literate to the extent required to live 'effectively' under contemporary conditions. Research and reports commissioned by governments claimed relentlessly that standards were falling, that far-reaching educational reform was needed, and that curriculum and pedagogy had to be overhauled in order to ensure that, at the very least, all students would acquire at least a *functional* level of literacy. 'Literacy' emerged as the key word here.

A third factor was the increasing development and popularity of a *sociocultural* perspective within studies of language and the social sciences (Gee

1996: Ch. 3; Gee *et al.* 1996: Ch. 1). During the 1980s and 1990s this impacted strongly on conceptual and theoretical understandings of practices involving texts. Early influential works drew on theory and research from different but broadly compatible fields. Gee (1996: Ch. 1) documents these very nicely. For example, Harvey Graff's book *The Literacy Myth* (1979) drew on revisionist history. Silvia Scribner and Michael Cole's *The Psychology of Literacy* (1981) drew on concepts and instrumentation that reflected pioneering work in social cognition by Vygotsky and Luria and developed a concept of 'practice' that has evolved into a key construct within sociocultural approaches to literacy. Ron and Suzanne Scollon's *Narrative, Literacy and Face in Interethnic Communication* (1981) worked at complex interfaces between linguistics, anthropology and epistemology to explore relationships among social practices, worldviews, orality and literacy. Shirley Heath explored the ways literacy is embedded in cultural contexts over an extended period using an ethnographic design and methods in her major study, *Ways with Words* (1983). Brian Street's *Literacy in Theory and in Practice* (1984) was strongly grounded in anthropology. Together with even earlier work done in history and cultural studies in Britain such as Robert K. Webb's *The British Working Class Reader* (1955) and Richard Hoggart's *The Uses of Literacy: Aspects of Working Class Life* (1957), among many others (see Lankshear 1999), these studies provided a strong base informed by research from which to challenge established approaches to teaching reading and writing in schools and the growing emphasis on 'literacy basics' and 'functional literacy' fuelled by the alleged literacy crisis.

In this context, 'literacy' emerged quickly and decisively as the key focus of formal education: the new 'bottom line'. With hindsight, this change can be viewed from several angles. First, the *educational language* associated with the development of competence with text changed, as we have already noted, from the language of 'reading' and 'writing' to the language of 'literacy'. The term began to figure prominently in school timetables and programme descriptions. The names of professional journals changed. For example, the *Australian Journal of Reading* became the *Australian Journal of Language and Literacy*, the *Journal of Reading* became the *Journal of Adolescent and Adult Literacy*, and the *Journal of Reading Behavior* became the *Journal of Literacy Research*. Likewise, areas of focus for professional and resource development were renamed. For example, 'emergent literacy' subsumed the conventional coverall term 'reading readiness', and the then new label 'writing readiness'; 'literacy development' was used in place of reading or writing development; 'literacy studies' instead of 'language arts' and the like.

The name change did not always count for much, since in many cases people continued doing in the name of 'literacy' much the same as they had always done as 'reading' teachers or researchers. The point is, however, that whereas 'reading' has traditionally been conceived in *psychological* terms, 'literacy' has always been much more a *sociological* concept. For example, 'illiteracy' and 'illiterate' usually carried social class or social group connotations. Being illiterate tended to be associated with being poor, being of marginal status and so on. In addition, the sociocultural approach to literacy overtly rejects the idea that textual practices are even largely, let alone solely, a matter of processes that 'go on in the head', or that essentially involve heads communicating with each other by means of graphic signs. From a sociocultural perspective literacy is a matter of social practices. Literacies are bound up with social, institutional and cultural relationships, and can only be understood when they are situated within their social, cultural and historical contexts (Gee *et al.* 1996: xii). Moreover, they are always connected to social identities – to being particular kinds of people. Literacies are always embedded in Discourses[1] (Gee 2000). Texts are integral parts of innumerable everyday '*lived, talked, enacted, value-and-belief-laden* practices' that are 'carried out in specific places and at specific times' (Gee *et al.* 1996: 3). Reading and writing are not the same things within a youth zine culture (see page 27), an online chat space, a school classroom, a feminist reading group, or within different kinds of religious ceremonies. People read and write differently out of different social practices, and these different ways with words are part of different ways of being persons and different ways and facets of doing life.

This has important implications. From a sociocultural perspective, it is impossible to separate out from text-mediated social practices the 'bits' concerned with reading or writing (or any other sense of 'literacy') and to treat them independently of all the 'non-print' bits, like values and gestures, context and meaning, actions and objects, talk and interaction, tools and spaces. They are all non-subtractable parts of integrated wholes. 'Literacy bits' do not exist apart from the social practices in which they are embedded and within which they are acquired. If, in some trivial sense they *can* be said to exist (e.g. as code), they do not *mean* anything. Hence, they cannot meaningfully be taught and learned as separate from the rest of the practice (Gee 1996).

By adopting and developing 'literacy' as their key word, socioculturally oriented theorists, researchers, and educators sought, among other things, to bypass the psychological reductionism inscribed on more than a century of educational activity associated with 'reading'. They wanted to keep *the social* to the forefront, and to keep the 'embeddedness' of literacy in larger social practices in clear view. This was often subverted, however, when reading specialists and experts simply adopted the term 'literacy' without taking up its substance.

Second, the scope and amount of *formal* educational activity in the name of literacy that was funded and sanctioned by official government policy, guidelines and directives reached impressive levels. Literacy quickly became a considerable *industry*, involving public and private providers of diverse goods and services at different rungs on the education ladder. Adult and workplace literacy programmes received formal recognition, funding, and credentialling in a manner previously unknown. Funding to providers was usually tagged to achievement outcomes and accountability procedures. In countries like Australia, national and state level policies actually factored workplace literacy competencies into the awards and remuneration system, providing incentives for workers to participate in work-related and work-based literacy programmes, many of which were conducted during company time. Adults and workers whose language backgrounds were not in the dominant/official language of the country were often specially targeted.

Resource and professional development activities mushroomed. Literacy educators and literacy programme providers sought curriculum resources, pedagogical approaches, and specialized training for their work. Armies of literacy consultants, resource developers, and professional development experts quickly emerged to meet the market for literacy goods and services. In keeping with the tradition of formal education, the belief that such work should have a grounding in research was also officially recognized and, to a greater or lesser extent, funded. Literacy soon emerged as a major focus within educational research. Once again, the Australian case ranks among the most complex and carefully staged responses to the belief that high levels of functional and work-related literacy on the part of all members of a nation's population is a precondition of successful transition to becoming a postindustrial economy and a knowledge society. At the end of the 1980s the Australian Language and Literacy Policy legislated for competitive research funding to support a national level research programme in the area of Child Literacy. During the 1990s, the National Children's Literacy Projects programme provided millions of competitive research dollars for targeted projects addressing diverse aspects of school age children's literacy. These funds counted toward the research quantum of individual universities, which in turn determined the level of government funding they received for general research activity. Research Centres and Schools or Departments specializing in (language and) literacy education became key planks in Education Faculty structures, and often emerged among the top research income earners within their faculties.

Third, at the same time as literacy assumed a larger and larger focal presence within the recognized role and scope of formal education, it also began to assume *loftier* status in terms of how it was defined and understood by many educationists. It was as if educationists who believed that education should involve much more and count for much more than was generally associated with the term 'literacy' responded to its new pride of place by building more into their conceptions of literacy in order to defend and preserve more expansive educational purposes and standards.

This trend is apparent in a variety of areas and initiatives. These include, among others, concepts and ideals of 'cultural literacy', 'critical literacy', 'technoliteracy', 'higher order literacies', 'three-dimensional literacy', 'powerful literacy', 'multiliteracies' and the like.

For example, the urgent interest shown, especially in the US, in relation to cultural literacy in the late 1980s and early 1990s was concerned with the kind of knowledge young people need in order to participate effectively in social life as active and informed citizens. Advocates of cultural literacy addressed the kinds of approaches and programmes schools should provide to this end. The association of cultural knowledge with literacy was, perhaps, made most clearly by E. D. Hirsch Jr in his highly influential book *Cultural Literacy: What Every American Needs to Know* (1987). Hirsch argued that students need to be familiar with a cultural canon in order to be able to negotiate their social context effectively. This canon comprises relevant cultural information that has high status in the public sphere. It is assumed that all members of society share this knowledge as part of their cultural heritage. Hirsch discerned cultural *illiteracy* among growing numbers of students who could not contextualize information or communicate with their fellows within the context of a larger national culture because they lacked the common cultural stock presumed to make such communication and meaning making possible. Hirsch regarded 'literate Americans' as those who possess a particular body of cultural knowledge, which he itemized in his book.

An interesting account that builds on a sociocultural perspective to develop a robust conception of literacy can be found in a 'three-dimensional' model (Green 1988, 1997). This view argues that literacy should be seen as having three interlocking dimensions of learning and practice – the operational, the cultural and the critical. These dimensions bring together language, meaning, and context (Green 1988). None has any priority over the others. In an integrated view of literate practice and literacy pedagogy all dimensions need to be taken into account simultaneously. The *operational* dimension focuses on the language aspect of literacy. It includes but also goes beyond competence with the tools, procedures, and techniques involved in being able to handle the written language system proficiently. It includes being able to read and write/key in a range of contexts in an appropriate and adequate manner. The *cultural* dimension involves competence with the meaning system of a social practice; knowing how to make and grasp meanings appropriately within the practice – in short, of understanding texts in relation to contexts. This means knowing what it is about given contexts of practice that makes for appropriateness or inappropriateness of particular ways of reading and writing. The *critical* dimension involves awareness that all social practices, and thus all literacies, are socially constructed and 'selective': they include some representations and classifications – values, purposes, rules, standards, and perspectives – and exclude others. To participate effectively and productively in any literate practice, people must be socialized into it. But if individuals are socialized into a social practice without realizing that it is socially constructed and selective, and that it can be acted on and transformed, they cannot play an active role in changing it. The critical dimension of literacy is the basis for ensuring that individuals are not merely able to participate in some existing literacy and make meanings within it, but also that, in various ways, they are able to transform and actively produce it (Green 1988; Gee *et al.* 1996). Hence, rather than focusing on the 'how to' knowledge of literacy, the 3D model of literacy complements and supplements operational or technical competence by contextualizing it with due regard for matters of culture, history and power.

During the past two decades various accounts have been provided of concepts like 'powerful literacies', 'higher order literacies' and, more recently, 'multiliteracies'.

The pedagogy of multiliteracies focuses strongly on how cultural and linguistic diversity and the burgeoning impact of new communications technologies are changing the demands on learners in terms of what we have identified here as the operational and cultural dimensions of literacies. Learners need new operational and cultural 'knowledges' in order to acquire new languages that provide access to new forms of work, civic, and private practices in their everyday lives. At the same time, as the proponents of multiliteracies argue, learners need to develop strengths in the critical dimension of literacy as well. Mary Kalantzis and Bill Cope (1996) make this very clear with respect to literacy demands in relation to work. They note that with a new work life comes a new language, with much of it attributable to new technologies like 'iconographic, text and screen-based modes of interacting with automated machinery' and to changes in the social relations of work (Kalantzis and Cope 1996: 5; see also Cope and Kalantzis 1999). This new work life can be even more highly exploitative and unjust than its predecessor. Accordingly, Kalantzis and Cope claim that when responding to radical contemporary changes in working life literacy educators need to walk a fine line. On one side, learners must

> have the opportunity to develop skills for access to new forms of work through learning the new language of work. But at the same time, as teachers, our role is not simply to be technocrats. Our job is not to produce docile, compliant workers. Students need to develop the skills to speak up, to negotiate and to be able to engage critically with the conditions of their working lives.
>
> (Kalantzis and Cope 1996: 6)

It is also very clear that literacies, conceived from a sociocultural perspective generally and a multiliteracies perspective specifically, entail a vast amount of knowledge. Being literate involves much more than simply knowing *how* to operate the language system. The cultural and critical facets of knowledge integral to being literate are considerable. Indeed, much of what the proponents of multiliteracies have explicated are the new and changing knowledge components of literacies under contemporary social, economic, cultural, political and civic conditions. In other words, being literate in any of the myriad forms literacies take presupposes complex amalgams of propositional, procedural and 'performative' forms of knowledge. Making meaning is knowledge intensive, and much of the knowledge that school-based learning is required to develop and mobilize is knowledge involved in meaning making.

The idea that literacies can be more or less 'powerful' was developed on a number of rather different fronts during the late 1980s and the 1990s. We will briefly mention two examples here. The first is the account provided by James Gee. The second is a view associated with a group of linguists in Australia whose work was extremely influential there during the 1990s.

For Gee (1990) a powerful literacy is not a specific literacy *per se* but, rather, a way of using a literacy. He defines being literate as having control, or fluent mastery, of language uses within what he calls secondary Discourses. Gee defines Discourses as 'ways of being in the world', which integrate words, acts, gestures, attitudes, beliefs, purposes, clothes, bodily movements and positions and so on. Discourses also integrate *identities*, in the sense that through their participation in Discourses individuals are identified and identifiable as members of socially meaningful groups or networks and players of socially meaningful roles (Gee 1990: 142–3). Language is integral to Discourses, but Discourses are always much more than language alone. Language uses – or what Gee calls the 'language bits' of Discourses – are 'connected stretches of language that make sense', that are meaningful within a Discourse (Gee 1990: 143). Language uses vary from Discourse to Discourse, but well-known examples include 'conversations, stories, reports, arguments, essays', as well as explanations, commands, interviews, ways of eliciting information and so on (Gee 1990: 143).

Gee distinguishes between a person's primary Discourse and its distinctive language use (which he mostly refers to as 'discourse' with a small 'd'), and their secondary Discourses and their respective language uses. Our primary Discourse involves 'face-to-face communication with intimates', and is the Discourse of our immediate group (Gee 1990: 143). Primary Discourses differ from social group to social group (e.g. by social class, ethnicity, etc.). We each belong to just one primary Discourse, which shapes who and what we initially are as persons. Members of all social groups that extend beyond immediate, face-to-face encounters also encounter secondary Discourses through their participation in secondary institutions, like schools, churches, sports clubs, community groups, workplaces and so on. These secondary Discourses have their own more or less distinctive language uses and they shape our identities in particular ways – as we take on their beliefs, purposes, ways of speaking and acting, moving, dressing and so on. According to Gee, then, since there are multiple secondary Discourses, and since literacy and being literate are defined in terms of controlling secondary language uses, there are multiple – indeed, *many* – literacies and ways of being literate. In all cases, however, being literate means being able to use the 'right' language in the 'right' ways within a Discourse. This corresponds roughly to command of the 'operational' and 'cultural' dimensions of literacy previously mentioned.

On the basis of these ideas, Gee defines *powerful* literacy in terms of employing a secondary language use as a 'metalanguage' for understanding, analysing and critiquing other Discourses and the way they constitute us as persons and situate us within society (Gee 1990: 153; see also Gee 1991: 8–9). By a metalanguage he means 'a set of meta-words, meta-values [and] meta-beliefs' (Gee 1990: 153). Practising a powerful literacy, so defined, can provide the basis for reconstituting our selves/identities and resituating ourselves within society.

To understand and critique a particular Discourse using a powerful literacy derived from some other Discourse requires one to understand both of these Discourses *as Discourses*: what they are, how they operate, what values and ways of being in the world they promote, how their 'language bits' reflect and enable this and so on. This is metalevel knowledge. In powerful literacy we draw on such knowledge to provide us with a reason, a basis, and an alternative in terms of which we can decide to opt out of another Discourse or work to change it.

A rather different account of powerful language was developed in Australia by a school of systemic functional linguists who became known among educators as 'genre theorists'. They adapted Michael Halliday's systemic functional linguistic theory and work in ways intended to invest it with socially transforming possibilities. Their underlying premise was that certain social groups and their characteristic genres enjoy more power than other groups and their genres. They associated social power with mastery of genres which, they believed, could be taught and learned under classroom conditions. They argued that powerful genres and their social purposes can – and *should* – be identified and taught explicitly to students, and particularly to students from marginalized and/or non-English speaking backgrounds. From this perspective, genre mastery and successful use of powerful genres depends on one's ability to make the 'right' linguistic choices according to immediate contexts and social purposes. The genre theorists argued that meanings – and the social effects of language use – depend directly on language choices, which in turn, depend on one's purposes. They maintained that language and literacy mastery is properly evaluated according to the repertoire of possible linguistic choices the language user is able to draw on appropriately and that a broad linguistic repertoire can be taught and refined explicitly in classrooms (cf. Christie 1987; Martin 1993; Martin and Rothery 1993).

From these and other perspectives, then, it was seen as important to ensure that literacy agendas were expansive, particularly in view of the attention literacy was claiming within education policy along with a great deal of government 'steerage' in terms of education applications.

A fourth development, during the 1980s and 1990s, was the application of the term 'literacy' to an ever increasing variety of practices, to the point where it now seems that practically any knowledge and learning deemed educationally valuable can somehow or other be conceived as a literacy. Sometimes this simply involved 'literacy' becoming a metaphor for 'competence' or 'proficiency'. Hence, concepts like 'computer literate' often just meant that someone was more or less proficient with a computer: they could perform commonly used operations, do basic troubleshooting and the like. 'Computer literacy' often stood in for some set of vaguely recognized sets of competencies that counted as being able to 'make sense of' and 'use' computers. The terms often mean something more precise than this, but talk of being computer literate has emerged alongside talk of being 'politically literate', 'maths literate', 'environmentally literate' and so on, as everyday terminology. This provides a rough index for just how focal literacy has become as a social issue and an educational ideal during the past two or three decades. In such uses, 'literacy' connotes the idea of being able to find one's way around some kind of system, and to 'know its language' well enough to be able to make sense of it. Such a system might be a technology, a domain of practice, a mode of thinking or reasoning and so on.

Getting closer to more literal associations with language *per se*, we nowadays hear frequent references to 'oral literacy', 'visual literacy', 'information literacy', 'media literacy', 'science literacy' and even 'emotional literacy'. These uses foreground the notion of being able to make meaning – as producer or receiver – from signs, signals, codes, graphic images and so on. In cases like 'science literacy', the concept implies being able to read and write meaningfully the language and literature of science. It is close to the idea advanced in the 1970s by philosophers like Paul Hirst (1974) with respect to knowledge and the academic disciplines. Hirst spoke of 'forms and fields of knowledge' – systematic ways of understanding the world, epitomized by academic disciplines – as having their own discrete 'languages and literatures'. To 'be on the inside' of a form or field of knowledge meant being able to 'speak' its language and 'read and write its literature'. The language comprised the procedures, techniques, standards, methods and so on used by expert practitioners. The literature comprised the products generated by faithful and competent practitioners who spoke the language in question.

In cases like 'media literacy' or 'information literacy' we sometimes find implications that we need to learn to 'read' media or information sources in specialized ways in order to 'get what is really there' and/or to avoid being 'taken in'. This is the idea that there are ways of deciphering media and information more or less *wittingly* or *critically* as an 'insider' or, at least, as an effective receiver or producer within the media spaces in question. To some extent this implies the ability to identify strategies and techniques being used to produce particular kinds of effects on what we think, believe, or desire.

An example here is provided by David Sholle and Stan Denski's (1993) account of television within their treatment of critical media literacy. They observe that television can be seen as 'a *pedagogical machine*' that operates to construct discourses 'that function primarily in the locus of a mode of transmission where "culture becomes defined solely by markets for culture" ' (1993: 309; original emphasis. The quotation is from Wexler 1988: 98). Sholle and Denski argue that if teachers are to educate learners to become media literate,

> we must attend to the multiple references and codes that position them [the learners]. This means paying attention to the manner in which popular culture texts are constructed by and construct various discursive codes, but also how such texts express various contradictory ideological interests and how these texts might be taken up in a way that creates possibilities for different constructions of cultural and political life.
>
> (Sholle and Denski 1993: 309)

A fifth change in emphasis is the recent tendency by literacy scholars and researchers to use 'new' in relation to 'literacy' and 'literacies'. This has occurred in two main ways, which we may call *paradigmatic* and *ontological* respectively.

The *paradigmatic* sense occurs in talk of the New Literacy Studies (Street 1993; Gee 1996, 2000) to refer to a specific sociocultural approach to understanding and researching literacy. In this sense, the *New* Literacy Studies comprise a new paradigm for looking at literacy as opposed to the paradigm that already existed that was based on psychology. The use of 'new' here parallels that which is involved in names for initiatives or movements such as the New School of Social Research, the New Science, the New Criticism (and New Critics) and so on. In all such cases, the proponents think of their project as comprising a new and different paradigm relative to an existing orthodoxy or dominant approach.

What we are calling the *ontological* sense of 'new' refers to the idea that changes have occurred in the character and substance of literacies associated with changes in technology, institutions, media, the economy, and the rapid movement toward global scale in manufacture, finance, communications and so on. These changes have impacted on social practices in all the main areas of everyday life within modern societies: in work, at leisure, in the home, in education, in the community, and in the public sphere. Established social practices have been transformed, and new forms of social practice have emerged and continue to emerge at a rapid rate. Many of these new and changing social practices involve new and changing ways of producing, distributing, exchanging and receiving texts by electronic means. These have generated new multimodal forms of texts that can arrive via digital code – what Richard Lanham (1994) calls 'the rich signal' – as sound, text, images, video, animations and any combination of these.

In this ontological sense, the category of 'new literacies' largely covers what are often referred to as 'post-typographic' forms of textual practice. These include using and constructing hyperlinks between documents and/or images, sounds, movies, semiotic languages (such as those used by the characters in the online episodic game *Banja,* or emoticons ('smileys') used in email, online chat space or in instant messaging), manipulating a mouse to move around *within* a text, reading file extensions and identifying what software will 'read' each file, producing 'non-linear' texts, navigating three-dimensional worlds online and so on.

The chapters that follow mainly address examples of literacies and issues about knowledge associated with the massive growth of electronic information and communications technologies and their increasing role and place within our everyday lives. To a large extent it is literacies in this post-typographic sense that schools have identified as their main challenge so far as incorporating 'new literacies' into their programmes and as media for learning are concerned.

At the same time, as our earlier reference to the 'multiliteracies' project suggests, new literacies associated with contemporary changes in our institutions and economy do not necessarily involve using new electronic ICTs, or, at least, the use of new ICTs may not be their most important aspect. This is especially true of some important work-related literacies, as recent work by Glynda Hull and colleagues makes clear (see, for example, Hull *et al.* forthcoming).

Without in any way wanting to underestimate the huge significance of post-typographic, electronically mediated literacies within everyday life, and their leading place within any useful conception of 'new literacies', we nonetheless want to stake a claim also for new literacies that are not necessarily associated with new ICTs. Consequently, to the two concepts of 'the new' that are already well established in the work of literacy scholars and researchers, we want to add a third for the purposes of framing this book. This third idea is more vague and impressionistic than the others, although we think it provides a valuable perspective from which to consider literacy work in schools under contemporary conditions. It is the idea of 'new literacies' as ones that are relatively new in *chronological* terms or, perhaps, that are new to being thought about as literacies – and, particularly, as literacies that schools should take into account. Examples of new literacies in this sense that we will address in the following chapters include scenario building and zines.

On the basis of these three ideas of the 'new', we have organized our discussion of new literacies and knowledge in classrooms in the following way. The book is organized in three parts and eight chapters. The first part addresses the theme 'What's new?' The key idea in this part of the book is that the far-reaching changes that have been going on in the world during the past twenty to thirty years are based on and reflect distinctively new ways of thinking and of going about things. New practices and new 'ways' are constituted by new *mindsets* and, in turn, they help to constitute new mindsets. We believe that there is something fundamentally inappropriate about trying to face *the new* by using perspectives – or what we refer to here as 'mindsets' – that have been forged in *the old*. Yet this is what we see everywhere in education – nowhere more so than in literacy education – and with very few exceptions. What happens when the new is faced through lenses and filters of the old? What does it look like in practice? What do new mindsets look like, and what sorts of things are involved in bringing new mindsets to bear on the interfaces between literacy, technology and social practices? These are the questions addressed in this introductory chapter and the two following chapters.

Chapter 2 explores the New Literacy Studies and the study of new literacies. To a surprising extent, those scholars who identify with the New Literacy Studies have to date not been very interested in what we regard as very important and influential new literacies. In fact, the writers who have thus far provided what we see as the most useful and illuminating accounts of new literacies, and who have best modelled instructive appropriations of new literacies, are mostly not literacy scholars or researchers at all. We believe it is time that literacy scholars working from a New Literacy Studies perspective begin to engage much more seriously with new literacies. In this chapter we draw on a combination of our own fieldwork and work done by people in fields other than literacy studies in order to identify a range of new literacies we think should increasingly be taken into account in literacy education and literacy research. These include literacies mediated by new information and communications technologies, as well as literacies that employ more conventional tools and forms of text.

The third chapter discusses literacy, mindsets and new technologies in schools. In areas outside education it is becoming quite common for writers to distinguish between mindsets forged in physical space and the mechanical age and those forged in cyberspace and the digital age. Margaret Wertheim (1999) and John Perry Barlow (in Tunbridge 1995) are among those who suggest how it may be inappropriate to confuse the spaces and misapply mindsets. In this chapter we take the 'mindset thesis' seriously, adapt it, and apply it to literacy education in school settings. We distinguish between 'insider' and 'outsider' mindsets with respect to new information and communications technologies. Drawing on this distinction we show how literacy education activities planned for students in classrooms in a diverse range of school sites bring the stamp of the 'old' to bear upon what should be 'new'. This chapter also provides examples of differences between looking at a series of patterns and principles pertaining to using new technologies in literacy work from the standpoint of 'insider' and 'outsider' mindsets respectively.

The second part of the book is organized around the theme of 'Staring at the future'. This is the idea that the future is already here, that we are literally staring at it, but that within school education we are not really engaging with it. The three chapters in this part of the book case study contemporary social practices within school and out-of-school contexts. Two of the chapters (Chapters 5 and 6) document practices that are emerging as exemplars of new ways of doing and being and new literacies integral to them. It builds on the ideas and examples addressed in the first part of the book, but projects them into spaces in the world beyond school and considers some of their implications for school education. This 'heart' of the book will provide vivid descriptions of some typical exemplars of new social practices and their literacies. They show us what 'the new' looks like in miniature, and draw our attention to some of the kinds of things we need to be aware of when making decisions about school-based learning. What does it mean to equip oneself for an attention economy? Where do digital display jackets and wearable computers fit into this? What are the meanings involved in being an 'urban creature' of the skim.com variety, and how are literacy and identity galvanized and mutually constitutive in this? What is a good citizen in the world according to eBay, and how and why do young (and not so young) people vigorously and enthusiastically pursue identities they value within such sites of practice? What are the literacies involved? How are they acquired? What should school be doing about them? Prior to discussing these examples of the 'genuinely new', however, we discuss in Chapter 4 what we regard as a 'faux new' phenomenon. This is Britain's National Grid for Learning, which has been developed as an elaborate resource intended to prepare learners for tomorrow by transcending 'yesterday's skills' (Blair 1997). We argue against any idea of the Grid having serious claims to involving new technologies and new social practices. Rather, we believe it is steeped in an outsider mindset and that it projects retrospective ways onto new technologies and into virtual spaces.

Chapter 4 critiques the approach taken in Britain by the National Grid for Learning to the challenge of using new technologies in the realm of formal education. The Grid is explored as a case study of 'faking it'. The chapter argues that the Grid basically imposes an outsider mindset on the use of the Internet for learning purposes. This effectively undermines the official reasons given for establishing the Grid in the first place. It runs the risk of providing young people with unfortunate experiences of Internet-mediated practices and, in the case of learners who have rich experiences of the Net, it risks offending their insider sensitivities and turning them off. The argument explores some of the contradictions that exist between the aspirations officially stated for the Grid as a learning resource, and the most likely outcomes of its uptake in classrooms.

Chapter 5, which looks at attention economics, information, and new literacies, is based on the idea that a new kind of economy – an *attention* economy – is emerging, and that it is likely to become increasingly central to the lives of many people in modern societies (Goldhaber 1997). Our argument explores three central questions. First, we ask what roles digital technologies can and do have for paying, attracting and maintaining attention. The second question asks what significance new literacies may have for participating effectively in an attention economy. Third, we ask what the answers to these previous questions mean for literacy education in classrooms. The tension between what the future may well look like and what is being done in schools to help prepare learners now for what they may be doing later runs throughout the argument.

Chapter 6 is called 'The Ratings Game: From eBay to Plastic'. It picks up on the allocation and pursuit of online personal ratings, which have become integral features of an increasing range of emerging social practices on the Internet. With the explosive growth of the Internet – particularly during the past ten years – practices involving peer review are becoming more significant within the everyday lives of ordinary people than we have previously known. Peer review and other forms of personal rating are becoming common within some unlikely domains of social practice. This chapter explores the phenomenon of online peer review within two very different kinds of social practice on the World Wide Web. It describes and interprets these practices and considers their possible relevance for education.

The first case involves the practice of reciprocal feedback between buyers and sellers on the massive online trading site of eBay.com. This is a context where participants can be excluded from further involvement in the eBay community if they exceed four negative ratings as a buyer or seller or both. On the other hand, obtaining high personal ratings appears to be emerging as a key dimension of personal identity constitution for many eBay participants.

The second case involves a multi-strand discussion board called Plastic (www.plastic.com), where participants can make postings relating to eight categories of topics (e.g. politics, media, work, film and TV). Those who post to the board are awarded ratings on two dimensions. One of these is 'karma', which rates the participant as an active member of the community relative to the number of newsworthy postings s/he has made to the site overall. The other is a peer ranking on a scale of –1 to +5 made by a changing group of moderators and other members of the Plastic community. This ranking practice is based on formal recognition by the site that users cannot read everything that is posted on a topic. With a peer ranking system in place, users can set filters to screen out postings that fall outside a ranking range of their choice. Hence, Plastic offers the ranking function as a means to assist users in practising selective reading and to help enhance the quality of postings to the site.

The final part of the book introduces the theme of 'Knowledge and change'. We identify changes occurring in the status, relations, and distributions of knowledge in a world where 'being digital' is increasingly the norm. The two chapters ask what these changes might mean for our long-standing concept of knowledge as 'justified true belief' and our established approach to curriculum with respect to the content and process aspects of justified true belief. We look at how social relations may change within inchoate and embryonic attempts to practise new ways of knowing within school settings. As is the norm throughout the book, these chapters draw extensively on recent research undertaken by us and our colleagues, with a particular emphasis on classroom settings.

Chapter 7 develops a concept we call 'digital epistemologies'. Some key assumptions underlying the theory and practice of curriculum up until the present are now being seriously challenged as a result of changes associated with increasing *digitization* of the world and our experience of it. The chapter explores four dimensions of change associated with intensified digitization and traces their implications for school education. The first dimension involves changes in 'the world (objects, phenomena) to be known'. The second concerns changes in our conceptions of knowledge and in processes of 'coming to know'. Third, we look at some changes in how 'knowers' are constituted that reflect the impact of digitization. Finally, the argument considers some changes in the significance of different modes of knowing and the balance among them that appear to be associated with digitization.

The concluding chapter addresses the theme of practising new ways of knowing with marginal learners. It case studies a research intervention based on ideas about mindsets discussed in the first part of the book. It describes an initiative undertaken on school premises but outside the formal curriculum. This aimed to develop some new pedagogical approaches to working with 'at risk' students that enabled productive dialogue across mindsets. Four 'tough' 14-year-old male students, excluded from their English classroom for unacceptable conduct, and uniformly identified as having literacy difficulties, were invited to work with a teacher, a teacher trainee, two researchers, and a research assistant in an activity to involve use of new technologies. Roughly envisaged as a potential model for building a programme of work collaboratively and 'up from the bottom', the project provided a context in which quite startling results emerged. By the end of the short duration project, all four boys had agreed to re-enter their conventional classroom to teach their peers what they had learned. The argument focuses on the potential for educationally fruitful changes in social relations of knowledge production that are associated with approaches to integrating new technologies into collaboratively planned work in a context of negotiation across explicitly recognized differences in mindsets.

In the course of developing the framework for this book we distinguished between two fundamental senses of 'new' as it applies to 'literacy studies'. The *paradigmatic* sense yields the idea of the New Literacy Studies. The *ontological* sense yields the idea of the study of new literacies. As suggested by our summary descriptions of the chapters that follow, this book will report some of our study to date of new literacies. At the same time, however, this study has been undertaken entirely from a New Literacy Studies perspective. We hope that the following chapters provide readers with a clear statement of how we understand and seek to contribute to the New Literacy Studies, *as well as* a clear statement of how we see some of the 'new literacies' at this point in their evolution. By way of a beginning, then, we turn in the next chapter to an account of the New Literacy Studies and the study of new literacies.

Note

1 From around 1992 Gee has distinguished between Discourse (with a capital D) and discourse. The former is the notion of ways of being in the world that integrate identities, and the latter refers to the language bits, or language uses, of Discourses.

CHAPTER 2

The 'New Literacy Studies' and the Study of *New* Literacies

Introduction

There is an interesting ambiguity and tension in the idea of 'new literacy studies'. From one standpoint the New Literacy Studies (NLS) refers to a new way of looking at literacy. This is sometimes referred to as a socio-cultural approach to literacy, or as socioliteracy studies. As such it is distinguished from 'old' approaches to studying literacy typically based in some kind of psychologistic or technicist paradigm. From a second standpoint, however, 'new literacy studies' can refer to studies of new forms of literacy. Rather than being about a new way of looking at literacy, this second idea is more about looking at 'new forms of literacy'.

This chapter begins from our observation that to date many people who 'belong to' and contribute to the NLS have not been very interested in what we personally have come to regard as important and influential new literacies. On the contrary, it seems to us that the sorts of people who have provided the most useful, helpful and illuminating accounts of new literacies, and who have best modelled instructive appropriations of new literacies, are, for the most part, not literacy scholars at all – whether by self-definition or in terms of formal recognition.

We believe that under contemporary conditions useful work in literacy at interfaces among schools, community, workplaces and other key sites of daily life *must* include serious engagement with a range of distinctively *new* literacies. These include literacies that are, in significant ways, new *in kind*. They also include other literacies that are *chronologically* new or that will in other ways be new to formal studies of literacy. From this perspective we find much that is valuable for informing school-based literacy education within bodies of literature and inquiry that have until now been strictly marginal to the NLS. In this chapter we will engage with some typical examples of this literature and take on board some of the challenges they present.

A small qualifying note is in order here. Any examples of 'new literacies' will inevitably be selective, partial and subject to disagreement on the part of others. Some 'new' literacies may come and go very quickly. Others will rise and rise. And under the fast-paced conditions of contemporary life, what appears new at a given point in time may be superseded and become 'old' very quickly. There are, then, risks involved in trying to identify exemplars of new literacies. We are aware of at least some of the risks and potential disputes involved here, and have done our best to select plausible candidates for new literacies. In the end, however, we think the most important point is to try and get the larger issues onto the educational agenda, since many attempts to respond to 'the new' in education seem to us not to go far enough. Many simply accommodate new motifs to old ways, as we will see at length in later chapters. Others seem to attend to the new within unduly narrow scopes of concern with, say, present and foreseeable future work or citizenship. Our view is that numerous highly influential (and powerful) literacies exist that enjoy high-profile places within contemporary everyday culture, but that are not in any significant way accounted for in school learning. The extent to which they can and should be addressed within formal education can only be raised once we have a sense of what they are. Our aim is to identify at least some plausible candidates to be taken into account.

Concepts of new literacies

As spelled out in the Introduction, we recognize two broad categories of new literacies. The first category, which we have identified as post-typographic new literacies, is well known, even if it is often not especially well defined or understood. These are literacies associated with new communications and information technologies or, in more general terms, the digital electronic apparatus (Ulmer 1987). The second category is a looser and more *ad hoc* category comprising literacies that are comparatively new in chronological terms and/or that are (or will be) new to being recognized as literacies – even within the sociocultural perspective. Literacies in this second category may have little or nothing to do with use of (new) digital electronic technologies. In some cases, however, they may well comprise new *technologies* in their own right. Since the latter is the less intuitive and less clear category we will briefly sketch a couple of examples of what we have in mind.

Scenario planning

Scenario planning has emerged during the past forty to fifty years as a generic technique to stimulate thinking about the future in the context of strategic planning (Cowan *et al.* 1998). It was initially used in military planning, and was subsequently adapted for use in business environments (Wack 1985a, 1985b; Schwartz 1991; van der Heijden 1996) and, most recently, for planning political futures in such countries as post-apartheid South Africa, Colombia, Japan, Canada and Cyprus (Cowan *et al.* 1998).

Scenarios are succinct narratives that describe possible futures and alternative paths toward the future, based on plausible hypotheses and assumptions. The idea behind scenarios is to start thinking about the future now in order to be better prepared for what comes later. Proponents of scenario planning make it very clear that scenarios are *not* predictions. Rather, they aim to perceive futures in the present. In Leonie Rowan and Chris Bigum's words (1997: 73), they are

> a means for rehearsing a number of possible futures. Building scenarios is a way of asking important 'what if' questions: a means of helping groups of people change the way they think about a problem. In other words, they are a means of learning.

Scenario planning is very much about challenging the kinds of mindsets that underwrite certainty and assuredness, and about 're-perceiving the world' (Rowan and Bigum 1997: 76) and promoting more open, flexible, proactive stances toward the future. As Cowan and colleagues (1998: 8) put it, the process and activity of scenario planning is designed to facilitate conversation about what is going on and what might occur in the world around us, so that we might 'make better decisions about what we ought to do or avoid doing'. Developing scenarios that perceive possible futures in the present can help us 'avoid situations in which events take us by surprise' (Cowan *et al.* 1998: 8). They encourage us to question 'conventional predictions of the future', as well as helping us to recognize 'signs of change' when they occur, and establish 'standards' for evaluating 'continued use of different strategies under different conditions' (Cowan *et al.* 1998: 8). Very importantly, they provide a means of organizing our knowledge and understanding of present contexts and future environments within which decisions we take today will have to be played out (Rowan and Bigum 1997: 76).

Within typical approaches to scenario planning a key goal is to aim for making policies and decisions *now* that are likely to prove sufficiently robust if played out across several possible futures. Rather than trying to predict the future, scenario planners imaginatively construct a range of possible futures. In light of these, which may be very different from one another, policies and decisions can be framed at each point in the ongoing 'present' that will optimize options regardless of which anticipated future is closest to the one that eventually plays out in reality.

Scenarios must narrate particular and credible worlds in the light of forces and influences currently evident and known to us, and which seem likely to steer the future in one direction or another. A popular way of doing this is to bring together participants in a policy- or decision-making exercise and have them frame a focusing question about or theme relevant to the area they are concerned with. If, for instance, our concern is with designing courses in literacy education and technology for in-service teachers presently in training, we might frame the question of what learning and teaching of literacy and technology might look like within educational settings for elementary school age children 15 years hence. Once the question is framed, participants try to identify 'driving forces' they see as operating and as being important in terms of their question or theme. When these have been thought through participants identify those forces or influences that seem more or less 'predetermined': that will play out in more or less known ways. Participants then identify less predictable influences, or uncertainties: key variables in shaping the future which could play out in quite different ways, but where we genuinely can't be confident one way or another about how they will play out. From this latter set, one or two are selected as 'critical uncertainties' (Rowan and Bigum 1997: 81). These are forces or influences that seem especially important in terms of the focusing question or theme but which are genuinely 'up for grabs' and unpredictable. The 'critical uncertainties' are then 'dimensionalized' by plotting credible poles: between possibilities that, at one pole are not too 'bland' and, at the other, not too 'off the wall'. These become raw materials for building scenarios: stories about which we can think in ways that suggest decisions and policy directions *now*.

A number of classic examples of scenario planning successes exist. One early and famous example concerns a petroleum company whose scenario planning entertained the possibility of a future change in the price of oil. This planning exercise occurred prior to the dramatic and world-changing oil shocks of the mid-1970s. At the time an oil price change, while possible, was practically unthinkable. Other companies certainly had not factored it into their way of thinking about the future. By dint of decisions made as a result of the scenario planning exercise, the company in question was well prepared for the unexpected, and dramatically improved its business position among oil companies after the OPEC countries acted to increase oil prices.

This is not to suggest that scenario planning is good just for business and profiteering activities. Rather, we think the kind of work that goes into scenario planning is exactly the kind of work that should be built into learning activities in schools, communities and workplaces. Since it is a form of reading and writing the world, it seems to us to qualify nicely as a new literacy: one that is comparatively new chronologically, and one that would most certainly be new so far as prevailing mindsets within the formal study of literacy is concerned.

Zines

This category of new literacies relates directly to a central motif of this book: namely, the issue of 'mindsets' that we will address in greater detail a little later. The rapidity and extent of change during the past twenty years has left many people who remain comparatively young in chronological terms out of touch with the tenor of the times. This manifests itself in diverse ways. One interesting but unfortunate example of this concerns the extent to which some progressive educators seem quick to dismiss or simply ignore a range of cultural forms as being apolitical – even regressive – because they fall outside the range of what progressives of their generation regard as being *political*. Zines – whether conventional print zines or electronic zines (ezines) – are a typical case in point.

'Zines' are the grunge frontier of publishing. Hard copy zines are typically hand-crafted, using found papers, card stock, typed texts, drawn or photocopied images, photographs, stickers, paper cutouts and so on. They are usually produced in small print runs, and mainly distributed via word of mouth. Generally they cost only one or two US dollars (or equivalent in the form of postage stamps or a 'trade' – someone else's zine in exchange).

Many are 'defiantly personal' texts 'which confidently explore their maker's passions, no matter how obscure they may seem' (Bail 1997: 44). They often articulate strong, counter-mainstream cultural themes or social activist projects (cf. Vale 1996, 1997). Mainstream discourses and values are subverted and pilloried in ways that can be breathtaking in their serious playfulness. In the 'Space and Technology' issue of *Mavis McKenzie*,

> Mavis writes letters to Hewlett Packard asking for advice about her ancient computer. She writes to a glass company about replacing the windows in her house with Windows 95. (They write back kindly advising her that Windows 95 is a software program.) She gets tickets to *The Price is Right* [one of those afternoon TV game shows]. Mavis has far too much time on her hands.
>
> (Bail 1997: 44)

Dishwasher Pete's zine, *Dishwasher*, presents a sophisticated and trenchant critique of and resistance to the McWork world.

> I'm addicted to that feeling of quitting; walking out the door, yelling 'Hurrah!' and running through the streets. Maybe I need to have jobs in order to appreciate my free leisure time or just life in general . . . Nowadays, I can't believe how *personally* employers take it when I quit. I think, 'What did you expect? Did you expect me to grow old and die here in your restaurant?' There seems to be a growing obsession with job security, a feeling that if you have a job you'd better stick with it and 'count your blessings'.
>
> (Dishwasher Pete in conversation with Vale 1997: 5, 6)

Generation X zinesters have evolved an array of distinctive trade-offs around the economics and politics of talent, passion and community. Bail (1997: 44) observes that

> Zines are cheap and fast. Yet their makers often struggle to pay for photocopying, stamps, even paper. I was showing a zine to a friend and coincidentally its producer was employed in her office mailroom. She'd always thought he was too talented for the job but suddenly realised why he stayed there. Zines are not easy to come by: producers [often] swap their publications with each other . . . Basically, you need to be in the loop to get the good stuff. It's give and take – those who contribute to the culture get the most from it . . . Nice to find a place with a generosity of spirit among peers . . . and to find a culture that hasn't been censored, sanitised and target-marketed.
>
> (Bail 1997: 44)

Zines are a medium for young people's opinions, thoughts, creativity, and for affirming a stance as active makers rather than passive consumers of culture.

We believe a case can be made for serious consideration of zines within progressive studies of new literacies. This would be similar to the ways critical historians of literacy have paid scholarly interest to progressive resistant textual productions of earlier times – particularly the working class underground press in the early industrial age. While we do not necessarily agree with the substantial positions advanced in some zines, the genre as a whole provides useful clues about some of the different ways young people understand and practise cultural politics. These often involve a blend of the anarchic, the edge-dweller, the intensely personal, the do-it-yourself ethic, dressed to spoof, the critique and subversion of mainstream culture and constructions of publishing. To that extent, zines reveal ideas about how many young people understand the nature and role of literacies in cultural and political practices.

The study of new literacies

There now exists a huge and growing body of literature that describes uses of new ICTs within school settings, including within literacy education specifically. It is highly questionable, however, whether much of this literature actually gets at anything that is significantly *new* so far as literacies and social practices are concerned. In other words, it does not follow from the fact that so-called new technologies are being used in literacy education that *new literacies* are being engaged with. Still less does it imply that learners are developing, critiquing, analysing, or even becoming technically proficient with new literacies.

In some of our other work (e.g. Lankshear and Bigum 1999: 454–6; Lankshear and Snyder 2000: Ch. 5; Goodson *et al.* 2002: Ch. 4) we have identified recurring features of new technology-mediated literacy practices in classrooms. These reflect a marked tendency to perpetuate the old, rather than to engage with and refine or reinvent the new. Many researchers have identified the 'old wine in new bottles' syndrome, whereby long-standing school literacy routines have a new technology tacked on here or there, without in any way changing the substance of the practice. Using computers to produce neat final copies, or slideshow presentation software for retelling stories, are obvious examples. In some cases, practices involving literacies that might reasonably be described as 'new' emerge within classroom activities, but at the same time appear very odd or 'unhinged' from the kinds of practices that are engaged beyond the classroom. Such practices are often 'solutions' to the demand that new technologies be employed in classroom programmes without the conditions existing for this to occur in sensible ways. Using email to share cryptic clues and interpretations of these clues among participating schools in an email-based competition requiring students to track down a 'criminal' is a case in point. So is inventing an activity for groups of students to write 'five-minute plays' taking turns to enter the text on the single laptop computer available from the class set of computers for each group of four or five students. Such examples are not so much instances of new literacies as pedagogical inventions born of necessity that infringe against the principle of efficacious learning (see p. 48).

Such subversions of 'the new' are not at all surprising when we take larger and underlying institutional characteristics of school into account. School routines are highly regular forms of practice that are intimately linked to what we call the 'deep grammar' of schooling, as well as to aspects of policy development and imposition, resourcing trends, professional preparation and development, and so on. In fact, we suggest that schools and classrooms are among the last places one would expect to find 'new literacies'. We can begin to see why this is so by considering two key elements of the deep grammar of school, which constructs learning as teacher-directed and 'curricular'.

First, schooling operates on the presumption that the teacher is the ultimate authority on matters of knowledge and learning. Hence, whatever is addressed and done in the classroom must fall within the teacher's competence parameters, since he or she is to *direct* learning.

Second, learning as 'curricular' means that classroom learning proceeds in accordance with a formally imposed/officially sanctioned sequenced curriculum which is founded on texts as information sources. Seymour Papert (1993: 9) observes the long-standing pervasive tendency in the education literature 'to assume that reading is the principal access route to knowledge for students'. The world, in other words, is accessed via texts (books; school is bookspace). This imposes a pressing and profoundly instrumental value and significance on the capacity to *read*. It also promotes and encourages a view of (school) literacy as *operational* in the first instance (which, unfortunately, is often the last instance as well): that is, reading as a matter of competence with *techniques* of decoding and encoding.

Current policies concerned with technologizing learning intersect, for example, with a teaching workforce that is largely un(der)prepared for the challenge of *directing* computer-mediated learning in the role of teacher as authority. In a climate of shortage, schools value almost any computer skills in teachers. In practice, this means that low-level operational or technical skills and knowledge predominate (Bigum 1997: 250). Not surprisingly, teachers look for ways to fit new technologies into classroom 'business as usual'. Since educational ends are directed by curriculum, and technologies are 'mere' tools, the task of integrating new technologies into learning is often realized by adapting them to familiar routines. One corollary of this is that making learners 'technologically literate' is largely reduced to teaching them how to 'drive' the new technologies. The emphasis is very much on technical or operational aspects: how to add sound, insert a graphic, open and save files, create a HyperCard stack and so on.

This logic can be seen as a specific instance of a much larger phenomenon: the systematic separation of (school) learning from participation in 'mature' (insider) versions of Discourses which are part of our life trajectories (Knobel 1999). School learning is learning for school; school as it always has been. The burgeoning take-up of new technologies simply gives us our latest 'fix' on this phenomenon. It is the 'truth' that underpins many current claims that school learning is at odds with authentic ways of learning to be in the world, and with social practice beyond the school gates. The reason why many school appropriations of new technologies appear 'odd' in relation to 'real world' practices – with which children are often familiar and comfortable – has to do with this very logic. It is precisely this 'deep grammar' of schooling that cuts schools off from the new (technological) literacies and associated subjectivities that Chris Bigum and Bill Green (1992) say educators are compelled to attend to. To put it another way, new literacies and social practices associated with new technologies 'are being invented on the streets' (Richard Smith, personal communication). These are the new literacies and practices that will (many of them) gradually become embedded in everyday social practice: the literacies against which the validity of school education will be assessed. But the 'deep grammar' of school is in tension here with its quest for legitimation in a high tech world – which is potentially highly problematic for schools.

Accepting the challenge of new literacies in the NLS

In the remainder of this chapter we lay out in a preliminary way some concepts and examples we think might help take us forward in studying new literacies in relation to school settings, as well as home, community, and workplace settings. These will be presented under three headings.

- The nature and significance of 'mindsets'.
- Some typical examples of new literacies.
- Descriptive, analytic and critical accounts of new literacies.

The kinds of concepts and examples below are further developed and extended in subsequent chapters.

The nature and significance of 'mindsets'

In recent work we have addressed some of the issues involved here by reference to a fruitful distinction advanced by John Perry Barlow (see Lankshear and Bigum 1999; Rowan *et al.* 2000; Goodson *et al.* 2002). We will look at Barlow's distinction in detail in the next chapter. For immediate purposes, however, it is sufficient to note that, in an interview with Nat Tunbridge (1995), Barlow spells out a distinction between two mindsets that are brought to bear on cyberspace specifically and spaces of digitized practices more generally. Barlow refers to these two mindsets as 'immigrant' and 'native' mindsets respectively. We prefer to call them 'outsider' (or 'newcomer') and 'insider' mindsets respectively, since the terminology of 'immigrants' and 'natives' might reasonably be seen as offensive by members of some social groupings.

Very briefly, Barlow distinguishes between those who have, as it were, 'been born and grown up' in the space of 'the Internet, virtual concepts and the IT world generally', whom he calls 'natives', and those who have, as it were, migrated to this space. The former (insiders) understand this space; the latter (outsiders/newcomers) do not. Barlow's distinction is between mindsets which relate to how this space is constructed and controlled in terms of values, morals, knowledge, competence and the like. Since 'newcomers' lack the experience, history, and resources available to them that 'insiders' have, they cannot – to that extent – understand the new space the way insiders do. On fundamental points and principles of cyber/information/virtual space, says Barlow, newcomers 'just don't get it' (in Tunbridge 1995: 4).

We may use 'newcomers' and 'insiders' as markers for two competing mindsets. One affirms the world as the same as before, only more technologized; the other affirms the world as radically different, precisely because of the operation of new technologies (Lankshear and Bigum 1999: 458). Of course, these distinctions are not the only way of 'carving up' the world, but we find them useful when talking about new technologies and education.

The 'deep grammar' of school – embedded in its administrative systems, policy development, curriculum and syllabus development, systemic planning and the like, as well as in its daily enactment within classroom routines and relations – institutionalizes the privileging of the new-comer/outsider mindset over the insider mindset. Many classroom constructions of literacy involving new technologies are classic instances of outsider understandings of literacy grounded in the familiar physical world (book space) being imported into cyber/virtual/information space. We will see numerous instances of this in examples covered in later chapters: including the large-scale example of Britain's National Grid for Learning. This generates familiar tensions for schools: tensions which may, however, be seen as choice points – where choice about mindsets is, in principle, open and up for grabs.

For example, schools already face sizeable cohorts of 'insiders' largely indifferent to and bemused by the quaint practices of schooling. This is a cohort that is in tune and largely at ease with the dizzy pace of change, with the development of new technologies, and with social and economic shifts that cause pain to many outsider/newcomers (Lankshear and Bigum 1999: 461).

Some typical examples of 'new' literacies

This section will provide a kind of 'operational definition' of how we see some of the territory of new literacies. It comprises a broad series of examples we find illuminating. They are only a very small sample of the kinds of textual practices we identify as new literacies and the larger Discourses in which they are embedded. We have aimed to span a wide range in terms of the cultural politics of new literacies, giving particular emphasis to practices that adopt an active or critical stance.

Multimediating: Michael Doneman

Michael and Ludmila Doneman are performance artists who use a range of digital technologies in their work with disadvantaged young people and indigenous people in Australia. They identify themselves as cultural *animateurs* (www.mwk16.com/pageSAC.html). In the following account of 'multimediating', Michael Doneman (1997: 131, original emphasis) emphasizes cultural production over consumption. In so doing he identifies what we see as an important principle of new literacies.

In matters of definition, why spend so much time on *multimedia* as a noun when we could be looking at *multimediating* as a verb? I can have almost any number of windows open – let's say I open a chat window (or I-phone or video chat), the Web, an ftp file transfer, a usenet news reader, a telnet MUD session, a low-end graphics app, a simple word processor, net radio or streamed video and e-mail. Let's say I am mixing-and-matching my time in each environment, communicating in different ways among different communities, cutting and pasting, sending and receiving simultaneously, producing and consuming simultaneously, role playing, documenting and archiving, selecting, discarding, maintaining, filtering, reciprocating, researching, criticising, responding, arguing, judging, broadcasting . . .

How is this multimediating constructing my world and my response to the world? How is it constructing and responding to *community*? How is it fitting me to operate effectively in the world?

Let's also say that I am doing this on-line activity from a workstation in the telecentre of a place like GRUNT [an inner city cultural youthspace located in a former warehouse], where there might be a rehearsal, music, informal chat, meetings and office work going on in *meatspace*. Other environments, other roles. Is the negotiation of these roles *on the fly* enabling or distracting me?

E-zining: Grrrowling with the Digitarts

Digitarts (digitarts.va.com.au) (*Digitarts* 2000) is an online multimedia project space originally constructed by young women for young women, exploring alternative perspectives on style, food, everyday life and commodities, and expressing different conceptions and constructions of female identity through poems, narratives, journal pages, how-to-do texts and digital images. To begin with, the project was dedicated to providing young women who are emerging artists and/or cultural workers with access to the knowledge and equipment necessary for the development of their arts and cultural practices in the area of new technologies. It aimed at challenging 'the "boys' toys" stigma often associated with electronic equipment', and to 'provide young women with access to information technology in a non-threatening "girls' own" space, to encourage involvement in technology-based artforms' (digitarts.va.com.au/gis/). In recent times, the brief of *Digitarts* has changed – possibly for funding reasons – and now includes socially and culturally disadvantaged young people of both genders. As the welcome page to the website puts it, 'Most people are happily oblivious to the inequities around them. We are not. Instead we look for the gaps, and seek to provide those missing out with access to knowledge and equipment in innovative and user-friendly ways.'

Despite changes, *Digitarts* remains a venue for emerging multimedia artists to showcase their work, a place for young people to display their burgeoning computer skills, and still seeks to attract young, traditionally disadvantaged people to new technologies by providing six- to eight-week webpage development courses for beginners. Other training provisions in the women-oriented days have included a 12-week advanced web-development course, and a 12-week digital animation course. The collaborative production of *GRRROWL* by young women around Australia (what the digitarts refer to as a 'semi-regular ezine'; digitarts.va.com.au/grrrowl.html) continues, still with its emphasis on women's experiences and skills. *GRRROWL* is available in at least 'six flavours' or issues: #1 machines, #2 fashion, #3 action, #3.5 party, #4 simply lifeless, #5 circle/cycle.

Two projects are typical of the early *Digitarts*. *Girls in Space* (digitarts.va.com.au/gis/) was prompted by the low visibility of young women in public spaces, and the lack of research in Australia about women's recreational and public space needs. It gathered information from young women who made use of public spaces and those who didn't, and made this information available to public policy makers. The information was also used to generate models of service and activity delivery designed to increase young women's participation in a range of public sites (e.g. recreation and public parks, sporting venues), and to promote collaboration between local government and community organizations. Spin-offs include an online gallery of poster art inspired in part by some *Girls in Space* participants' reflections on women and public spaces (see: digitarts.va.com.au/masses/gallery.html), and an online pyjama party (reported in *GRRROWL* at digitarts.va.com.au/grrrowl3.5) which explores real and virtual spaces in participants' lives.

A second project involves the ezine *GRRROWL* (digitarts.va.com.au/grrrowl). This is an ongoing, collaborative publishing endeavour. One of its early issues focused on grrrls and machines. Each contributor constructed a page that is either a personal introduction – much like a conversation between newly met friends – or contains poems or anecdotes about women and technology. Hotlinks to similar websites on the Internet also define each writer's self, and her self as connected with other selves. Issues of *GRRROWL* provide alternative readings of fashion trends and body image, perspectives of contemporary culture and everyday life and the like.

GRRROWL #4 (digitarts.va.com.au/grrrowl4) investigates the theme

'Simply Lifeless'. It documents online the everyday lives of young women in Darwin and Brisbane. Its thesis is: 'Our culture informs our everyday activity. Our everyday activity informs our culture.' The issue celebrates the 'everyperson' (cf. de Certeau 1984; Duncombe 1997), with eight young women, ranging in age from 12 years to 25 years, broadcasting by means of webpages 'snapshots' of their lives – including digital videos of key elements (composing music on a much-loved guitar, a daughter feeding a pet chicken, etc.), or hypertext journals that span a day or a week of her life and that also include personal, digital images (family album snaps, etc.), hand-drawn graphics, digital artwork and so on (see, especially, 12-year-old Gabriell's page: digitarts.va.com.au/grrrowl4/gabriell/typicalday. html). By documenting the 'banal' and 'everyday', this issue of *GRRROWL* aims at 'increasing the range of criteria by which our cultures are measured and defined' (digitarts.va.com.au/grrrowl4).

Each *Digitart* project engages its participants in developing a range of 'operational' technology and literacy skills needed to produce effective webpages (e.g. becoming fluent in webpage design skills, Hypertext Markup Language (HTML) and Virtual Reality Modelling Language (VRML), scanning images, hyperlinking files, digital photography and image manipulation, developing electronic postcards and 'mail to:' forms online, embedding digital video clips in webpages). Items in the *Digitarts* portfolio are steeped in cultural analyses of everyday life, as well as in processes that properly blur the relationship between effective webpage construction in cyberspace and meaningful social practices in 'meat space'. This includes broadcast publishing of online magazine-type commentaries, the use of the Internet to establish and nurture interactive networks of relations between like-minded people, and the exploration and presentation of cultural and community membership and self-identity through writing, images, and hyperlinks. *Digitarts'* work has an overt critical dimension by virtue of its keen-edged critique of 'mainstream' Australian society. For instance, the editorial in the third issue of *GRRROWL* explains how to override/subvert the default settings on readers' Internet browser software, and encourages young women to override/subvert other socially constructed 'default settings' that may be operating in their lives. It challenges social scripts which allocate various speaking and acting roles for young women that cast them as passive social objects or as victims (e.g. 'This is not about framing women as victims – mass media vehicles already do a pretty good job of that'; *Girls in Space*), and that write certain types of girls (or grrrls) out of the picture altogether. *Digitarts* offers a coherent alternative to the commodification of youth culture – i.e. youth as a market category – by making space for young women, and now young men, to become *producers*, and not merely consumers, of culture in the way it privileges the personal over the commercial (cf. Doneman 1997: 139; Duncombe 1997: 68, 70).

Meme-ing: David Bennahum

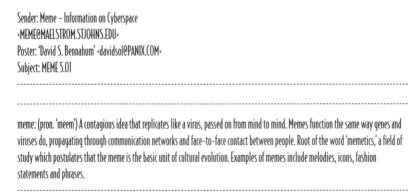

Sender: Meme – Information on Cyberspace
<MEME@MAELSTROM.STJOHNS.EDU>
Poster: 'David S. Bennahum' <davidsol@PANIX.COM>
Subject: MEME 5.01

----

meme: (pron. 'meem') A contagious idea that replicates like a virus, passed on from mind to mind. Memes function the same way genes and viruses do, propagating through communication networks and face-to-face contact between people. Root of the word 'memetics,' a field of study which postulates that the meme is the basic unit of cultural evolution. Examples of memes include melodies, icons, fashion statements and phrases.

David Bennahum is the author of *Extra Life: Coming of Age in Cyberspace* (1998). We learned about his book through his regular MEME newsletter (see the MEME website, including back issues: memex.org).

Meme-ing is a powerful metalevel literacy; an enactive project of trying to project into cultural evolution by imitating the behavioural logic – replication – of genes and viruses. It involves at least two necessary conditions: susceptibility (for contagion) and conditions for replication to occur. Susceptibility is tackled by way of 'hooks' and 'catches' – something that is likely to catch on, that gets behind early warning systems and immunity (even well-developed critical consciousnesses can get infiltrated by the Nike icon or the Coca-Cola white swirl on red). Electronic networks provide ideal contexts for replication.

Examples of successful memes and their respective 'cloners', 'high-profile carriers' or 'taggers' include: 'cyberspace' (William Gibson), 'screenagers' (Douglas Rushkoff), 'GenX' (Doug Coupland), 'the information superhighway' (Al Gore), 'global village' (Marshall McLuhan), 'cyborgs' (Donna Haraway), 'clock of the long now' (Stewart Brand and colleagues), 'digital divide' (Clinton administration), 'complexity' (the Santa Fe Group), D/discourse (James Gee), and so on. The principle that lies behind meme-ing, so far as generating active/activist literacies is concerned, is simple yet fundamental: If *we* don't like *their* contagious ideas, *we* need to produce some of our *own*.

Blogging: personal weblogs from Jane Doe to Andrew Sullivan

In a May 2002 online archive of *Wired*, a writer for *The New York Times*, Andrew Sullivan, suggested that 'blogging' – the practice of publishing personal weblogs – is changing the media world. He goes so far as to suggest that blogging could 'foment a revolution in the way journalism functions in our culture' (Sullivan 2002: 1).

Weblogs are online personal diaries or journals that are added to by the owner anywhere from every now and then to multiple times a day. Sullivan traces their history from the mid-1990s, when blogging was confined to small-scale 'sometimes nutty, sometimes inspired writing of online diaries' (2002: 1). Today, however, the Internet is home to blogs covering diverse topics and types. Sullivan notes examples ranging from tech blogs, sex blogs, drug blogs and onanistic teenage blogs to news and commentary blogs. The latter comprise sites that are 'packed with links and quips and ideas and arguments' that as recently as 2001 'were the near monopoly of established news outlets' (2002: 1). While they are often still 'nutty', and can be painfully banal, prejudiced, angst-ridden, or downright nasty, they can also be erudite and scale the pinnacles of sophisticated commentary and critique. Weblogs transcend traditional media categories. In the broad area of journalism, for instance, they may be as 'nuanced and well-sourced as traditional journalism' yet have 'the immediacy of talk radio' (Sullivan 2002: 1).

Furthermore, blogging is in tune with the tenor of the times. Blogs invoke the personal touch and put the character and temperament of the writer out front, rather than disguising it behind a façade of detached objectivity underwritten by the presumed editorial authority of the big formal newspaper or network. Sullivan, whose own blog reaches an estimated quarter of a million readers monthly and has become economically profitable, claims that Net Age readers are increasingly sceptical about the authority of big name media. Many readers know that the editors and writers of the most respected traditional news media are fallible and 'no more inherently trustworthy than a lone blogger who has earned a reader's respect' (Sullivan 2002: 1).

In general, blogs mix comment with links, in varying ratios. Although there are any number of services online that help users create the basic HTML code and 'look' of their blogs (e.g. Williams 2002), there is no content formula, and personal style and nature of the topic appear to be key variables in whether a blog privileges commentary or links, or effects a reasonable balance. Chris Baker (2002: 1), writing in the same issue of *Wired*, notes that an index of blogs created at MIT 'tracks top blogs based on how many people link to them' (see blogdex.media.mit.edu). Baker identifies a number of current high-profile 'power bloggers', briefly describes the theme or purpose of their blogs, and reports their respective ratios of comments to links. At one pole of Baker's selection is the blog of Australian illustrator and Web designer, Claire Robertson (www.loobylu. com), which 'serves up a breezy diary accompanied by exquisite illustrations', with a ratio of 20 comments to every link (Baker 2002: 1). At the other end of the spectrum we find the blog of Jessamyn West, the 'hippest ex-librarian on the Web' (Baker 2002: 1). West is credited with 'bringing the controversy and intrigue of library subculture to life' (Baker 2002: 1) and, not surprisingly perhaps, provides an average of five links for each commentary.

The vast majority of bloggers, however, are individuals writing for relatively small audiences on themes, topics or issues of personal interest to themselves. Chris Raettig's popular weblog drew international attention in 2001 with an enormous collection of corporate anthem sound files he had gathered (and had been sent by others) that were, as he put it, 'so bad, they were good' (Raettig 2001: 1). Raettig is a 22-year-old software programmer and developer living in London, and his blog – titled *i like cheese* (chris. raettig.org) – features livecam images of his studio apartment; links to a digital photo 'warehouse' he has established and which documents everyday moments in his life; hyperlinks to the technology development company he is partner in, the corporate anthem webpage, alternative rock music, and suchlike; and his journal entries. The principal theme that loosely ties his blog entries together is new technologies, with recent diary entries including commentaries on the relaunch of his corporate anthems webpage on the zdnet.org website and the renewed international media interest this created; a trip to Cambridge to meet with owners of a technology start-up company; a review of his day; ideas for large-scale Internet-based projects; and comments on the current health of the Web industry in general.

At a rather different point on the politico-cultural spectrum we find the blog of Asparagirl, a 23-year-old Web designer who works for IBM. Her blog (asparagirl.com/blog/) was recently showcased in a *Washington Post* article on weblogs (Kurtz 2002: 1). It attracts over 1000 daily visitors and presents self-styled 'solipstic' commentaries that engage with themes, issues and events such as the nature of the Internet (e.g. issues concerning the joys of interactivity and the need for privacy); issues concerning statecraft and the Palestinian–Israeli conflict written from her perspective as a Jewish-American; meeting other bloggers at a party; the latest bubblegum collector cards that feature victims of the 11 September attacks on the US; meta-comments on the content of other people's blogs, and so on.

Map rapping: the Global Business Network

The Global Business Network (GBN 2002) is, among other things, an originating force behind the practice of scenario planning (www.gbn.org). Founded in 1987, GBN is a network of organizations and individuals 'committed to re-perceiving the present in order to anticipate the future and better manage strategic response' (Rowan and Bigum 1997: 76). In some ways the organization approximates to an actor network. Its services include a 'WorldView program' where members are brought together via meetings, publications, and online conferences, and a training service – Learning Journeys – which introduces members and the public to the use of scenarios within their own organizations and contexts.

The GBN site contains a Scenario Planning section which describes how scenarios are crafted and used, together with reports of several projects and examples of the kind of thinking scenarios promote and demand. Its 'map rap' page by Peter Schwartz (no date) – and originally one of the site's earlier 'front pages' – exemplifies a new literacy in the way we are thinking of here. It employs new technologies to communicate new ways of reading and writing the world that challenge old/outmoded or no longer efficient mindsets.

> If you were an explorer in the early 1700s this map, by cartographer Herman Moll, might well have guided your explorations of North America. It is, for the most part, recognizable to modern eyes, except for one thing – it shows California as an island [see Figure 2.1].
>
> This error was the result of good Cartesian reasoning: Spanish explorers coming from the south had encountered the tip of the Baja Peninsula; voyaging further north they sailed into the Straits of Juan de Fuca. When they connected the first point to the second they created the Gulf of California.
>
> (Schwartz no date)

As Schwartz puts it, this would be merely a historical curiosity were it not for the missionaries sent from Spain to convert the heathens in New Mexico. After landing in California, they prepared to cross the Gulf as their maps instructed: they packed up their boats and carried them up over the Sierra Nevada and down the other side, and found . . . not sea, but the longest, driest beach they'd ever seen.

When they wrote back, protesting that there was no Gulf of California, the mapmakers replied: 'Well, the map is right, so you must be in the wrong place' (or words to that effect). This misunderstanding persisted for 50 years until one of the missionaries rose high enough in the Church

Figure 2.1 Early map of California
Source: Schwartz (no date: 1)

to be able to persuade the King of Spain to issue a decree to change the maps.

As Schwartz reminds us, once you come to believe in a map, it's very difficult to change it, and, if your facts are wrong, then you'll be relying on a map that's wrong too. One aim of the Global Business Network is to 'challenge "mental maps" ' (Schwartz no date) that blind people to the lie of the land rather than helping them get to where they want to go. Thus, 'through the process of scenario planning and strategic conversation, GBN can help decision makers develop more subtle, flexible maps that enable people to navigate the uncharted territory of the future' (Schwartz no date).

Culture jamming: Adbusters

At Adbusters' Culture Jamming Headquarters (www.adbusters.org), a series of elegantly designed and technically polished pages present information about the organization and its purposes, describe an array of culture jamming campaigns, describe the Adbusters' paper-based magazine, and target worthy media events and advertising, cultural practices, and overbloated corporate globalization with knife-sharp critiques in the form of parodies that act as exposés of corporate wheelings and dealings, and/or online information tours focusing on social issues. By turning media images in upon themselves, or by writing texts that critique the effects of transnational companies, the Adbusters' culture jamming campaigns scribe new literacy practices for all people. An early image from a critique of a past trend to claim an 'equality' ethic in the fashion world shows how combining familiar images and tweaking texts can produce bitingly honest social commentaries that everyone everywhere is able to read – a kind of global literacy (see Figure 2.2).

The nature of culture jamming and the philosophy that underlies it, together with many practical examples of how to enact culture jamming literacies, are described in *Culture Jam: How to Reverse America's Suicidal Consumer Binge – And Why We Must* (Lasn 1999), written by Kalle Lasn, publisher of *Adbusters* magazine and founder of the Adbuster Media Foundation. The potential effectiveness of culture jamming was

Figure 2.2 Adbuster spoof advertisement
Source: http://adbusters.org/spoofads/fashion/benetton/

clearly demonstrated recently. An email posting in January 2002 to the Culture Jammers Network informed recipients that Adbusters' activities had come under increased scrutiny following 11 September 2001. According to the posting,

> Recently, our Corporate America Flag billboard in Times Square, New York, attracted the attention of the Federal Department of Defense, and a visit by an agent who asked a lot of pointed questions about our motivations and intent. We wondered: What gives? 'Just following up a lead from a tip line,' the agent admitted.
>
> (Adbusters 2002: 1)

Adbusters were clearly worrying people in high places. They observed that any campaign daring to question 'US economic, military or foreign policy in these delicate times', or any negative evaluation of how the US is handling its 'war on terrorism', runs the risk of being cast as 'a kind of enemy of the state, if not an outright terrorist' (Adbusters 2002: 1).

Adbusters' response was to mobilize Internet space to engage in a classic act of cyberactivist literacy. The posting asked other Culture Jammers whether their activities had received similar attention, noting that they had received messages from other activist organizations that had found themselves under investigation 'in a political climate that's starting to take on shades of McCarthyism' (Adbusters 2002: 1). Noting that they could live with vigilance, but that intimidation amounting to persecution is 'another bucket of fish', Adbusters established its own 'rat line' and invited others to publicize instances of state persecution, using a medium that has immediate global reach.

> If you know of social marketing campaigns or protest actions that are being suppressed, or if you come across any other story of overzealous government 'information management,' please tell us your story. Go to <http://www.adbusters.org/campaigns/flag/nyc.html>.
>
> (Adbusters 2002: 1)

Shortly after this occurred, Adbusters was contacted by Miramax, a Disney corporation, and informed that the corporate US flag billboard was hindering filming sequences in Times Square. Miramax requested Adbusters either to take the billboard down for a few weeks, cover it up, or replace the corporate logos Adbusters had inserted in place of stars on the flag with the original stars. Adbusters decided to reject all three options. Instead, they invited Internet users to produce their own spoofs on the corporate flag theme. The result was a series of high-quality spoofs which Adbusters published on their website, together with their own commentary on Miramax's intervention (www.adbusters.org/campaigns/flag/nyc/). In the context of the US war on (other nations') terrorism, the corporate flag campaign lifted adbusting as a new literacy to a new plane.

Communication guerrilla literacies

Digital hacking is one of a number of practices identified by Michael Doneman (1997) as being part of a suite of 'communication guerrilla' activities. Originally, as with journal hacks who would churn out texts to deadlines, hacking meant nothing more than writing a computer program. Over time, however, 'hacking' has become associated in the popular mind as the practice of breaking into computer networks in order to read or tweak data on machines to which one has no authorized access. Doneman (1997: 139) draws on Umberto Eco's concept of 'communications guerillas' to describe an 'emerging opposition to the pervasive and coercive use of information imagery by powerful groups'. According to Doneman, communications guerillas are committed to urging people to read media and other messages in ways that open onto critical – and multiple – analyses and interpretations of these messages and, hence, multiple active responses generated by the readers and not by the message writers. As Doneman explains:

> These guerrillas are not always young people or outlaws, but often enough they are – often enough for us to consider much of the following list (downloaded from the Net) as aspects of emerging youth cultures:
>
> - **Hacking** – the infiltration and manipulation of systems.
> - **Subvertising** – the production and dissemination of anti-ads [cf. Adbusters in the previous section].
> - **Sniping** – late night raids on public places (as in the work of Australia's own BUGA UP [Billboard Utilising Graffitists Against Unhealthy Promotions www.buga-up.org]).
> - **Media hoaxing** – the hoodwinking of journalists [Dishwasher Pete once sent a friend in to be interviewed in his place on the David Letterman Show. The behind-the-scenes people twigged that Pete's friend was not Pete, but the show was about to go to air and there was nothing they could do. See Vale 1997: 18 for a detailed account].
> - **Audio agitprop** – the deconstructing of pop music and challenging of copyright laws [music file websites are a good example of this].

- **Academy hacking** – cultural studies conducted outside university walls by insurgent intellectuals [e.g. zinesters].
- **Subcultural bricolage** – the refunction, by societal 'outsiders', of symbols associated with the dominant culture (as in the 'voguing' of poor, black, urban drag queens).
- **Slashing** – the renewing of tales told for mass consumption (as in the pornographic and often homoerotic Kirk/Spock stories published by male and female Trekkies in Star Trek fanzines [and ezines]).
- **Transmission jamming** [e.g. Adbusters].
- **Pirate radio and TV broadcasting.**
- **Neo-situationist demonstrations** (as in late-night dancing in ATM lobbies).
- **Camcorder counter-surveillance** (as in the celebrated tape of the police bashing of Rodney King).

All of these activities [involve] the introduction of *noise* to the signal in order to 'restore a critical dimension to passive reception'. All are examples of the potential power, for good or ill, of the notion of *interactivity*.

(Doneman 1997: 139)

Descriptive, analytic and critical accounts of new literacies

New literacies are complex and diverse. Within education research contexts we need to find ways of researching these literacies that do them justice, that do not water them down, or leach the colour from them. We think that to be useful, the investigation and interpretation of new literacies should involve descriptive, analytic and critical accounts.

Descriptive

The field needs rich descriptive sociological accounts of new literacies. Ideally these will be produced as much as possible by insiders who can 'tell it like it is practised' – avoiding the risk faced by academic literacy scholars and researchers of getting tripped up on self-conscious allocations to categories. For people like ourselves this might mean that more of our work will assume a kind of 'brokerage' role – sifting through what is already available and working to find ways of projecting this work usefully into literacy education and research spaces.

Several years ago, Douglas Rushkoff published his first book, *Cyberia* (1994). While this has a degree of analysis and comment running through it, it is first and foremost an attempt to describe a world. As a description of a domain of social practice it differs markedly from, say, the kind of account Stephen Duncombe provides of zines (1997). We see both kinds of book playing important roles in informing educational practices generally and literacy education in particular. The kind of account Duncombe provides is work we believe is urgently needed on behalf of the growing range of new literacies. At the same time, we personally learned a great deal from Rushkoff's book (and his subsequent works) in the way of the knowledge it offers of emerging social practices that we think is indispensable for literacy scholars and educators. This included insights into Discourses that are increasingly central to the lives of young people. It also included insights into aspects of subjectivity, identity formation, existential significance, worldviews, and so on, as seen from the perspective of participants. This kind of material speaks directly to the sorts of issues raised by educationists who are concerned about things like the presence of aliens in our classrooms (Green and Bigum 1993). Generation X books, such as those written by Douglas Coupland (1991, 1995, 1996, 2000), also provide the kind of verité descriptions educators can learn much from.

We welcome the growing body of work done by 'new literacies' insiders and see much value in bringing this work into the gamut of study of new literacies as an important 'data base' for dealing with educational issues at the interfaces of work, community, schools and homes.

Analytic

Different forms of analytic work are relevant to studying and documenting new literacies. Analytic tools from formal academic and scholarly work might be applied to the kinds of descriptive studies noted immediately above (remembering, of course, that such descriptive accounts will always and inescapably involve a degree of interpretation and analysis). This would involve taking the descriptions as a kind of 'secondary data' and making further 'sense' of it in various ways. At one level of analysis one might identify and relate the Discourse and discourse aspects of a set of social practices (i.e. the ways of speaking, acting, believing, thinking, etc. that signal one as a member of a particular Discourse, along with the 'language bits' of this Discourse; Gee 1996). At a different analytic level, the work might involve a form of sociological imagination (Mills 1959): exploring how subjectivity and identity are related to participation in or membership of Discourses in which new literacies are developed, employed, refined and transformed.

As an example of the kind of analytic work that might be done from the standpoint of sociological imagination we can take a case like David Bennahum's book, *Extra Life* (1998) that we mentioned earlier in this chapter. Grounded in Bennahum's experiences of growing up in a digitally saturated environment, *Extra Life* has been nicely described by Douglas Rushkoff as a '*Catcher in the Rye* for the Atari Generation'. Bennahum locates computers and computing practices within key phases and events in his adolescence and adult life in New York City. For example, a particular computer teacher, the computing classroom, and experiences within his computing classes emerge as pedagogical oases in the desert. There is more than a hint that Bennahum's interest in computing may have helped prevent him going down a road of delinquency and precocity that brought sticky ends to some of his adolescent peers.

Bennahum describes an array of Discourses to which he was apprenticed: for example, the Jewish faith, downtown Manhattan street culture, school- and home-based computer nerd culture, teenage sex and romance and, eventually, sophisticated forms of Discourse in cyberspace. From the analytic perspective of sociological imagination, the book provides, among other things, rich data for relating the emergence of a particular kind of symbolic analyst and knowledge worker and the kinds of subjectivity that support creating and maintaining a list like 'meme' to participation in various computing culture Discourses. When the links to Bennahum's 'meme' list and his home page are taken into account, it is possible to generate and reflect on a diverse range of ideas about how a stratum of the Atari generation builds networks, employs marketing strategies, maintains support systems and so on.

Bennahum is an author, cyber-activist, public intellectual, member of a cyberculture 'elite', and a symbolic analyst and knowledge worker of high order and standing. How Bennahum became an insider to particular Discourses, and how this afforded him various 'tracks' so far as access to peer groups, employment, and making his way within an emerging global order are concerned, offer some crucial insights for contemporary literacy educators.

With respect to the Discourse–discourse relationship, and a close focus on the language bits within larger social practices, the world of new literacies is rich, varied and easily accessed. We hint at some of the possibilities for investigation and reflection in our chapter on online ratings practices (see Chapter 6).

Critical–evaluative

Two types of critical–evaluative accounts of new literacies seem especially important in relation to literacy education – bearing in mind that, as the outcomes of the practice of *critique*, 'critical' accounts span the range from strongly positive or affirmative to strongly negative or condemnatory.

One type involves taking an ethical perspective toward new literacies, such that we can make *sound and fair* judgements that have educational relevance about the worth of particular new literacies and the legitimacy of their claims to places within formal literacy programmes. The matter of mindsets arises again here. Engaging in critique of new literacies should also be taken as an invitation to examine our own mindset as much as an invitation to judge a practice. The educational literature on practices involving new technologies and, more generally, on popular cultural practices is replete with what seem to us to be straightforward *dismissals* of new ways of doing and being from the standpoint of unquestioned outsider perspectives. Such critiques are more likely to obstruct than enable progress in curriculum and pedagogy. On the other hand, the kind of critique of the D/discourses involved in the design and production of a particular range of computing games provided in Allucquère Rosanne Stone's chapter on 'Cyberdämmerung at Wellspring Systems', in her book, *The War of Desire and Technology at the Close of the Mechanical Age* (1996), may be invaluable for literacy educators. Stone provides a stunning account of life inside an electronic games production sweatshop. The chapter disrupts concepts like 'symbolic analysis', presents a new line on what lies behind the text, and takes a sober look at the theme of gender and power in the world of new technologies.

The second kind of critique we have in mind involves taking a curriculum and pedagogy perspective based on the criterion of *efficacious learning*. From a sociocultural perspective,

> the focus of learning and education is not children, nor schools, but human lives seen as *trajectories* through multiple social practices in various social institutions. If learning is to be efficacious, then what a child or adult does *now* as a learner must be connected in meaningful and motivated ways with 'mature' (insider) versions of related social practices.
>
> (Gee *et al.* 1996: 4)

For literacy education to be soundly based, we *must* be able to demonstrate the efficacy of any and every literacy that is taught compulsorily. This, of course, immediately questions the basis of much, if not most, of what currently passes for literacy education. The criterion of efficacy applies very strongly to attempts to promote new literacies in classrooms. As we have argued elsewhere (Lankshear and Snyder 2000; Goodson *et al.* 2002), and will see again in specific cases in later chapters, efforts to incorporate new ICTs into language and literacy education are often misguided from the standpoint of efficacious learning. Often they enlist learners in characteristically 'schoolish' practices that have little or no present or future purchase on life outside the classroom.

In the following chapters we aim to provide accounts of new literacies and knowledge in the context of rapidly changing technological, economic, social, and cultural conditions that pay balanced attention to these descriptive, analytic and critical–evaluative facets of studying new literacies. We begin our pursuit of this aim in the next chapter, with a discussion of literacy, mindsets, and new technologies in schools.

CHAPTER 3

Atoms and Bits: Literacy and the Challenge of Mindsets

Introduction

At the present time schools and classrooms can be seen as a specific instance of a general phenomenon that involves a 'fracturing of space' and a striking divergence in mindsets (Lankshear and Bigum 1999: 457). The fracturing of space refers to the dramatic emergence and explosion of *cyberspace* as a distinctively new space that coexists with physical space. The divergence in mindsets is between those who, in various ways, continue to view the world from perspectives based on the constitution and mastery of the physical world, and those who approach the contemporary world as something that is inherently different from how it was before. The contemporary world *is* different, in ways that have a lot to do with the impact of the ongoing information technology revolution and a new informational or cyberspatial paradigm emerging with it (cf. Lankshear and Bigum 1999). In this chapter we look at some of the things that make the contemporary world significantly different from how it was even 30 years ago, and suggest a few points at which these differences impact on literacy education.

From atoms to bits

It is now becoming quite common to find books and articles about themes related to 'cyberspace' and drawing a distinction early on between 'atoms and bits' (e.g. Negroponte 1995; Gershenfeld 1999). These can be thought of as different kinds of 'stuff'. Atoms belong to the physical world we have always known, and to the world which can be captured in 'analogue' forms. Bits belong to the digital world. They are 'states of being' like 'on or off, true or false, up or down, in or out, black or white' which can be represented in binary code of 0s and 1s in a colourless, sizeless, weightless form that can be 'moved' at the speed of light (Negroponte 1995: 14).

We are used to dealing with atoms. Over the centuries humans have developed concepts, frameworks, laws, assumptions and procedures and so on for handling the myriad aspects of the physical world. Thinking in atomic terms has become a kind of 'baseline' in our conventional mindsets. Many things are changing, however, as our everyday environments become increasingly digitized. This invites us – indeed, *challenges* us – to develop new conceptual, belief and knowledge orientations and approaches to our everyday worlds.

In *Being Digital* (1995), Nicholas Negroponte gives the example of checking in at a place where he was asked if he had a laptop computer with him. He was asked how much it was worth (in case it was lost or stolen). Negroponte valued it at $1–2 million. The check-in person disputed the possibility of the machine having such a high value, and asked what kind it was. On being told she assigned it a $2000 value. Negroponte says this exchange reflects the distinction between atoms and bits as different kinds of stuff.

Not unreasonably, the person in the position of responsibility for property was thinking in terms of atoms, in the form of the physical computer. The laptop was atom stuff, of a particular make and vintage, and its value as such was $2000. Being 'digital' in his perspective on the world, Negroponte regarded the value of the machine almost entirely in terms of its 'bits'. That is, he thought of the machine in terms of its 'contents' in the form of ideas or patents potentials and the like that were 'contained' (even the language gets tricky) as binary code some'where' on the hard disk. Depending on what was on the disk at the time the value of the 'computer' could have been practically anything at all in dollar terms, not to mention in terms of potential human benefits and the like.

At a very simple level, this can be seen as an example of a divergence in mindsets that relates to the contemporary fracturing of space (cf. Wertheim 1999). To get a better sense of what is involved, it may be helpful to look at some historical aspects of the social, economic, cultural, and technological 'lives' of atoms and bits from the past 200 years.

Industrialism and informationalism: from steam to semiconductors

In the early 1970s, scholars like Daniel Bell (1974) and Alain Touraine (1974) began mapping contours of a qualitative shift they saw occurring from the paradigm of an industrial society toward the emergence of a paradigm of a postindustrial society based increasingly on information and oriented increasingly toward services. Postindustrialism emerges with a shift in the 'economic tilt' (Lyon 1988: 3) from manufacturing toward the provision of services. Within this context, more and more productive activity is underpinned by the application of scientific and technological knowledge and information, which is mediated by information technology. Knowledge and information increasingly displace labour and capital as the central variables in economic activity. Non-material, non-physical stuff moves to centre stage as the key factor in economic growth and wealth accumulation.

Twenty years after the publication of Bell's and Touraine's work, Manuel Castells (1996) described and explained the emergence of a new mode of development. Castells's work benefits from hindsight of the incredible explosion of applied theory and knowledge that has been realized in the form of digital electronic information and communications technologies and their applications. Castells describes what he calls the 'informational' mode of development – or, 'informationalism' – that has occurred in the context of 'the information technology revolution' (Castells 1996: Ch. 2). He distinguishes the *information technology* revolution from preceding *industrial* revolutions.

Drawing on work of historians of technology (e.g. Forbes 1958 and Mokyr 1990), Castells identifies two industrial revolutions during the eighteenth and nineteenth centuries. The first, during the latter part of the eighteenth century, was mainly characterized by the emergence of machines to replace hand tools, as well as by the invention of the steam engine, spinning machinery, and new processes in metallurgy. The second revolution, during the latter part of the nineteenth century, involved development of internal combustion engines, electricity, scientifically based chemicals, and the emergence of new communications technologies in the form of the telegraph and telephone (Castells 1996: 34). Castells identifies these as industrial *revolutions* in the sense that a sudden, unexpected surge of technological applications transformed the processes of production and distribution, created a flurry of new products, and shifted decisively the location of wealth and power in a planet that became suddenly under the reach of those countries and elites able to master the new techno system.

(Castells 1996: 35)

Notwithstanding the diverse array of new industrial technologies and inventions involved, Castells (1996: 38) identifies the 'fundamental innovations' in generating and distributing *energy* as comprising the heart of these industrial revolutions. Energy – *power* – was the process at the core of all industrial processes. Industrialism involved processes mediated by capital and by human labour that applied power to material resources. Initially this was steam power, followed later by electricity and nuclear power. Industrialism used power to apply mechanical processes to physical stuff that was moved physically through physical space. This was true even of aspects of industrial production, distribution and exchange that were less 'heavily' industrial. Castells notes, for example, that electricity was essential for connecting the new telephony and telegraphic communications technologies into large-scale systems that had wide reach.

The contemporary information technology revolution, however, has taken an inherently different form from its industrial predecessor. Castells (1996: 41–3) identifies transistors and semiconductors of increasingly microscopic construction as the key inventions at the heart of the information technology revolution. Information technologies are the contemporary equivalent of power within the industrial revolutions. There is a very important difference, however. As we have noted, within the industrial revolution the key inventions and technologies were applied to physical stuff. They operated mechanically within an environment of physical stuff. The applications of the defining inventions and technologies of the contemporary information technology revolution are quite different. New digital electronic technologies are being applied to *nonphysical* stuff: to ideas, information, theories, data, and so on. Moreover, these applications are being made within environments and via processes that are not usefully thought of in physical terms (at least, not first and foremost), even though physics – for example, electrical impulses travelling at the speed of light – *is* involved.

Applications and environments in the contemporary information technology revolution

This section looks in a little more detail at some key features of how defining technologies and inventions of the current information technology revolution are being applied. We will also briefly describe some of the main features of the environments in which these technologies are taken up and applied. By means of such descriptions the kinds of differences between spaces of *physical stuff*, on one hand, and *information* or *cyber* spaces on the other, and the relevance of these differences to the issue of mindsets, will become more apparent. We will address four key features here. There are many others, but those we take up here are sufficient for our purposes and are especially relevant to issues about literacy education.

The new technologies are applied in the first instance to what can broadly be termed 'information' which, as a catchall concept, covers 'data', 'ideas', 'images', 'symbols', and even 'theories'. The manipulation and analysis of symbols in various forms is playing an increasingly important role in the organization of work and in the enhancement of economic productivity. As levels of material production fall as a proportion of gross national product (GNP) within modern economies, levels of information processing production increase. Robert Reich (1992: 177) noted a decade ago that in advanced economies trade in 'data, words, oral and visual representations' is accounting for both an increased proportion of GNP and an increasing proportion of the workforce. Hence, as Castells notes, it is not simply that the new technologies are being applied to non-physical raw materials, in the form of information. It is also that 'information' in some form or other is to an increasing extent the *product* or outcome of the production process. 'To be more precise', says Castells (1996: 67), 'the products of new information technology industries are information processing devices *or information processing itself*' (our italics). With the addition of human action, the new technologies transform the *processes of information processing*. As information processing becomes increasingly networked electronically, it becomes more possible and easier to apply 'progress in technology, knowledge, and management to technology, knowledge, and management themselves . . . [in a] virtuous circle' (Castells 1996: 67). Of course, it is true that sooner or later these knowledge products in the form of new theories, new ideas, new representations of best practice and so on get applied to processes involving manipulation of physical stuff within processes designed to produce physical stuff. But it is the ideas and knowledge – the non-material outcomes – that are seen and treated as being the highest sources of added value, and the precondition of economic, social, and cultural progress.

The overall logic of the situation puts a higher and higher premium on metalevel processes and capacities. Knowledge work is now unquestionably regarded as the highest order of productive activity. This is activity and production that belongs to the non-material realm. It means, in short, that the most potent and valued forms of literacy will be – and in the foreseeable future will continue to be – those that tend toward the highest order manipulation of symbols to generate the 'data, words, oral and visual representations' Reich was referring to. There is an important point to note here so far as literacies, symbol manipulation and value are concerned. This is that the valuing of such metalevel productions and manipulations should not be seen simply in economic terms. We are currently well on the way into the maturation of a 'meta era' in which metalevel 'smarts' are valued across a wider front and are becoming increasingly the sources of status, prestige and other social goods (Gee 1991) in *non-economic* as well as economic terms. The Internet is a space that is actively employed by all kinds of people to peddle their symbolic manipulations of various kinds. There may not be a lot of economic return in, say, an Adbusters spoof, or a smart meme. But the social goods and potency that accrue on other terms (e.g. political mobilization, cultural transformation, the creation of communities around a idea) can be enormous and highly sought after.

Second, if we take 'cyberspace', broadly understood as the space of the Internet and innumerable intranets, servers and computers, to comprise the general environment of the information technology revolution, it is fair to say that we often find non-material and non-quantifiable values coming to the fore. This is prefigured in Castells's account of the different ends or performance principles around which technological processes are organized within industrialism and informationalism respectively. According to Castells, 'industrialism is oriented toward economic growth, that is, toward maximizing output' (1996: 17). By contrast,

> [i]nformationalism is oriented towards technological development, that is toward the accumulation of knowledge and towards higher levels of complexity in information processing. While higher levels of knowledge may normally result in higher levels of output per unit of input, it is the pursuit of knowledge and information that characterizes the technological production function under informationalism.
>
> Castells 1996: 17–18)

Similarly, a vast amount of activity in cyberspace is consciously directed toward non-material goals, and successful or satisfying participation identified in terms of qualitative values. Two different kinds of example will serve to indicate the scope of this point.

1 One concerns Sherry Turkle's (1995) studies of people's lives on the screen in spaces like MOOs and MUDs (Multi-Object Oriented Domains and Multi-User Domains). These online areas are dedicated to dialogues and chat among members and are organized into distinct topographical spaces like rooms, public areas like cafes and town squares, and, in some cases even entire worlds. Reflecting on Turkle's account, Margaret Wertheim (1999: 289) notes the extent to which 'cyberspace beckons as a place where they might build a better "life"' than they see as being likely for them in the physical domain of their lives. This, she observes, seems especially true for young people in so-called 'advanced' countries where many, if not most children born into middle class homes will fail to match their parents' living standards. For these children, cyberspace offers valued experiences of satisfactions and success. Not surprisingly, many young people invest a great deal of time, energy, and self there. Wertheim cites two of Turkle's subjects who identified MUDs (online chat spaces in the form of spatially structured multi-user 'dungeons' or domains) as offering them more than their material world. One stated in so few words that 'MUDs got me back into the middle class': not literally, of course, but, as Wertheim notes, in the sense that in his online MUD world 'he and his friends are energetic and productive cyber citizens' (Wertheim 1999: 289).

2 A different, but often-related angle on the non-material ends and values of much activity in cyberspace is provided by current interest in the Internet as a medium par excellence of attention flows, and as a space ideally constituted for attempts to gain and maintain attention. Michael Goldhaber (1997), among others (e.g. MacLeod 2000), has gone so far as to talk of an emerging attention economy within which the central scarce resource will be attention. The idea of an attention economy is premised on the fact that the human capacity to produce material things outstrips the net capacity to consume the things that are produced – such are the irrational contingencies of distribution. In this context, 'material needs at the level of creature comfort are fairly well satisfied for those in a position to demand them' (Goldhaber 1997: 1). For this powerful minority of the world's people, the need for attention becomes increasingly important, and increasingly the focus of their productive activity. According to Goldhaber, when our material desires are more or less satisfied, such that we do not feel pressures of scarcity (such as being

afraid of hunger or lack of shelter), we are driven increasingly by 'desires of a less strictly material kind'. Several such desires, he believes, converge toward a desire for attention. These include, for example, a desire for meaning in our lives. For many people a sense of meaning is bestowed by receiving attention from others. Goldhaber claims that people in postindustrial societies will increasingly live their lives in the spaces of the Internet, and that these lives will fall more and more under economic laws organic to this new space. Goldhaber (1997, 1998a) argues that the basis of the coming new economy will be attention and *not* information. Attention, unlike information, is inherently scarce. This, says Goldhaber (1998b: 1), is because 'each of us has only so much of it to give, and [attention] can only come from us – not machines, computers or anywhere else'. But like information, attention moves through the Net. Goldhaber identifies cyberspace as being where the attention economy will come into its own.

Third, Castells makes an important and interesting point relating to the application of new technologies that has far-reaching implications for the issue of mindsets as well as for issues pertaining to literacy education. He argues that new electronic ICTs are not simply *tools* (or technologies in the sense of material tools). They are also, and crucially, *processes* to be developed. This second sense gives us the idea of technologies in the sense of non-material *ways* of thinking, doing, being, organizing, believing, and so on. This is the idea of technologies as discursive modes and formations.

Castells's point has to do with the nature and role of knowledge and information within the current revolution. According to Castells, the information technology revolution and the emergence of a knowledge society are defined not so much by the centrality of knowledge and information – since new forms of knowledge and information are important in *all* such moments of major productive and developmental change. Rather, they are defined more by the way knowledge and information are applied to knowledge generation and information processing/communication devices. Castells refers here to a 'cumulative feedback loop between innovation and the uses of innovation' (1996: 32). He notes that since the 1970s

> the uses of telecommunications technologies have gone through three distinct stages: automation of tasks, experimentation of uses, reconfiguration of applications. In the first two stages technological innovation progressed through learning *by using* . . . In the third stage, the users learned technology *by doing* and ended up reconfiguring the networks, and finding new applications.
>
> (Castells 1996: 32)

Everyday diffusion of new technology amplifies its powers as it is appropriated and redefined by users through doing – which is what Castells means by identifying the new information technologies as processes to be developed as well as tools to be used. Successful new applications add economic and technological value, bestowing advantage and elite status on their inventors. This is because of the close relationship that now exists between creating and manipulating symbols (cultural activity) and the ability to produce goods and services (productive or economic activity). Within the contemporary context, then, elites learn by doing, not by using – where elites are construed as those who generate high-value additions. By the same token, users can *become* doers 'by taking control of technology, as in the case of the Internet' (Castells 1996: 32).

Fourth, two further and related points about the *environments* of the information technology revolution are worth nothing here. The first is that the virtual environment or domain of cyberspace seems to be practically limitless – capable of almost infinite expansion. Its growth is limited in physical terms only by the capacity to generate additional server space and bandwidth. To all intents and purposes these will constitute no significant limitation whatsoever in the foreseeable future. Cyberspace can and will continue to grow and grow. Hence, there is in theory and, foreseeably, in practice, 'room' for anyone and everyone to participate to the fullest extent of their interests and capabilities. That is, there appears to be no inherent self-limiting tendency in cyberspace. One person's 'being there' does not limit the capacity of being there for any other person in the ways that it can and does within certain kinds of physical environments where participation is keenly sought (such as labour markets, arable land, prestige golf courses, etc.). In the case of labour markets, for example, laws of supply and demand and institutionalized arrangements governing paid work operate in tandem with the finitude of physical resources and other dimensions of material possibility (e.g. limits to how much of a product can actually be consumed). Under these circumstances unemployment, underemployment, and forms of employment that underutilize people's productive capacities emerge as abiding conditions of labour within capitalism. Indeed, modes of production like capitalism can be seen as human inventions that have evolved in order to handle physical limits in ways that will produce certain kinds of outcomes (like profit, ownership, accumulation, and so on). It is true that under current and foreseeable conditions the growth of cyberspace sooner or later relates more or less directly to the operations of capitalism. There is no sign at present, however, that this relationship will tend toward limiting participation. Indeed, rapid steps are being taken to try and recruit as many people as quickly as possible to information space. The Internet certainly spawns all manner of elitisms and hierarchies and, as we will see in later chapters, practices that sort out those with soft skins from those whose skins are tougher. The 'endless room' available within virtual environments in theory and in practice, however, works against the principle of excluding people on the grounds that not everyone can be accommodated. There may be other grounds for wanting to exclude certain people and certain forms or levels of participation. But the capacity to accommodate all is not among these reasons. One person's full participation in cyberspace does not contradict the prospects for other people's full participation. For example, information is unlike physical resources, which, because they consume space, are finite. Information is not subject to scarcity laws. The fact that one person consumes a particular piece of information does not prevent another from using it. In the world of physical resources, however, the fact that one person consumes a resource often makes it unavailable for others.

The second point about the environments of the information technology revolution is that they tend toward endless proliferation of information. Information, of one kind and quality or another, grows unfettered at the speed of light and the pace of keystrokes. Much of this is 'private' information that is not intended to be publicly available. But even within the domain of information produced for public access, the amount of information coming at us makes it impossible to attend to it all and, often, even to all of that which is relevant to some interest we have defined and are following via specialized information services. Still less is it possible to deal with it as fully and as closely as we might want. Amid the exponential growth, far beyond saturation, of publicly available information, it is important that we be able to develop means and strategies for handling it in workable and effective ways.

The matter of mindsets

On the basis of the kinds of points we have spelled out in the previous section, a number of writers are arguing that different kinds of mindsets attach appropriately to physical spaces and virtual/cyber or information spaces respectively. They argue, in effect, that for the potential and integrity of new kinds of spaces to be realized as far as possible, and for human potential likewise to be optimally realized through participation in these new spaces, it is important that we adopt mindsets that are appropriate to these areas. In particular, these authors argue, it is important not to impose on a space some mindset that is appropriate to a different kind of space but not to this one. In this section we will consider some work that has been done on mindsets and related concepts, beginning with further elaboration of ideas advanced by John Perry Barlow, which we mentioned briefly in Chapter 2.

As we saw in the previous chapter, Barlow provides a basis for distinguishing between a general mindset that sees the contemporary world as being essentially the same as before, just more 'technologized', and a mindset that approaches the world as having changed fundamentally in important respects under the impact of the information revolution. Barlow points toward this general distinction by making three more specific distinctions of his own. Each of these is relevant to themes we develop in later chapters.

First, Barlow distinguishes between paradigms of value he sees operating in physical space and information/cyber space respectively. In physical space, says Barlow, controlled economics increases value by regulating scarcity. To take the case of diamonds, the value of diamonds is not a function of their degree of rarity or actual scarceness but, rather, of the fact that a single corporation owns most of them – and, hence, can regulate or control their scarcity. Within this paradigm, scarcity has value. We might note here how schools have traditionally operated to regulate scarcity of credentialled achievement – including allocations of literacy 'success'. This has maintained scarce 'supply' and, to that extent, high value for those achievements that are suitably credentialled. In the economy of cyberspace, however, the opposite holds. Barlow argues that with information it is familiarity, not scarcity, that has value. With information, 'it's dispersion that has the value, and it's not a commodity, it's a relationship and as in any relationship, the more that's going back and forth the higher the value of the relationship' (in Tunbridge 1995: 5). The implication here is that people who bring a scarcity model of value with them to cyberspace do not understand the new space and will act in ways that diminish rather than expand its potential. For example, applying certain excluding conditions to the use of information (e.g. copyright restrictions) may constrain the dispersal of that information in ways that undermine its capacity to provide a basis for *relationship*. This would in turn undermine the potential of that information to work as a catalyst for generating creative and productive conversations, the development of fruitful ideas, the emergence of effective networks, and so on. The kind of value Barlow sees as appropriate to cyberspace has to do with maximizing relationships, conversations, networks, and dispersal. Hence, to bring a model of value that 'belongs' to a different kind of space is inappropriate and creates an impediment to actualizing the new space.

Barlow's second distinction is between different ways of looking at well-known issues and concerns associated with cyberspace. He uses the now-aged examples of pornography on the Internet and Bill Gates's apparent manoeuvre to gain control of the Internet by bundling Microsoft Network with Windows 95/98. There are very different ways of looking at these concerns depending on whether one comes from the physical space–industrial mindset or from the alternative mindset associated with understanding cyberspace.

With respect to pornography on the Internet, Barlow rejects the imposition of gross filters. To begin with he believes ultimately they cannot work – because, he says, Netspace cannot be controlled in that way. The more elaborate the filter, the more elaborate will be the search to find ways around it, and the more powerful these resistances become. Barlow advocates more local and individualized filters that work on the principle of people taking responsibility for their choices and deciding what 'noise' they want to filter out. He reasons as follows:

> If you have concerns about your children looking at pornography the answer is not to eliminate pornography from the world, which will never happen; the answer is to raise them to find it as distasteful as you do.
>
> (Barlow in Tunbridge 1995: 5)

Similarly, with the fear of Microsoft controlling Netspace, the point is that the Internet 'is too complex for any one person or organization to create the software for it' (Barlow in Tunbridge 1995: 5). Barlow claims that software development will continue to be organic, to be shared and dispersed. Short-term domains of control and influence will undoubtedly exist, but they cannot become total or monopolistic – due to the very nature of the space. The growing popularity of non-commercial resources like the Linux line of shareware provides an ongoing case in point.

Barlow's third distinction is the one we emphasized in Chapter 2. It is between people who have been born into and have grown up within the context of cyberspace, on one hand, and those who come to this new world from the standpoint of a lifelong socialization in physical space, on the other. We will refer here to the former as 'insiders' and the latter as 'outsider–newcomers'. This distinction marks off those who 'understand the Internet, virtual concepts and the IT world generally' from those who do not: that is, it distinguishes mindsets (Barlow in Tunbridge 1995: 5). Newcomers to cyberspace don't have the experiences, history, and resources available to draw on that insiders have. And so, to that extent, they cannot understand the space as insiders do. Barlow believes this distinction falls very much along age lines. He says that, generally speaking, people over the age of 25 [in 1995] are outsider-newcomers. Conversely, 'if you're under 25 you're closer to being an [insider], in terms of understanding what it [i.e. the Internet, virtual concepts and the IT world generally] is and having a real basic sense of it (Barlow in Tunbridge, 1995: 5). In short, then, Barlow is suggesting that without the appropriate mindset people will, and do, approach the tools and environments of the new technological revolution in inappropriate ways. Moreover, he believes that in the current context, legions of 'outsiders' ('immigrants') are doing precisely that.

From a more conventionally academic and scholarly standpoint, Richard Lanham (1994) looks at very different ways of approaching what we might call data space. He is especially concerned with the question of strategies for dealing with vast volumes of data. An address to a conference of librarians provided a context for Lanham to explore different ways of thinking about electronic data and how to manage it. While he does not explicitly refer to these different kinds of approaches as different *mindsets*, his ideas can usefully be understood as such. We will look at Lanham's ideas in greater depth in Chapter 5 on the theme of attention economics. For immediate purposes a brief overview of his position will suffice.

Lanham approaches the issue of how to deal with vast amounts of data via the concept of attention. He sees attention as being the key to managing data flows productively, but notes that attention is an increasingly scarce resource. Indeed, he identifies attention as the most precious resource in what he calls an *economy* of attention. This is where differences in mindsets emerge. Lanham describes attention as a non-material (or what he calls 'immaterial') resource. When the most precious resource is non-material, however, 'the economic doctrines, social structures, and political systems that evolved in a world devoted to the service of matter become rapidly ill-suited to cope with the new situation' (Wriston cited in Lanham 1994: 1). In a manner reminiscent of Barlow, among others (cf. Goldhaber 1997), Lanham insists that we cannot continue to apply concepts, laws, practices and the like that were developed to deal with the economic world of goods to the emerging economic world of information.

Lanham provides examples from the world of librarians of points at which it is necessary to abandon concepts and practices developed to deal with the material economic world of goods and to develop and apply different 'concepts, laws and practices' to the world of information. He argues, for example, that a theory of communication grounded in the world of material 'stuff' simply will not do under present and foreseeable conditions. He argues that a theory of communication based on stuff has 'spatial' and 'style and expression' characteristics that will not work in data space.

A theory of communication based on stuff presupposes a model of simple exchange, whereby a package of thought and feeling is transferred from one body and place to another or others. In the case of librarians, their past role was to lend out books as a means of 'facilitating thinking done elsewhere' (Lanham 1994: 1). In the words of one of Lanham's correspondents, this is a role of 'maintaining the signifiers, and leaving the decryption of the signifieds to the readers' (Lanham 1994: 1). Lanham disagrees wholeheartedly. On the contrary, he says, in the world of superabundant information thinking requires access to what he calls 'attention structures'. These help us attend to the floods of information as data that we face. The problem is that in the midst of massive data flows we may not always have the time or know-how to construct the kinds of 'human-attention structures' that would render data useful to us in the various spheres of our lives. An expert and specialized role emerges of developing attention structures that will present data to consumers in ways that help them identify where and how this data will be useful to them, and how to use it to serve their purposes.

Lanham believes that librarians are among those whose role in the information age is, at least in part, to help develop attention structures that others (in this case, those who use library resources) can employ in order to turn information made available by librarians into something they can use beneficially. According to Lanham, librarians and libraries find themselves in the middle of a world where thinking involves generating attention structures. Librarians who continue to cling to the old role will miss the point of their vocation in the information age. To date, says Lanham, most seem to have done precisely that. Libraries – especially academic libraries – have mainly limited themselves thus far to developing online 'hubs' that contain everything from password-accessed article services through to lists of free online journals and useful search engines.

With respect to style and expression, says Lanham, the communication paradigm from the world of stuff employs a 'Clarity–Brevity–Sincerity' style of prose and expression (1994: 1). Lanham argues that this model no longer applies. With respect to style and expression the logic of the transaction within an economy of attention is no longer 'simply the rationalist market . . . beloved by the economists of stuff' (Lanham 1994: 1). Rather, people bring with them to the free market of ideas 'a complex calculus of pleasure' and 'make all kinds of purchases' (Lanham 1994: 1). Those who produce the kinds of resources available in libraries (and elsewhere) need to identify and employ new forms and modes of style and expression to meet the demands of a changing market. This aspect goes to the heart of new literacies, where exponents of memes, adbusts, and the like were among the earliest to have seen the point.

Finally, it is useful to consider how some of the most influential 'movers and shakers' operating on the Internet and in information spaces more generally manifest a broad mindset that exemplifies Castells's idea of 'elites' who innovate by 'doing' in ways that 'reconfigure the networks', and who otherwise 'take control of the technology' and 'find new applications'. Jeff Bezos, founder of Amazon.com, provides a good example here. Robert Spector's (2000) account of the creation and rise of Amazon.com provides some interesting insights into how Bezos thinks about information space and how to 'live' there. Spector describes how Bezos was wanting to establish the kind of enterprise that Amazon.com has since become, and had made it known to corporate headhunters that he wished 'to hook up with a technology company, where he could chase his real passion [of] "second-phase" automation' (2000: 16).

Bezos describes second-phase automation as 'the common theme that has run through my life' (cited in Spector 2000: 16). By first-phase automation, Bezos means 'where you use technology to do the same old . . . processes, but just faster and more efficiently'. Within the e-commerce field barcode scanners and point-of-sale systems would be typical examples of first-phase automation. In such cases, the e-commerce enterprise would be using the Internet to do 'the same process you've always done, but just more efficiently' (Spector 2000: 16).

First-phase automation was not of interest to Bezos. He wanted to do more than simply transfer life as it is done in a physical space to the online world of the Internet. Instead, he prefers to think in terms of second-phase automation. This is 'when you can fundamentally change the underlying . . . process' – in his case, a business process – 'and do things in a completely new way'. For Bezos, second-phase information is 'more of a revolution instead of an evolution' (Spector 2000: 16).

To a large extent, buying a book on Amazon.com *is* a qualitatively different experience from buying a book in a conventional store. For example, Amazon invites consumers to reconstitute themselves in certain ways. Each webpage for each book has space for readers to post reviews of the book, an evaluation rating scale for readers to post their rating of the book, and a facility for readers to say whether they found a particular review useful (and the same holds for all other items sold through Amazon.com, such as music CDs, movies, electronic components, kitchenware, etc.). To this extent, consumers are being invited *also* to become critics, reviewers or commentators. The practice of inviting reader/user-consumers to submit reviews can be seen as part of Amazon.com's suite of strategies for encouraging customers to buy as much product as possible. Amazon.com goes so far as to offer cash prizes to customers who write the first customer review for certain listed books and the other products sold through Amazon.com.

So far as the book side of its operation is concerned, Amazon's mission is 'to use the Internet to transform book buying into the fastest, easiest, and most enjoyable shopping experience possible' (Amazon.com 2002: 1). In line with this the company also supplies a rating for each item based on customer evaluations and a ranking number that indicates how well the book is doing in sales from the website in comparison with other books. Amazon.com also recommends books you might like, based on your previous purchases or on information you have provided, and offers an alerting service to let you know when new books are available, using key-words you key into the service sign-up form.

In Chapter 6 we will look at another enterprise, eBay.com, which has also aimed to project online commercial transactions into a qualitatively different cultural space from that of conventional transactions. In terms of the mindsets behind them, examples like Amazon.com and eBay stand out starkly from examples of e-commerce that have simply replicated concepts and practices from the physical commercial world to online environments. The latter may, of course, serve short-term bottom-line purposes very well, and to say that a company has engaged only in first-phase automation on the Internet is not to condemn it. It is, however, to say that it has been content to approach the online world as simply a technologized extension of the physical world.

The challenge of mindsets for literacy education

In this chapter so far we have briefly described some of the differences recognized by leading researchers and scholars as existing between the paradigms of the industrial revolution and the information technology revolution. These paradigms generate qualitatively different *modus operandi* and conceptual schemes that support different kinds of worldviews, social and cultural practices, subjectivities and so on. In the current conjuncture, new technologies are associated in complex ways with new ways of organizing human activities in economic, cultural, political and social spheres. They are associated with the emergence of new kinds of relationships, new kinds of experiences and conceptions of space and time, and the like. The new world that is emerging is, however, approached and understood, and responded to, in very different ways and from very different perspectives by different people.

Besides briefly describing some aspects of difference between the two paradigms and their respective 'worlds', we have offered brief sketches of broadly competing mindsets brought to bear on the contemporary world. We acknowledge that the notion of 'mindsets' we are employing is a crude and rather blunt instrument, and that mindsets themselves are much more intricate, complex, multiple and subtle than our overview of them here suggests. By the same token, we believe that the same blunt instrument we are employing is nonetheless a fruitful heuristic device for thinking about literacy and literacy education under contemporary conditions. We think it is also useful for thinking about how literacy education is itself thought about by different people. If a blunt and crude tool has potential and serves a useful purpose it can always be sharpened and further refined to make it more sophisticated and effective. The point is to have something useful and usable to start with. That is what we have aimed to provide here: nothing more; but at the same time, nothing less.

We want now to put our accounts of the 'worlds' of 'atoms and bits' and contending mindsets to work on aspects of literacy and literacy education. Clearly, the situation is not one of either/or options: adopt one mindset or another. We are witnesses to a fracturing of space, not a displacement of one space by another. The challenge is how to live in physical space and, to an increasing extent, in cyberspace and the datasphere. A sound education will cater to both, and will do so in informed and principled ways.

In the remainder of the chapter we draw on the ideas advanced above to look at some key themes in literacy education in ways that illustrate the kinds of things that are at stake between different mindsets. We begin by considering some ideas advanced by Chris Bigum and Colin Lankshear about how a range of patterns and principles derived from empirical study of computer uses in literacy education mean very different things from the standpoint of different mindsets (see Lankshear and Bigum 1999). Following this we will look at some implications of our argument for the themes of 'relevance', 'access', and 'marginality' in the context of literacy education.

Reading principles across mindsets

During 1996–97 a team of researchers from four Australian states conducted a government-funded study of literacy, technology, and learning.

This included empirical investigation in 20 classrooms from 11 partici-pating schools within three states (Lankshear *et al.* 1997; Lankshear and Bigum 1999; Lankshear and Snyder 2000). Data analysis and findings from the study gravitated around three major issues. The first concerned the situation of teachers with little experience of new technologies trying to integrate them efficiently and meaningfully into classroom practices when they lacked experience of efficient meaningful uses in their own lives. The second concerned the uneven involvement of teachers within individual schools in efforts to integrate new technologies into learning. As a result, students would have rich experiences one year with no follow-up the next. Finally, there was an issue of the kind of things being done with the new technologies in the classrooms. In terms of the 3D model of literacy described in Chapter 1, much learning involving new technologies operated on merely one dimension, exhausted by a focus on operational aspects to the exclusion of cultural and critical dimensions. Moreover, from the perspective of the concept of efficacious learning noted in the previous chapter, many of the uses made of new technologies in the sites appeared odd, mys-terious, and 'unreal'. There were many instances of characteristically schoolish practices, unhinged from mature or insider versions of social practices in the world beyond school. Finally, the study found many cases of the 'old wine in new bottles' syndrome. Teachers, not surprisingly, seemed often to be looking for technological applications that fitted their pedagogical styles and, more generally, with classroom business as usual.

The original study (Lankshear *et al.* 1997) advanced four preliminary principles the team believed should guide further developments in efforts to integrate new technologies into classroom learning: 'teachers first', 'complementarity', 'workability' and 'equity' (cf. Bigum and Kenway 1998). In subsequent reflection on these principles, two of the original team members briefly considered how these principles could be read in very different ways from 'outsider–newcomer' and 'insider' mindsets respectively (Lankshear and Bigum 1999). We will illustrate the kinds of different readings from the two mindsets by reference to the principles of 'teachers first' and 'workability'.

'Teachers first' asserts the need to address teachers' needs in learning new technologies, and their relationship to language and literacy *even before* addressing the needs of students. For teachers to make sound edu-cational choices about using new technologies in classroom practices they must *first* know how to use them (and any benefits of doing so) for their own authentic purposes. Teachers need support in making use of new tech-nologies to enhance their personal work before learning to use them in their teaching.

Affirming that teachers need to be put first flows directly from the insider mindset (that is, it involves the idea of teachers becoming 'insiders' to practices, as far as possible and as quickly as possible). It is easy, however, for the intent of this principle to be subverted. This may occur by developing practices that *appear* to put teachers first, but that in fact are short-term professional development activities designed in such ways that they will put teachers into classrooms with improved technological skills and understandings, yet *within the confines of a newcomer–outsider worldview*. Within 'systems thinking' it seems to be assumed that having 'put teachers first' for a time (the duration of professional development support) the problems of teaching about and with new information and communications technologies (ICTs) are thereby solved.

From an insider perspective this can never be so. Even if it *were* somehow possible, it would not be desirable. An insider perspective emphasizes the importance of addressing the ongoing needs of teachers, but at the same time points to the importance of developing new kinds of alignments, and associations between outsiders and insiders. Traces of such inclinations were evident in some of the study sites. Typically, however, the larger constraints of schooling based upon a traditional outsider mindset – such as the teacher being the ultimate authority – render such practices fragile and, usually, ineffectual in the long run.

The principle of 'workability' builds on the crucial criterion for implementing any new technology within educational settings – does it improve the teaching and learning cycle? It requires that the use of any hardware or software improves, helps, or supports the work of teachers or students, and affirms the work of teachers and students as a priority in deciding whether or not to adopt a given technology. Any adoption of new technology requires a principled approach that acknowledges the actual costs involved in taking it on.

More than 25 years ago Joseph Weizenbaum ([1976] 1984) wrote persuasively about the dangers of using computers to do things solely on the basis that they *can be done* using a computer. Weizenbaum distinguished between computing 'cans' and computing 'oughts'. This involves the idea that applying computers to a task is a *moral* issue that should *not* be determined essentially on grounds of *efficiency*. From an outsider perspective workability is almost entirely a matter of efficiency. It is very much more than this to insiders, however. From an insider perspective 'workability' also includes a sense of elegance, beauty (Bennahum 1998; Gelernter 1998), appropriateness and other criteria, which newcomers may see at best dimly when they look in from outside. The two broad mindsets – insider and outsider – yield two quite different notions of workability.

From the kind of new literacies perspective we are advancing here, and as Bigum and Lankshear argue, the test for teachers is not so much whether the computer can do the job. Rather, it is about the extent to which the practice *includes* the sensibilities of insiders (in this case, 'savvy' learners). This is not easy, and is always confounded by prevailing views that teachers, schools, adults, parents, and systems 'know what is best'. In our terms here, this is 'outsider' ideology perpetuated in the interests of outsiders. Against this, we would endorse the idea that 'for perhaps the first time in human history, new technologies have amplified the capacities and skills of the young to such an extent that many conventional assumptions about curriculum [and pedagogy] become inappropriate' (Lankshear and Bigum 1999: 460).

Relevance, access and marginality: some implications of the argument

The ideas we have argued for in this chapter have implications for how we understand and address issues of 'relevance', 'access' and 'marginality' in literacy education. We will consider some examples here, drawing particularly on the notion of contending mindsets and on recent research in which we have been involved.

Relevance

We will consider three aspects of relevance here.

First, in terms of Lanham's arguments we may need to think beyond our current conceptions of orientations and techniques within literacy education for dealing with information. At present, so far as literacy educators consider approaches to handling information at all, this is largely limited to various versions of critical literacy and (often-vague) notions of information literacy. These are important aspects of literacy education and merit continued development. Often, however, they betray versions of the outsider mindset. Hence, future work should aim to reconstitute them in ways that build on insider perspectives. At the same time, we need to recognize, with Lanham (1994), that before we even get to organizing, managing, and critiquing information, we must increasingly have *structures* available to us for attending to information in the first place. We may be so deluged by information that attending to *any* of it becomes burdensome.

There are at least three sides to the issue of attention structures. As *producers* or *disseminators* of information we may stand a better chance of having others attend to our information if we can 'house' it within effective attention structures. As *brokers* or *mediators* of information, as in the case of Lanham's librarians, we can facilitate attention on the part of consumers of information produced by others by developing effective attention structures for presenting it. To date literacy researchers and educators know little about what this involves, although some of Lanham's examples provide places from which to start conceptualizing the work to be done. Finally, as *users* or *consumers* of information we need to know how to recognize, create, and work with ready-made attention structures. To some extent Amazon.com's book ratings system functions as an attention structure. So does the facility provided on the webpage for each book that identifies other authors whose books were purchased by buyers of the book on that page. Likewise, the system of ratings for buyers and sellers participating in the eBay.com community (see Chapter 6) might be seen as a kind of attention structure. Knowing (how) to use ratings in order to make informed eBay transactions is a key element of participation. To what extent and how they should deal with such things as eBay-like rating systems and other kinds of attention structures within classroom learning is an issue literacy educators will have to face in the years ahead when considering what is relevant to literacy education.

Second, it is hard to escape the conclusion that school literacy has been used, and continues to be used, as a powerful mechanism for mediating the supply and demand of social goods. Throughout the period of mass schooling, literacy has evolved as a medium for excluding certain people from particular kinds of opportunities and options, and for helping to legitimate such exclusion. In settings where 'the good life' has been associated so closely with the capacity to consume material commodities and services, constructions of school literacy have worked very effectively to help structure, legitimate, and explain unequal access to and distribution of social goods. School constructions of literacy built on particular interest-serving notions of what is relevant have effectively excluded entire groups of people from full participation in school routines and reward systems, defined many students as remedial (hence, unworthy), and blocked paths to all manner of future opportunities. They have done this by defining literacy in terms of criteria, genres, tastes, standards and so on, which systematically privilege a minority of class/language/ethnicity (and, some would add, gender) -specific groups, and disadvantage others. These criteria, tastes, genres, and standards have defined what is (and is not) *relevant* in school literacy education.

While there have never been just grounds for constructions of school literacy that favour particular groups, there *has* been a kind of (wretched) coherence in how they operate. The most prized material goods available for distribution are finite. It is in the interests of social order and peaceful acceptance of differential allocations of social goods that they should appear to be legitimate. As part of a credentials system linked to allocations of social goods, constructions of school literacies have been an important and integral element of elaborate mechanisms that simultaneously exclude and purport to legitimate that exclusion. While literacies that exclude may have their peculiar coherence in 'meatspace', the underlying grounds for this coherence do not apply in cyberspace. In fact, the opposite is the case. In cyberspace, 'spaces' for full and rewarding participation are virtually infinite, and they beg inclusion. To a large extent, the kinds of criteria used in school literacy to define relevance (and thereby serve to label, exclude, and to privilege and marginalize) do not apply to the social practices of cyberspace. Participation can be peer aided, can find its way around faulty spelling, can lean heavily on use of icons, sound/audio, graphics, and so on. Pronunciation need not be an issue. Moreover, it is rare to encounter youngsters who wanted to, but could not, find their way around video games and other pursuits no less demanding than what is required for successful participation in all manner of personally rewarding practices on the Internet and in other digitized domains (Howard 1998; Gee forthcoming).

A 'will to inclusivity' is evident within insider constructions of cyberspace. Moreover, involvement in virtual communities has proven capacity to afford rewarding and satisfying personal benefits ranging from incomes to companionship to senses of personal success and adequacy. Such considerations encourage us to consider relevance in literacy education from a mindset like that attributed by Barlow to insiders ('natives'), rather than the outsider ('immigrant') mindset that continues to dominate contemporary education policy and literacy education. The potential of such an approach, and some of the advantages it may have, was brought home to us powerfully in a recent intervention study in which we were involved (see Rowan *et al.* 2002).

This study was framed as a preliminary attempt to develop an approach to curriculum and pedagogy informed by applying Barlow's distinctions to the notion of mindsets. It was intended to explore possibilities for counteracting disadvantage in literacy education by undertaking small-scale teaching and learning projects involving the use of new ICTs. These were designed in ways markedly different to conventional classroom approaches.

- Learning groups were conceived as small 'clusters'. A cluster would ideally contain four to six students identified by the school as being disadvantaged in some way, a teacher, a teacher in training, and one or two cultural workers from the community who had a demonstrated supportive orientation toward young people. This structuring was designed to maximize both a mix of 'outsider' and 'insider' mindsets and the prospects of members negotiating across mindsets.
- Learning sessions were to take place outside school hours and outside the designated curriculum, although on school sites.
- The learning activity was to comprise a previously undetermined project, which would be conceptualized and undertaken collaboratively within the cluster and completed in 20 hours of face-to-face activity within a semester (with as much work done between sessions as participants were motivated to do). The clusters would begin 'from scratch'. The only parameters would be to come up with a collaborative task involving new ICTs, to which all participants were committed, to which all felt they could contribute, from which all felt they could learn, and which would produce some kind of 'literacy-related' outcome.

One of the four sites that comprised the overall study spoke powerfully to the issue of relevance in literacy education. This was the Yanga Headlands State High School site, which provides the focus in Chapter 8 (see also Rowan *et al.* 2002). In this site the English coordinator and school vice-principal, Lucy, who became the teacher participant, invited four 14-year-old male students (all Year 9) to participate. Their subject teachers regarded all four as 'trouble', and as having significant problems with literacy. At the time of the intervention, they had been excluded from their regular English class and were being taught by Lucy as a small group, doing projects on things they were interested in. They had recently worked on producing a magazine based on their shared interest in motorcycles. The boys concurred in their teachers' appraisals of them, and in interviews and conversation gave numerous examples of their disruptive behaviour in class. At the start of the project each expressed negative opinions of his abilities with respect to literacy and classroom learning generally.

The other members of the cluster (Lucy, two academics involved in conceptualizing the project, a student teacher and a research assistant) provided an open and supportive collegial environment. The group decided to collaborate on building a website about motorcycles. Only one member of the group (an academic) had previous expertise with webpage construction. During the project the students mastered basic concepts and tools of webpage design and construction. They admitted to having previously been dismissed from a keyboarding class where they 'played up' over being required 'to just tap, tap, tap at keys'. They also admitted they had been barred from using the school computers to access the Internet for 'breaking the rules'. Amidst fears about pornography, school duty of care, accountability requirements and so on, the school had instigated a 'licence' system to regulate student use of the Internet. The rules the boys had broken were conditions for obtaining and keeping their 'licence'.

At the conclusion of the project all four agreed willingly to serve as peer tutors to teach what they had learned to their classmates in regular class lessons (at the start of the project they had flatly refused to be involved in any such programme of peer instruction). They developed a strategy for doing this that would match availability of machines to class times and sizes. Some of the Web work they produced for the project was very good in conceptual, technical and aesthetic terms. Possibly of greater interest was the considerable evidence that emerged incidentally during the sessions of their literacies and literacy-related knowledge (see Chapter 8). These included unprompted displays of very sound understandings of copyright regulations, the importance of context in writing, diverse functions of the Internet and its relationship to everyday social practices and the importance of webpages being fast-loading in order to 'hold people's attention'. One student, Jarrod, made this comment in the context of advising the others not to put too many pictures onto each page. He grasped what matters on the Internet, where speed is everything (Johnson 1997) and attention the goal (Goldhaber 1997).

With regard to relevance in literacy education, this study reminded us that schools have always traded on their capacity to provide students with literacy skills necessary for contemporary living. Schools argue that they are best placed to teach students about where and how to give their attention to what is worth knowing. If this has ever been true, it must surely now be in serious doubt. At present schools demonstrably do *not* teach effectively, or even seriously promote, many of the literacy skills and understandings students need in their lives *now and in the future*. One consequence of this is continued exclusion, failing, and negative labelling of very many students who, in fact, have abundant control of language uses needed for negotiating the spaces in which they will spend much of their time. More problematically, forms of curriculum irrelevance and associated exclusion locks many such students out of subsequent opportunities to acquire literacies involved in diverse practices they could choose to participate and excel in, given the option.

Third, although we have touched briefly in this chapter on the economics of attention in relation to literacy by reference to Richard Lanham's work, there are other relevant perspectives on the emergence of an attention economy. This wider area of concern about the economics of attention has important and far-reaching implications for relevance in literacy education. We will deal at length with the theme of the attention economy and new literacies in Chapter 5. In anticipation of this we merely note here that some views of what will be required to participate effectively in an attention economy imply that a range of new literacies *not currently addressed by schools* are likely to become especially valuable. These include some of the new literacies briefly described in the previous chapter: notably, 'multimediating', 'meme-ing', 'e-zining' and 'culture jamming'. They also include other new literacies that are addressed in subsequent chapters: for example, what we call 'contact displaying', 'scenariating', 'transferring attention', and 'framing and encapsulating' (see Chapter 5). The importance of these and other new literacies may well and truly eclipse much of what we have hitherto considered most important to an effective literacy education.

Access

With respect to literacies involving new technologies, access may have less to do with physical availability of computing hardware and software than is commonly assumed from the standpoint of mindsets constituted under the regime of physical space (where access readily implies access to material things). A second site (Marshall State School) from the literacy, technology and disadvantage project that included Yanga Headlands provides some helpful correctives here.

Marshall is a relatively new and rapidly growing elementary school in an expanding middle and upper middle class suburb in the capital city of an Australian state. Sixty per cent of the school families are formally designated 'upper middle class'. At the time of the study (1999) the school had recently installed 12 state of the art Pentium II PCs to serve staff and student computing purposes in a designated space adjacent to the library – which became the space used in the study. The computers were all connected on an Ethernet LAN to a powerful server running the then latest version of Windows NT. The computers were loaded with standard applications including word processing and basic graphics/desktop publishing software. The server included a CD-ROM stack, so students could access data-based CD-ROMs (notably Microsoft resources like *Encarta*, *Dangerous Creatures* and *Minibeasts*). Control of the server, computer and network was invested in a full-time teacher aide based in the library.

The server was located in a room adjacent to the main library. This was kept locked during the project sessions. Education Queensland was the service provider for the school's Internet connection. Despite this wealth of digital technologies, however, student access to the computers and the Internet was extremely limited and tightly regulated. Students could access only 'preselected' or what the school called 'supervised' websites. These comprised sites carefully screened by teachers or the librarian, and which they had then downloaded and saved onto the network server. Students then accessed that website via the server; in other words, the computer was not actually online when these students visited each pre-downloaded website, which in turn meant that many of the hyperlinks in any given text would not work because they required access to other online websites. This also meant that 'web surfing' or using Internet search engines could not be done by students.

Teacher access to the Internet was less restricted, however few – if any – teachers appeared to make use of the Internet services at school. Emphasis in the school appeared to be on passive 'browsing' and closely circumscribed information gathering by students. Interviews revealed that many students in the class from which the student participants were selected (and, indeed, students of the school at large) had Internet access at home. Interview data also indicated that there was a very low level of operational/technical knowledge of computers among the staff and the librarian disliked and resented the computers, claiming they were taking over her library and turning it into a lab.

The four students in the cluster came from Years 5 and 6. During the process of negotiating weekend access for the project, the Principal had made it clear that he wanted the group to produce a school website. After the project had been negotiated, availability of the school space and equipment for the project was limited to two weekends. This permitted only about half the number of hours originally envisaged for the activities. To the researchers the school-computing ethos represented an almost extreme caricature of Barlow's 'outsider' mindset perspective. The study offered up some revealing insights into the issue of access. One especially telling vignette involving Caleb, one of the Year 6 students in the study, shows how processes and practices grounded in constraints imposed from an outsider mindset can actually undermine insider knowledge which could otherwise have been used to support effective learning.

Caleb enjoyed home access to the Internet. He regularly emailed his cousin, Mitchell, and would join him in the Yahoo chat space on the Internet (chat.yahoo.com). Caleb knew such things as how to 'ping' (his use of the term) someone in a chat space so that the message becomes private and no one in the space other than the intended recipient can read it. Besides his facility with popular digital communications applications like email and chat, Caleb knew how to follow hyperlinks and locate websites from Uniform Resource Locators (URLs). He also had a 'feel' for the logic of URLs. However, he was much less familiar with strategies for locating information, like the use of search engines. He had not learned how to do this at home. More significantly, the tight surveillance of the Internet at school and the artificial process of 'web searching' actively withheld constructive usable opportunities to become proficient with information searching. Caleb told one of the researchers how he went to use the Internet for a project on medieval times. He recounted how he keyed what he thought seemed a likely URL – www.medieval.com.au – into the 'go to' space of his Internet browser. But he received back the message 'Your URL could not be retrieved'. He gave up at that point, telling the researcher that 'it didn't work' because there must not be any information about medieval times on the Internet, and that he had not subsequently tried to use the Internet for school project purposes.

From an outsider mindset access is about availability of hardware and software – particularly under 'safe' conditions. When viewed from an insider perspective on access, the kind of practices promoted at the resource-rich Marshall State School contributed to counterproductive effects. Implementing control over 'safe conditions' in accord with an outsider mindset contributed to *undermining* access as understood from an insider perspective. From the latter, access is about being able to get at authentic spaces and uses, and being able to actualize the power of the technologies and use them for doing well what they can be used to do well. In the Marshall case, the school practice unwittingly subverted 'insider-like' knowledge (to get information you key in a URL, rather than use an online search engine). As we have seen, Caleb was already a proficient and enthusiastic user of online chat space and email for authentic personal purposes. Moreover, he also had home access to the Internet, which he could have used to search for schoolwork-related information. All he needed was a basic introduction to search engines and online surfing. The school had tacitly withheld this, while inadvertently communicating a misleading experience of how to access information.

(Dis)advantage and marginality

The previous vignette also indicates how we may need to rethink aspects of advantage and disadvantage in literacy education in a context where learners will increasingly have insider-like knowledge of new literacies and social practices associated with digital technologies. Subjecting students to mystifying or inefficient uses of new ICTs in classrooms may actually *disadvantage* (e.g. by confusing them, alienating them, etc.) learners who have previously acquired a degree of knowledge and mastery of relevant applications in other settings.

From the opposite standpoint, it is often argued that there is a case to be made in equity terms for incorporating new ICTs into classroom learning in order to provide opportunities for students who lack alternative opportunities to use new technologies. While this idea may be sound *in principle*, its intent will be undermined if student learning opportunities are hostaged to outsider mindsets and minimalist applications of hardware, software, and peripherals. As Castells reminds us, elites learn by doing. To be provided, compulsorily, with opportunities that are constrained to being a user (and, in all likelihood, a user confined to 'schoolish' uses and/or the minimal standard 'packaged' uses touted by producers) may do little or nothing to promote the interests of designated equity groups.

One implication is to provide learners with opportunities for learning by *doing*, in Castells's sense. This means at least two things. First, it means allowing students to learn how to get the most out of new ICTs within contexts of 'high-end' social practices; for example, conducting research and other forms of symbolic manipulation and analysis within contexts offering access to genuine expertise. This will call for reconfiguring *schools* and their relationships to their communities, not merely reconfiguring literacy education (Bigum *et al.* in process). Second, it means allowing students maximum space to *experiment* with new ICTs in ways that are conducive to working out new kinds of things they could be used for and new kinds of adaptations. This may require schools to enter partnerships with individuals and agencies that can enable these things under suitable conditions, and will doubtless entail some risks. Here again, we might profit from starting to try and understand what is at stake across different mindsets. We should be wary of administrations and political 'visions' that burden schools with fears of students accessing vicious websites while gutting the curriculum of the kinds of learning opportunities that look beyond 'values' like efficiency, performativity and cost-benefit maximization, and toward the kind of personal development advocated by Barlow. Such 'outsider' logic will always privilege 'gross filters' over educational opportunities for young people to learn how and why to find distasteful things distasteful (to the extent that they truly are). Of course, were young people to have such opportunities, efficiency, performativity, cost-benefit maximization and the like might well become early casualties.

Our argument from competing mindsets suggests new ways of thinking about marginalization besides those we have properly become accustomed to in relation to social, economic, and cultural inequities. We must now also take seriously the idea that the sensitivities of very many young people who are 'insiders' to Discourses associated with having grown up within (and *only* within) the contemporary information technology revolution can be marginalized when formal learning is dominated by outsider mindsets. As we will see in the next chapter, a disturbing example of this is provided by the ongoing implementation in Britain of a National Grid for Learning.

PART 2

Staring at the Future

CHAPTER 4

Faking It: The National Grid for Learning

When is 'new'?

We began this book with a working concept of 'new' in relation to literacies. This was based on three ideas. We referred to these respectively as 'paradigmatic', 'ontological' and 'chronological' senses of 'the new'. Subsequently, however, we have used the idea of competing mindsets to distinguish broadly different approaches to social practices mediated by new ICTs. At the most general level these mindsets can be described as different orientations toward the contemporary world. One mindset affirms the world as the same as before, only more technologized; the other affirms the world as radically different, precisely because of the operation of new technologies. Some variations around this broad distinction were entertained in Chapter 2. One of these was the distinction Jeff Bezos draws between first- and second-phase automation. First-phase automation involves using new technologies to do old processes more quickly and efficiently, whereas second-phase automation involves fundamentally changing the underlying process of an existing practice and, instead, doing things in a new way.

Such ideas introduce a complication to the working concept with which we began. Specifically, to what extent do we want to call a new literacy *new* if it still bears the stamp of an outsider mindset and/or essentially replicates old textual practices through the medium of new technologies? If an activity comprises 'classroom writing as always done', except that now we are using a computer, then in Bezos's terms it is basically the same practice. If, further, we consider literacies from a sociocultural perspective as always being embedded in social practices, we might reasonably ask whether a literacy can be new in any significant sense if the practice remains the same ('old'). We might regard it as an extant literacy but with a new gadget added on. Certainly, our usual meaning of 'add on' in relation to educational processes intimates that nothing significantly new has occurred.

Personally, we are less concerned with whatever the answer to this question might be than we are with the issue of what is at stake educationally when the question is posed. This chapter will try to illustrate what is at stake by looking at the creation in Britain of a National Grid for Learning.

Introduction to the National Grid for Learning

Britain's National Grid for Learning 'opened for business' in late 1999 as a 'government initiative [designed] to help learners and educators in the UK to benefit from information and communications technology' (BECTa 2001a: 1). The Grid comprises a 'vital part of government commitment to creating a connected learning society in which learning is increasingly accessible and adapted to individual needs' (BECTa 2001a: 1). According to Prime Minister Tony Blair,

> Not only will digital technologies become a normal part of everyday life, but Britain's international competitiveness will increasingly depend on the way in which we adopt them. Used well, they have the potential to improve achievement in our schools and colleges, to boost the prospects of British industry and commerce, to offer opportunities to all learners and particularly to those who would otherwise be excluded, and significantly to enhance our quality of life. In parallel, the Government is investing very substantial new resources in a programme to raise standards in schools and increase opportunities in lifelong learning. The National Grid for Learning will play a crucial part in this process.
>
> (Blair 1999: 1)

Policy aspirations are that the Grid will help raise education standards by providing teachers, students and education institutions with access to information and communications technologies (ICTs). Although this chapter will focus on the Grid in relation to school-age users, it has a much wider brief than formal education alone. Key targeted user groups include teachers and students from primary schools, secondary schools and tertiary education, industry personnel, communities, and people involved in lifelong learning.

The Grid comprises computer hardware, software and peripherals, Internet connections and local area networking hardware and software. The British government had consigned more than £650 million to support Grid development up to 2002, and as of mid-2001 had pledged a further £710 million for 2003–04 (Heller *et al.* 2001: 1). Expenditure covers physically equipping schools, colleges, libraries and community centres with computers and Internet connections, providing Internet-based content, and enabling teachers and lecturers to access professional development resources. By late 2001, computers in UK schools totalled almost 1.1 million at an average of 34 desktop computers per school – although 25 per cent of these computers are identified as being 'ineffective for curriculum use' (BESA 2001: 1). By 2002, according to government estimates, almost all schools in the UK now have Internet access, with an average of 75 per cent of computers in each school linked to the Internet. In these schools almost half the students use the Internet daily (BESA 2001: 1).

Government hopes the Grid will offer four key resources to support school-based learning. These are highly interactive, global, and well-informed learning activities for in-class use; indices and links to 'worldwide sources and data' to support homework; information services (e.g. parental access to general school information); and chat space for teachers to share teaching ideas and experiences (Blair 1997). Design and development of the main website for the Grid – the National Grid for Learning 'portal' – has been assigned to the British Educational Communications and Technology Agency, known as BECTa (www.becta.org.uk). BECTa's other responsibilities include monitoring Grid use and safety, and coordinating diverse input and services from public and private bodies, organizations and individuals. As of March 2002, no readily accessible information based on sustained research was available on the effectiveness of using the Grid in school contexts. BECTa has begun assembling reports of research relevant to evaluating the Grid as a learning resource (BECTa 2002a), but to date no substantive investigation of classroom use of the Grid has been reported and assessment of school-related computer use at home has been superficial at best. Most of the studies reported have been general surveys of a quantitative nature as distinct from attempts to evaluate the quality of learning as impacted by the Grid (see, for example, BECTa 2002b).

At the same time, some scholars have expressed early reservations about the capacity of the Grid to match the hype and expense invested in it with expansive and enriched learning opportunities, let alone on an equitable basis (e.g., Selwyn 1999, 2000a, 2000b; Ruth *et al.* 2000). Indeed, in arguments that prefigure some of the lines we will develop here, Neil Selwyn and colleagues argue that the policies shaping the Grid's ongoing development and implementation continue to be housed within 'a restrictive technocratic and determinist discourse of the "technical fix" ' (Selwyn *et al.* 2001: 225), and examine the Grid's role in 'extending and reinforcing existing power configurations in education' (Selwyn 2000b: 243).

The Grid today

Between September 2001 and March 2002 we documented some key elements of the Grid relevant to classroom learning. After describing the front page of the portal, we will focus on some offerings for early years literacy, as well as on the GridClub and Grid Safety pages. These provide especially revealing insights into what the National Grid for Learning *means* for school education during the primary or elementary school years.

The Grid portal is arranged according to three specific, cross-referenced and user-targeted categories: 'WHAT are you looking for?', 'WHERE are you?' and 'WHO are you?' (see Figure 4.1 below). The 'What' category presents a menu of hyperlinks organized into subcategories that include: 'Learning Resources', 'Games & Quizzes', 'Lesson Plans & Worksheets', 'Subscription Services', 'Reference Material', 'Libraries & Archives', 'Museums & Galleries', 'Government Information', 'Advice', 'Learning Opportunities', 'Jobs' and 'On-line Purchasing'.

The 'Who?' link on the front page of the Grid portal takes the user to a menu of subcategories that include: 'Children', 'Parents', 'Teachers', 'Students', 'Lecturers', 'Adult Learners', 'Community Support', and 'Managers & Governors' (NGfL 2002a: 1). The 'Children' subcategory comprises a list of websites ranked according to target age ranges. The age ranges used on the Grid portal are: 0–7, 7–11, 11–14, 14–16 and 16+. Recommended websites include online tutorials and quizzes in all school subject areas, online museums (e.g. information pertaining to Ancient Egypt, online art and archaeology museums), online information sites (e.g. data pertaining to the UK government), the BBC education pages, and suchlike.

The 'Where' button takes the user to a clickable map of the United Kingdom plus a menu of hyperlinks to information relevant to users in Scotland, Wales and Ireland, as well as to the nine regions in England. The map or menu can be used to 'find resources that are relevant to your region, such as community grids for learning, local projects, museums or libraries' (NGfL 2002b: 1). Each member country and each region of England is responsible for developing a section of the National Grid for Learning specific to its cultures, populations, contexts and school systems, in accordance with rules, regulations and visions set down by the UK government. Community groups and schools may contribute content to the Grid, along with commercial content providers who span regions and countries. Each of these 12 geographical categories is subdivided into menus of links pertaining to national sites, community grids, libraries and archives, and museums and galleries.

As shown in Figure 4.1, the front page of the Grid portal website is divided into three columns. The first contains two sets of menus. One comprises the three main organizing devices (What?, Where?, and Who?). The

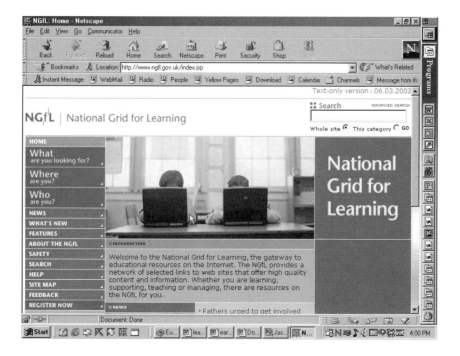

Figure 4.1 Portal for National Grid for Learning
Source: www.ngfl.gov.uk

other set focuses on information that supports the Grid itself. This includes a link to a News section containing education-related news items (e.g. a story on fathers being encouraged to become more involved in their sons' education). Other sections include a 'What's New' link showcasing websites recently added to the Grid network; a 'Features' link concerned with current events in the academic year (e.g. exam and exam revision), and that regularly features the favourite websites of different teachers and schools; a link to background information on the Grid itself; a link to a Grid network search engine service; a 'Help' section; a site map link that takes the user to a hyperlinked list of Grid portal categories and sub-categories; provision for user feedback on the Grid portal and network content; and a link to that portion of the Grid concerned with establishing clear guidelines as to what counts as safe and proper practice within the Grid.

The centre column is devoted to content listing. This generally comprises hyperlinks to websites that form part of the overall Grid network (which extends far beyond the actual portal website). These content lists vary according to which category and subcategory the user is accessing. The remaining column provides related links to content in the 'What's New' and 'News' sections of the Grid portal. At the time of writing, the right hand column within the 'Children' subcategory of 'Who are you?' listed links to a meningitis information website, a new Roald Dahl website, and a news item about students performing mystery plays in a cathedral.

For a more detailed sense of the Grid, we will now describe some key features of the websites specifically devoted to learners themselves and to issues of safety and propriety in the Grid.

Early years literacy

By clicking on the 'Children' subcategory of the 'Who are you?' link on the front page, users can select between resources aimed at children under 11 years in age and at children aged 11 to 14 years respectively. The under-11 sub-category menu contains eight options: 'Early Years', 'Art & Music', 'English', 'Health & Wellbeing', 'History & Geography', 'Maths', 'Science' and 'Sports, Clubs & Hobbies' (NGfL 2002c: 1). At the time of writing, the 'Early Years' section contains 25 links to websites within the Grid network. At the time of writing, only four of the 25 showcased sites from the Grid portal can reasonably be identified as aiming directly at a young audience and containing content that may readily be accessed and used by youngsters. These are *Buses of Sunnydown Garage* (www.

sunnydownbuses.com), *Let's Discover* (www.letsdiscover.org.uk), *Channel 4Learning* (www.channel4.com/learning), and *Early Birds Music* (www. earlybirdsmusic.com). Of these, only the first three are relevant to our focus on children's literacy.

We will consider here some typical resources identified as suitable for children in the 'up to 7-years-old' age grouping within the early years section on the portal, and analyse what parents and teachers are likely to encounter in their initial forays to locate material suitable for young children to use. Most activities for young children on Grid-endorsed websites fall into one or other of two categories: namely, *print-and-complete* or *click-and-action* exercises. The former involve printing out online worksheets for children to complete offline. Typical tasks include matching objects, spotting differences between two similar images, tracing over or joining dotted lines, cutting out shapes, categorizing functions (e.g. 'Which of these fly?' or 'What sound do I make?'), and hand colouring outline images. For example, the *Channel 4Learning* site (Channel 4Learning 2002a) preschool section largely comprises print-and-complete tasks linked thematically by reference to muppet characters from *The Hoobs* television programme for preschoolers. These activities generally require adult intervention to explain what to do (by reading activity suggestions accessed via an 'ideas' button). Hence, the 'What would you call these things?' page (Channel 4Learning 2002b) presents young users with four 'fantasy' animals that need identifying names (see Figure 4.2) and instructs parents or caregivers to have the child 'invent new words for fantasy things' (Channel 4Learning 2002c: 1).

It is difficult to imagine young children working on their own intuiting the goal of this activity. This locks them into a form of dependency on adults at odds with learning to become independent users of the Internet. The activity in Figure 4.2 is a typical example of what is available for young children on this website, and the additional suggested activities associated with this worksheet underscore the website's assumption that children and parents will sit and work together at the computer. These activities include:

- Make up some new words to the last line of a familiar nursery rhyme and say it to your child, e.g.:

  Jack and Jill went up the hill
  To fetch a pail of water
  Jack fell down and broke his crown
  And Jill was filled with laughter.

Figure 4.2 Printable activity example (image produced by Sheila Fraser and designed by Lucy Mackenzie for SFTV on behalf of 4Learning)
Source: www.channel4.com/learning/microsites/H/Hoobs/activities/108_activity. shtml

See if your child notices the difference! Perhaps they could also make up their own last line.

• Let your child enjoy saying some long words, for example the names of dinosaurs. Find some dinosaur books in the library and help your child to say their names.

(Channel 4Learning 2002d: 1)

Such activities are linked to a set of educational aims that straddle Channel 4's television and Internet-based endeavours. These aims have been derived directly from the Early Learning Goals set down for the Foundation stage of the UK government's National Curriculum for children aged 3 to 5+ years (see Qualifications and Curriculum Authority 2000). These goals promote 'Knowledge and Understanding of the World', 'Mathematics Development', 'Emotional, Personal and Social Development',

'Communication and Language', 'Expressive and Aesthetic Development', and 'Physical Development and Movement'. The suite of activities associated with Figure 4.2 is intended to deal with 'communication and language' and 'expressive and aesthetic development' aims. This is a troubling prospect indeed. Such activities appear to be desperate afterthoughts that are at most tenuously linked with the original worksheet.

The second category of prevalent activities on Grid-endorsed sites is what we call 'click and action' activities. These involve children clicking on an item or pressing a key on the keyboard in order to complete a task (which generally brings about some kind of 'active' response on the screen). Typical examples are found on the *Let's Discover* website. Developed by the Museum for Children, Halifax, in collaboration with a multimedia company, the site aims at being a 'one-stop resource for adults to plan and prepare curriculum-driven visits for children aged 3–8' (Eureka! and Publitek New Media Limited 2001a: 1). It offers a teaching idea archive and provides six 'clickable' learning games (their term) for children to complete: three related to reading and writing, two to maths and one to 'healthy eating'.

The website aims to make learning fun, and claims that

the on-line activities will ensure more enthusiastic, productive and stimulating visits to museums and galleries. The varied content will encourage children to explore and investigate subjects for themselves, building not only academic knowledge but also self-esteem and confidence.

(Eureka! and Publitek New Media Limited 2001b: 1)

Yet, all the literacy-related activities require only low-level responses from youngsters. For example, the first literacy activity invites children to key a letter. An image of something whose name begins with the keyed letter appears on the screen (e.g. 'A' will produce an apple). This is followed by the name of the item (e.g. 'apple') which slowly appears letter by letter. A range of related sound effects accompanies this sequence, and simple animations accompany most images. There is no active 'game' dimension to this exercise. The letter formation 'activity' is even less cognitively demanding. Here too, children are invited to press a letter on the keyboard. The letter appears in the nationally approved beginner's handwriting script on a screen ruled up to look like a beginner's handwriting workbook. The letter is blue, and a red dot slowly traces over the letter in black – using the correct entries and exits, directions and retracings as taught at school. A full set of printable letter formation practice sheets is also available on this website.

The sentence formation activity begins with an image of a young boy 'standing' on a blue background. Beneath is the word 'Jesp', and to the right is a short list of highlighted, clickable verbs (e.g. jumps, sings, laughs, sleeps). Clicking on a verb removes the highlighting and places it next to the word 'Jesp'. Unselected verbs disappear and a list of prepositions appears to the right of the verb. Selecting a preposition brings up a list of nouns and articles (e.g. the house, the garden). Selecting a noun sets a simple animation in motion that has Jesp carry out the task described in the now-finished sentence. 'Jesp sings under the house' has an animation of Jesp standing beneath the image of a brick-red house, with musical notes streaming from his open mouth. Interestingly, there is no accompanying audiofile that 'reads' the sentence for the child, although Jesp sings 'When you're happy and you know it' whenever a sentence containing the word 'sings' has been constructed. Neither is there a function enabling children to add vocabulary or images of their own to the exercise. Some of the sentences are awkward rather than humorous and risk sending the wrong message about what counts as a 'good' sentence (e.g. 'Jesp laughs on the house', 'Jesp sings over the house', 'Jesp sings under the garden'). Indeed, the activity is little more than a series of digital worksheets with very little to recommend it as 'making learning fun' or 'building not only academic knowledge but also self-esteem and confidence' (Eureka! and Publitek New Media Limited 2001b: 1).

One of the very few Early Years websites hyperlinked to the Grid portal clearly intended for younger children to use more or less unassisted by adults is *Buses of Sunnydown Garage* (Arber 2001). This site is organized around an 'automotive' motif, and presents a series of narratives about a community of buses that live in and work out of Sunnydown Bus Station. Some of these are click and advance stories where readers click on hyperlinks to move from one frame or page to another – in the manner of slideshow presentations. There are 13 stories about these (anthropomorphized) buses. Five stories are described by the author as interactive. The eight non-interactive (or what the author calls 'for reading') stories each involve a single webpage of text, with hand drawn and coloured illustrations located at strategic points throughout the story. The interactive stories are generally a sequence of static hand-drawn and hand-coloured images – although some do have simple animation (e.g. flashing police lights). A caption-like sentence or two accompanies each image, and the reader advances the story by clicking on the 'forward' hyperlink in the bottom right-hand corner of the page. The 'for reading' stories contain much more print than pictures, while the reverse is true for the click-and-advance stories.

While the overall do-it-yourself feel to the website is appealing, the stories resemble many basal reader texts in terms of strange or oversimplified sentence constructions, simple storylines, illustrations that add little or nothing to the meaning of the written text, awkward chronology and so on. Most of the 'interactive' stories have associated 'literacy activities' as well. For example, a story about a bus named Geoff comes with a retelling exercise. Four pictures from the story are presented in the order in which they appeared and users are instructed to retell the story in their own words. Other exercises employ printable worksheets associated with specific school subject areas. For example, in addition to the retelling exercise (which is also printable), the activities associated with 'literacy' include a story sequencing activity worksheet and a story prompt worksheet that comprises a difficult to decipher picture – especially when printed out – and ruled lines for writing on.

GridClub

GridClub (2002) is one of the very few websites dedicated to learners themselves. Most topics on Grid-endorsed sites are addressed to teachers, governors/managers and parents. GridClub pitches at learners aged 7–11, and is introduced as being fun, safe, and 'designed for kids to use at *home* or school' (2001a; original emphasis). The GridClub grew out of a government and media company initiative to encourage the development of 'exciting, dynamic facilities' (DfEE 1999: 2). It was envisaged from the outset as 'an interactive facility for young learners combining broadcasting, the Internet and other powerful learning resources which will be fun to use and help young people to succeed in homework, examinations or simply discover more about the world' (DfEE 1999: 2), and lauded as an exemplary website for children to use (cf. Holder 2001). Promotion on the website claims that every effort has been made by GridClub creators to engage children in this age range by using cartoons and online games, and by encouraging their own hobbies and special interests outside school. Teachers have designed all the interactive games, ideas and activities on the GridClub site. These address Key Stage 2 of the National Curriculum. The GridClub site currently has three main areas. 'Have a Go' and the 'Look it Up' reference section are open to anyone. The third area comprises the clubs themselves. These are open only to children aged 7–11, and children can join only through their schools.

'Have a Go' contains literally hundreds of activities and exercises related to National Curriculum subjects (e.g. pertaining to scientific principles of angle and force) (GridClub 2001b). 'Look it Up' includes an online dictionary, thesaurus, and 'clickable' atlas. *Homework High* (2001) is a recent addition to this reference section. It is organized according to secondary-school subject areas. *Homework High* is sponsored by Learn.co.uk – a commercial online index to teaching resources. Each area in this section allows students to post a homework-related question. These are responded to by 'resident experts'. Within the English subject section the following questions posted by readers were typical during the period we sampled from the site (*Homework High* 2001: 1):

- I have a 700–1000 word essay to write about *Great Expectations*. I need to know what to write about for the question 'What changes do you see Pip go through up to chapter 19?' I need to write about various different types of change and give references to them in the book. I have been told that chapter 19 in particular is a significant chapter concerning change. Thank you for your help.
- Is Philip Larkin essentially pessimistic? Help Please!!!!!!!!
- What is a proscenium arch stage?
- Hi I have to write a story on Harry Potter. Can you help?
- I have got my year 10 english exam on friday and was wondering if you could give me any info on this poem and short story: 'Telephone Conversation' by Wole Soyinka.

Questions and answers are archived and searchable. Each subject section also includes a chat service.

Restrictions on access to the clubs section of the GridClub website make it difficult to describe the individual clubs in close detail (GridClub 2001c). Clubs include Outdoor Adventure, Animals, On the Move, Collectors, Sports and Football, among others. Some clubs, like Outdoor Adventure, appear mainly to be for chatting about activities and interests. Others, like the Animals Club, provide members with information on a range of topics relevant to the club. They also include games on their website, and give members opportunities to interact online about their shared specific interests in what are labelled 'mini-clubs' (e.g. saddle club, dinosaur club). Each club is overseen by 'grown up club leaders' (GridClub 2001c: 1).

A tension exists between the formal purpose of GridClub and much of what we could find on the site. GridClub's purpose is to provide young students with online spaces to pursue their own interests. It seems, however, that much of the site is dedicated to 'learning activities' that are constructed in characteristically 'school-like' ways. The 'Tell Tales' (or subject English) category within the 'Have a Go' section of the website is a case in point. The 'Owl stories' – promoted as 'four great stories to keep you amused' (GridClub 2001d) and connected with the Literacy Hour initiative – are really drill-and-skill activities in narrative guise. The first of the four Owl stories, *Ozzie Takes a Ride* (Oz New Media 2001), aims at Year 3 students. The text itself is reminiscent of slideshows, with one fixed backdrop following on from the other in a linear, sequential manner. Although some of the images involve simple animation, the interface looks and feels like a teacher-made resource, rather than a slick, seamless, attention-grabbing production such as those found in, for example, Dorling Kindersley or Bröderbund CD-ROMs.

Ozzie Takes a Ride never misses an opportunity to create 'teachable moments'. A typical example occurs when Ozzie the cat and Archie the dog are playing badminton. As the shuttlecock is hit between the two players, it first sails over the clothesline 'net' with a big smile on its face, saying 'happy'. The next screen shows the same shuttlecock flying back over the net with a frown and saying 'unhappy'. The following screen seizes the moment by asking: 'Did you see what happened when *un-* was added to *happy*? The word *unhappy* was created, which is the opposite, or antonym, of *happy*' (original emphases; Oz New Media 2001: no page). This is repeated for the 'dis-' prefix. At this point, the 'story' becomes an exercise in making the antonyms of a given set of words by clicking on the appropriate 'un-' or 'dis-' prefix. It then moves onto a classifying activity, followed by an exercise requiring the student to distinguish between examples of rhymes and cinquains. Next follows an exercise on using the table of contents in a book to 'zero in on' needed information. This is followed in turn by a brief history of bone collecting, and so on. The narrative 'glue' holding the drills together is, at best, thin.

Safety and propriety in the Grid

BECTa has been assigned the task of establishing clear guidelines as to what counts as safe and proper practice within the Grid. Two main roles are involved. One is to define, monitor and, so far as possible, exercise control over acceptable content generated by schools, local councils, commercial ventures and so on within Grid-linked sites. The other involves providing guides to appropriate use of Grid content. This partly consists of explaining intellectual property rights and guides to 'fair use' of content found on the Grid (many Grid-linked sites have been built and are maintained by commercial outfits averse to plagiarism). Beyond this, the concern with propriety has been extended imposing conceptions of appropriate practice in a wider and more invasive sense (see below).

To pursue these ends, BECTa has produced an information website known as *Superhighway Safety* (BECTa 2001). Britain's Minister for Early

Years and School Standards, Catherine Ashton, outlines the mission to be served by the site and its services as follows:

> This Government wants everyone to have access to the wealth of cultural, scientific and intellectual material to be found on the Internet. But we are equally determined to ensure that students are protected from unsuitable material and that we all use the equipment we have properly. We all share a responsibility to make sure that students' use of the Internet is appropriate and safe.
>
> (Ashton 2002: 1)

With respect to protecting learners from 'unsuitable material' on the Internet several responses have been made. One is Gridwatch (2001). This details 'a vision for the roles and responsibilities of teachers, parents and students' when using the Grid (DfES c.2001: 8; Ashton 2002: 1). Gridwatch is a service for reporting unsuitable material encountered on the Grid, as well as for users to offer feedback on the quality, currency and accuracy of information available on Grid-linked sites. Other safety measures are promoted as well:

- 'Walled gardens'. This is a paid subscription service that 'offers subscribers access to collections of pre-selected Web sites. Walled Gardens offer the highest form of control and protection against users intentionally or inadvertently accessing inappropriate material' (DfES c.2001: 3).
- Filtering and site-blocking software. These software programs search for potentially unsavoury words in webpage and email texts and block access to email or websites where they are found.
- Usage tracking software. This enables teachers to 'track' the websites students have visited or tried to visit.
- Firewalls. These are programs that sit on a network and block or control entry to and exit from areas they are protecting.
- 'User contracts with children' (Ashton 2002: 1) and signed 'codes of conduct' for all learners. Users under 18 years of age need to have their signed codes of conduct countersigned by caregivers (DfES c.2001: 1).
- Impressing on students the importance of never giving out their personal details (name, age, address, etc.) in their emails or online chat.

The Superhighway Safety site also lists diverse non-Grid websites dealing with the safety of children on the Internet for teachers and parents to read, and presents examples of what its creators regard as excellent practice. Denbigh School offers a typical case.

> Denbigh School, a technology college for 12- to 18-year-olds in Milton Keynes, uses an Internet filtering system to prevent students from

accessing inappropriate web sites – and not just those that might feature sex or violence. 'No football sites are allowed either,' says deputy head Chris Woods. 'Otherwise the kids would just waste time.'

(DfES c.2001: 13)

Elaborate measures are described and recommended for promoting and maintaining propriety in a wider sense. *Superhighway Safety* urges 'regular checks by teachers of incoming and outgoing [e]mail [that] will reveal cases of inappropriate use' (DfES c.2001: 5), and suggests teachers should 'often monitor chat spaces, remotely and in person' (DfES c.2001: 20). It also strongly advises schools to include automatic disclaimers at the end of each email sent by students in order to protect the school. It further suggests that 'schools may want to restrict some pupils to using internal email only, whilst providing others with greater access' (DfES c.2001: 5). A range of information is disseminated to teachers on a regular basis, urging caution and the direct teaching of (social) rule-governed technology use. Email has been particularly targeted in terms of safety concerns and measures. BECTa and the DfES discuss email use predominately in terms of emailing 'partner schools', thereby implying a norm for practice. BECTa has also produced a seven-page information sheet, *Using Email in Classroom Projects at Key Stage 2* (BECTa 2001b). Besides listing what email offers to teaching and learning and providing practical application suggestions, the sheet encourages whole-class discussion to consider the 'pleasures and pitfalls of e-mail' and to establish 'ground rules for e-mail use' (BECTa 2001b: 1). It goes on to say that these rules should include an understanding of the following points (BECTa 2001b: 2):

- Language use in e-mail should be appropriate for a general audience. E-mail should be available to be read by the entire class and both teachers [of the partnered classes]. E-mail is not a private medium.
- Names or pen names must be included on each e-mail sent, and the e-mail should be addressed to a specific recipient in the partner class.
- Responsibility for who will check mailboxes should be established.
- It is necessary to decide whether e-mail should be stored electronically and where, or whether e-mail should be printed out and, if so, where copies should go.
- There should be sanctions if the rules are broken, and that the rules and sanctions are in place to protect and support people in both [partner] schools.

The *Superhighway Safety* website (BECTa 2001c) provides a number of examples, like the following, of what these rules look like in practice.

Ambleside Primary School in Cumbria, which was highly commended in this year's ICT in Practice Awards, provides one e-mail address for each class. Teaching staff believe this improves security, making it easier to supervise children and that the lack of individual addresses has not hindered pupils from making full use of the Internet on a variety of online projects such as communicating with individual penpals from around the world, contributing to the school's award-winning website, and whole classes working with classes at schools in other countries.

The school has developed its own set of rules to ensure the privacy and safety of pupils when using e-mail, the Internet and the World Wide Web.

These rules stipulate that children are not allowed to engage in conversation or dialogue with others on the Internet without per-mission or supervision from their teacher. All e-mails to classes are moderated by the class teacher.

Children are also taught never to reveal personal details, such as home addresses and telephone numbers, when they are communicating with other Internet users. If they ever receive a message that makes them feel uncomfortable or upset, they are told to report it to a teacher.

As a further precaution, downloading of files is restricted to staff (or children under supervision) and children have no access to newsgroups.

Any other school that wishes to obtain an individual class or staff e-mail address must first contact Ambleside's ICT co-ordinator.

Parents are encouraged to take similar precautions and invest in security software when using the Internet at home with their children.

Ambleside's Internet service provider (ISP) is Schoolzone which offers a variety of packages and security features including filtering.

Figure 4.3 Pupils using email at Ambleside Primary School, Cumbria
Source: DfES (c.2001: 16)

Assessing the Grid

Our choices of material to convey a sense of the Grid have been as fair and representative as possible. It is impossible for a brief descriptive overview to paint a comprehensive picture. Even so, the picture conveyed by our data resonates strongly with examples that abound in research-based accounts of Internet practices in classrooms and of typical government initiatives to promote Internet-enhanced learning opportunities. We are confident that the aspects described in this chapter are indicative of a general mindset to be discussed in the following sections under three broad headings.

- The language of the Grid's creators.
- Potential for counterproductive outcomes.
- Risks of promoting non-efficacious learning.

Two brief comments are warranted before taking up this discussion. First, it is clear that the Grid is ripe for sustained research, but that to date little has been published in the way of substantive evaluation and critique. Second, as with policy critique and similar activities, we are mindful that what is advocated is by no means necessarily what occurs in practice. For example, teachers who are 'insiders' will be able to find their way around many of the issues and concerns we address in the sections that follow. Such teachers will be able to find ways to extend trust to students around pursuits like emailing and Internet browsing that minimize the risk of those stereotypical dangers imagined by those who drive *Superhighway Safety* actually occurring. David Bennahum's (1998) account of his computing teacher, Mr Moran, is an outstanding portrayal of how the time-worn stereotypical 'worries' of the Gridmeisters can be transcended by teachers who have sound and informed pedagogical understandings and a working knowledge of new ICTs. Unfortunately, we cannot presume such teachers to be the norm. By the same token, we despair at the thought of teachers coming to classroom uses of new technologies being saddled with the kind of mindset that pervades the official view of the Grid. While the policies, recommendations, guidelines and information sheets peddled by the Grid establishment do not necessarily issue in practice that conforms to the letter, they certainly *do* create a powerful ideological representation of Internet learning uses, and all such representations exercise constraining effects at the level of practice.

The language of the Grid's creators

The language used by Grid personnel is replete with talk of 'policing', 'protection', 'controlling' and the like. This spells trouble for expansive educational visions. It begins with the very name 'Grid'. Grids are uniform. They imprint patterns of regularly spaced horizontal and vertical lines forming enclosed squares. The idea of a learning grid evokes notions of regularity, uniformity, boxes and cells, the imposition of order on a space, and the desirability of being able to *fix* something – or somebody – in relation to particular points or norms.

Sadly, there is some coherence here. This is what *learning itself* becomes like when mapped out as a national curriculum. Key learning stages and designated standards become encoded as a system so that regiments of functionarios can check student after student against criteria from which efficiency measures can be calculated and compared in the name of performativity (Lyotard 1984). The Grid is neatly matched to the lock steps of standards-based instruction, where 'delivering learning content' simultaneously becomes pretext and context for an administration to demonstrate fiscal accountability by showing how standards get met with ever-increasing efficiency. This alienates learning – turning it away from authentic engagement with the world in ways that can actualize human powers. Learning becomes a process of wearing a path through regular and regulated points in a grid. To the extent that teachers and learners do not *actively* resist the lines being closely mapped out for them when education is constituted as a site of performativity, learning literally becomes gridlocked.

The same mindset that produces the notion of a 'grid' in the first place is evident also in the free and unapologetic references to 'policing' and 'protecting' that pepper the webpages concerned with safety and propriety on the Grid. BECTa acknowledges that a major part of its role involves 'helping to police content' (BECTa 2001a: 1–2). Unfortunately, 'policing' is the right word. Take, for example, the scope and nature of the kind of ground rules for using email proposed by BECTa. Even on a conservative assessment, these are draconian. They make sense only on a basis of presuming that learners have delinquent proclivities that need intense surveillance and to be subjected to random checks.

The language of recommended ground rules for emailing in school is precisely the language of policing, surveillance and presumed delinquency or aberrance: 'random checking', 'restrictions', 'rules and sanctions', 'supervision', 'security' and so on. Here it is worth recalling the direction pointed by the example of excellent practice of using filters to prevent students accessing inappropriate sites noted above. In the hands of outsiders, 'inappropriate sites' quickly come to refer not simply to sites that feature sex and/or violence, but to *football* sites as well. (Gauging the precise point at which 'the draconian' becomes 'the totalitarian' need not detain us here.)

Of course, there is more to these points about the *language* of the Grid than the words alone. This language, like all language, is embedded in and reflects a discursive orientation toward the world. It is born of and begets social practices – ways of doing things, ways of being, and ways of shaping what other people do and become. Here again, Barlow's distinctions are useful since they concern modes of controlling values, morals, knowledge, competence, and the like.

As noted previously, Barlow speaks specifically to the issue of *pornography* on the net. The way he addresses the issue, however, can apply equally to concerns expressed on behalf of Grid Safety about the possibility of students accessing websites involving sex and violence (and even *football*). Barlow's rejection of approaches that impose gross filters, in favour of developing more localized filters that work on the principle of individuals and groups taking informed responsibility for their choices and deciding what 'noise' they want to filter out, is, precisely, an *educative* stance. It is the kind of stance we should be requiring educators, education administrators, and educationists to be advocating and adopting with respect to issues and concerns like 'safety on the Grid'.

Strategic approaches that use filters and other material forms of control (like random checking) carry over to cyberspace various models, approaches, concepts, and orientations that have evolved in physical–industrial space. Their perpetrators typically come to cyberspace and, more generally, to the information technology revolution from the standpoint of a lifelong socialization in physical space. Those in positions of power bring their mindsets to new times and new spaces and impose their language, values, and preferred practices on them. This is what we see writ large in the *police* and *protect* operating logic of the Grid.

Our point here begins from Barlow's suggestion that we educate (he uses 'raise') young people in ways that promote in them strong ethical senses of what is distasteful. Then, and only then, can they deploy the kinds of filters that can ultimately be counted on in cyberspace. Our fear, however, is that the kind of protection logic operated by Gridmeisters is symptomatic of the extent to which bureaucratized, performativity-oriented school systems have actually *given up* on educating and moved to other ground. 'Protecting' becomes 'conforming with practice guidelines that constitute lists of procedures for enacting accountability with respect to duty of care'. This is no guarantee of safety. It is the easy way out, the defaulter's default mode. To be safe people ultimately must learn how to protect themselves – be this physically, morally, or whatever. The operating logic of the Grid actually impedes this. It imposes forms of control that try to eliminate risk, but do so at the cost of obliterating 'pedagogical moments' conducive to learning how to 'keep ourselves safe' in the rich sense with which education should be concerned.

Potential for counterproductive outcomes

At numerous points and on different levels the operating logic of the Grid contradicts and undermines the ends and outcomes it purports to enable. Some of the recommendations made in the name of 'policing and protecting' are very likely to have counterproductive outcomes in terms of other Grid goals. Consider, for instance, the advice given on *Superhighway Safety* that schools include automatic disclaimers at the end of each email message sent by students (in order to protect the school). This conflicts with the emphasis found elsewhere on students learning *not* to identify themselves in any way in their emailing and online chat activities. Such seemingly small contradictions have a habit of replicating, until a system trips itself up. Hence, the suggestion on *Superhighway Safety* that schools may want to 'restrict some students to using internal email only, while providing others with greater access' is in tension with the government's stated aim of enhancing educational outcomes through access to ICTs. The will to police and punish conflicts here with the will to enhance. Such contradictions abound in the Grid.

The kinds of counterproductive outcomes that readily arise from a clampdown mentality around computing were exemplified in Caleb's futile web search for information about medieval times described in Chapter 3. By turning 'web searching' into a tightly surveilled and artificial practice, school practice contributed to Caleb's misunderstandings about the nature of URLs, Internet domains, use of search engines, and other aspects integral to effective use of the Internet to locate information. Given the current constitution of the Grid, it is *reasonable* to expect large-scale 'Caleb-like' instances to occur. Indeed, it would be *unreasonable* to expect otherwise. The learners most likely to be disadvantaged here are those who most rely on schools for opportunities to use the Internet.

The issue of counterproductivity looms large when we compare policy aspirations with how the Grid has unfolded. Tony Blair's observation that Britain's international competitiveness will increasingly depend on how its citizens adopt digital technologies (1999: 1) is pertinent here. For example, by making available a range of 'off the shelf', 'one size fits all' resources, the Grid may well help thwart professional development of teachers in areas of symbolic work like designing resources in the light of conceptual and theoretical understandings they embrace. The kind of competitive edge mentioned by Blair has much to do with high-level symbolic analytic work. Encouraging development of symbolic analytic talent within school education presupposes that teachers are disposed to model such talent as often as possible. Along with the generalized political and administrative fetish for standardized quick fix packaged programs, resources, and remediation services that currently besets performativity-driven public education, the Grid works against enhancing teacher work at the level of symbolic analysis.

Finally, with respect to counterproductivity, we should not be surprised if younger learners find little on the Grid that appeals to them or engages their attention for long. Within the relatively minute proportion of Grid-recommended material designed for and pitched directly at young users – e.g. *The Buses of Sunnydown Garage*, the *Let's Discover* literacy activities – we find a striking absence of links to resources developed *by* children *for* children.

Elsewhere (Lankshear 1997: Ch. 7; Goodson *et al.* 2002), we have described a website called *Alex's Scribbles – Koala Trouble* (Balson and Balson 2001). Designed and produced by Alex (5 years old when he began his website) and his father, the site presents a series of 13 stories written from 1996 to 1999 about Max, the koala, and the adventures he has with his mother and various friends. The *Koala Trouble* stories are simple narratives requiring readers to solve problems and to 'click' on image-mapped hypertext links to help Max and his friends in a range of sticky situations.

Besides the Max stories, the website had a feedback section where children (and adults) from around the world could (and in their thousands, did) email Alex in response to the stories they had read. Another section of the website was given over to classrooms in other countries, such as Singapore and the US, where readers 'hosted' Max on his 'round the world' trip. This section showcases classroom accounts, stories and pictures describing Max's adventures in their part of the world.

The website began as a response to Alex's boredom at 4 and 5 years of age with most of the material on the Internet. Before the end of 1997 *Koala Trouble* had hosted '*1,000,000 kids of all ages* since it first went up on the Internet'. During 1999 it was estimated that 'the number [was] closer to two million' (Balson and Balson 1999: 1, emphasis in original). *Koala Trouble* has received numerous prestigious awards and accolades. Alex and Max received email correspondence from children and adults all around the world. Messages were often imaginative and creative (adding episodes to Max's adventures, or imagining him in the homes of the correspondents). This correspondence affirms the compellingness of the website and exemplifies authentic uses of email as a communication medium.

In its current state, the Grid offers young learners little or nothing similar in intent or kind to *Koala Trouble*. More importantly, it offers little to encourage the development of 'Alex-like' young people. Yet, we would argue, the Grid's aim to help promote development of learners with 'good understanding of ICT' and who 'adopt digital technologies' in ways that will shape future leading edges has a lot to do with encouraging 'Alex-like' activity now. At present the Grid constructs 'good understanding of ICT' in terms of being able to 'drive' the equipment safely, or with adequate protection. As Castells (1996) makes clear, however, the greatest added value associated with new ICTs involves seeing them as *processes to be developed*, rather than as tools or applications to be mastered at the level of use. People like Alex display good understandings of ICT as 'processes to be developed'. This, however, is patently what the Grid in its current conception and state does *not* promote and, indeed, runs the acute risk of *actively undermining*.

Risks of promoting non-efficacious learning

Many limitations we find in the Grid are not confined to it alone. Rather, they are instances of more general limitations we associate with conventional views and practices of school-based learning grounded in 'psychologistic' models. Viewed from the standpoint of a sociocultural approach, much of what the Grid offers seems beholden to pedagogical concepts and approaches likely to generate non-efficacious learning.

Once again, the 'exemplary' case of Denbigh School applies here. The view expressed there about blocking football sites (or similar kinds of Internet resources) should worry any educator committed to efficacious learning. Internet-based football sites are among the very kinds of stimuli that can readily support meaningful learning for entire strata of learners (including many to whom 'inclusion' policies purportedly relate). For example, from exposure to well-designed and produced websites young people can assimilate sound understandings of mature practices that make for effective website development of their own. We saw this in Jarrod's observation (see Chapter 3) that webpages had to be fast loading to be effective, although Jarrod had no prior experience of constructing webpages. Likewise, to those with interests in the game, football sites provide rich possibilities for achieving meaningful and motivated connections between what students do as learners now and insider versions of related social practices. Such practices may range from being a valued supporter of a football club to becoming a professional football player or working for a football club. Other related practices may include designing, marketing and selling football memorabilia, becoming an archivist, and so on. For a pedagogically adept teacher, it should be more difficult *not* to be able to turn access to a football site on the Internet toward efficacious learning for particular students than to be *able* to. The same holds for all kinds of interest sites that appeal to learners operating from varying gender, ethnic, social class, religious, and cultural subjectivities. Interestingly, while the Grid is intended to facilitate lifelong learning, it identifies a practice that negates the idea of life being a trajectory, and of learning being properly concerned with building understandings of possible and viable trajectories, as *exemplary*.

The approach to email taken on the *Superhighway Safety* and related sites likewise infringes against principles and practices of efficacious learning. Email is the most widely used Internet application in the world (Shapiro and Rohde 2000: xviii). It tends also to be among those applications most maligned in classroom practices. Using email in classrooms is widely constructed as 'writing to penpals via the Internet'. To suggest that it should be used principally to communicate with students in another class is to miss the point of most insider uses of email. Email use among adolescents and children is generally reported as a medium for communicating with friends and family, for sharing and accessing information such as text and music files, for participating in discussion lists and such like.

Rules of email use promoted by BECTa and the DfES, and some practices identified as exemplars of conforming to them, similarly distort the medium. Claiming that email is not a private medium is incorrect. It is not solely or 'by nature' a private medium. Neither, however, is it solely or 'by nature' a public medium. Rather, emailing assumes numerous forms according to the social practices of email users. It is no less (or more) a private medium than the telephone. Vast numbers of people use emailing for private purposes, including when they send messages from public facilities. Email intended for general audiences is generally sent by means of the multiple recipient function, analogously to how memos or newsletters get sent to general audiences.

Similarly, such practices as providing a single email address for an entire class of students and designating one person to log-on and collect the email for the class seem misplaced. The latter sits uneasily with the policy aspiration that all learners master a range of information and communications technologies (BECTa 2001b: 1). The former, exemplified in the Ambleside School vignette supplied by DfES, is wrongheaded. This is *not* how institutions beyond school (other, perhaps, than prisons) behave. Such practice contributes to preparing learners for a world that is *not* a world they are likely to live in. It generates distorted conceptions of social practices outside the artificial learning environment of the classroom. It would make better sense for each partner class involved in the 'pen pal-ing' of email to *fax* one another. This would at least approximate to mature versions of social practices involving fax machines. A single fax number per work unit or institutional division is normal. Moreover, the hard copy format of a fax message sent to a number serving multiple persons discourages prudent people from transmitting sensitive material that can be viewed by all and sundry.

The Grid runs serious risks of dumbing learners (and teachers) down and 'subtracting value' from learning opportunities. The 'activities' from the *Let's Discover* site described earlier are a case in point. The idea that, for example, youngsters could experience engagements that reduce them to keying a letter (any letter) and waiting while a name for an image slowly spells itself out as being stimulating and edifying is a disturbing thought. The same holds for the sentence formation 'activity' and most of the maths 'activities' on this same website. Young learners inhabit a world of burgeoning new literacies (Howard 1998; Lankshear and Knobel 2001; Alvermann 2002) that differ in kind, scope, and purpose from conventional literacies and familiar language uses forged in pre-digital times. In its 'early years' fare, the Grid does not engage with new literacies at all. It does not even acknowledge them. Resources like *The Buses from Sunnydown Garage* narratives merely provide opportunities to use a mouse minimally in the course of projecting conventional established language uses into electronic spaces.

This is not the stuff of a learning society as conceptualized in policy statements pertaining to the Grid. It runs directly counter to Tony Blair's claim (1997: 1), that 'children cannot be effective in tomorrow's world if they are trained in yesterday's skills'. In the case of the Owl stories, learners are being encouraged to use poorly conceptualized programs as well as to practise decontextualized literacy skills by means of 'yesterday's literacy drills'. The same applies to other examples, such as the Channel 4 'literacy' activities. The government's conception of a learning society calls for much more sophisticated literacy understandings and learning practices than the 'old basics' promoted in the Owl Stories, within the *Let's Discover* website, and throughout Grid space generally (cf. Lankshear 1998; Rowan *et al.* 2002).

Finally, with respect to critique of the Grid, we may consider an issue concerning the *Homework High* page. Having access to a facility for posting homework-related questions to be addressed by 'resident experts' is potentially very valuable for students. It can provide direct access to mature forms of thinking, evaluating, writing, etc., within an area of social practice. On the other hand, however, the value so far as effective learning is concerned of encouraging students to post questions and requests like the majority of those we reported above (page 92) is highly dubious. If learners want to learn to use the Internet effectively to discover what a proscenium arch stage is, it is more appropriate for them to know how to go to a good quality search engine, and to learn something about conducting efficient searches in the process. What could and should a 'resident expert' provide in response to requests like: 'Is Philip Larkin essentially pessimistic? Help Please!!!!!!!!' or 'Hi I have to write a story on Harry Potter. Can you help?'

It appears to us that in its current and foreseeable states of development, the Grid is more likely to impede than enable efficacious learning. The *mindset* informing its design and construction militates against its being 'reformed' in ways likely to support expansive educational goals and to attract and sustain the interest of learners with alternative access sources to online environments. Unfortunately, the Grid and the mindset it betrays are things we think teachers and learners with an eye to today and tomorrow would be better off without.

Thinking anew, thinking relationally: schools as knowledge producers for their communities

At the beginning of this chapter we said it is less important what particular answer is given to questions like 'when is a literacy *new*?' and '*what* is a new literacy?' than to see what is at stake when the issue arises in relation to concrete cases. The National Grid for Learning has provided the case in this chapter. Our arguments incline us personally to regard the practices and literacies coalescing around the grid as 'faux new'. They replicate long-established practices and prejudices in a context of using new technologies. Aspirations that the Grid will transcend the logic of preparing learners for tomorrow's needs by teaching yesterday's skills seem misplaced. The Grid is 'faking it'. It is an outsider imposition on what should increasingly become insider spaces.

This, of course, raises the question of what it might look like for schools to pick up new ICTs from something more closely approaching an insider perspective. There are many possibilities here, some of which we will explore in later chapters. To conclude this chapter, however, we will look briefly at one possible contender. This builds on recent work by Chris Bigum (2002), who looks at some 'design sensibilities' (Schrage 1998) that currently shape how new ICTs are used in schools and suggests a constructive alternative that has strong insider resonances.

Design sensibilities are skews or biases in how we understand technologies and affect how we use them. Three design sensibilities reflected in much of the take-up of new technologies in schools are that 'IT is an educational good', that 'new technologies can be seen in terms of earlier technologies', and that the Internet is about information delivery. The first encourages the 'domestication' of new ICTs to pre-existing curriculum activities. Since 'education' = 'curriculum activity', and since IT is an educational good, then using IT will help us to do better what we already do. The second is the kind of view that sees the word processor as a kind of typewriter or pencil. It encourages using computers to produce final versions of essays or projects (where 'rough copies' have been produced in pen or pencil first). The third is associated with seeing a school webpage as a medium for providing information about the school, for posting completed assignments, and so on. It should be clear that the Grid is best understood in terms of such design sensibilities.

Other design sensibilities, however, may be more appropriate so far as schools are concerned. Given that the biggest impact digital technologies have is on *relationships* between people and between people and organizations, Bigum suggests an alternative design sensibility based partly on *relationships*. Schools should consider how new ICTs might be used productively in terms of relationships that could be developed and mediated using new technologies, rather than in terms of information delivery or of doing old things in new ways. In addition, in contexts of superabundant information, point of view – like attention – becomes a scarce resource for handling information and using it effectively (Bigum 2002).

These two ideas underpin very different possibilities for what schools might do and be, and for what learning might become. Bigum explores these in terms of the school's potential relationship to its community as a producer of knowledge, doing full-fledged research that enhances a community's point of view. He argues that communities will increasingly need and benefit from having good quality knowledge about themselves. Such knowledge provides a local community with a sound basis for reading and responding to global and informational influences it encounters. Community self-knowledge, in other words, provides a *point of view* or a form of *expertise* from which to interpret and respond to more global forces pressing upon it. Producing, accumulating, and disseminating local knowledge will consequently become increasingly valuable to communities as they become caught up more and more in global-level trends and processes.

To become knowledge producers for their communities, however, schools will have to move from the 'pretend' space of current forms of curriculum-based learning to doing *investigatory* work that is regarded as genuinely useful and valuable by external (community) groups. This means transforming learning into processes of doing *research* that meets standards of quality, rigour and relevance acknowledged by the community – work in which new ICTs can play an important role. Such work will go beyond the fragmentary kind of involvement schools sometimes have when students contribute to larger research projects (e.g. on environment, traffic flows) by collecting data (e.g. rainfall, counting vehicles) to be used in the studies. Rather, schools will need to see research in its full sense and range of activities as something they are good at and through which they can relate and contribute to their community. This is not beyond schools and students. Bigum documents the case of a primary/elementary school in a small town that has adopted an approach whereby requests made of the school for expertise or knowledge are framed in terms of the possibility of students making the response.

> On one occasion a group of local principals visited the school to inspect the approach the school was employing in its use of ICTs. While teachers structured the day and spoke on some occasions to the group, there were three workshops for principals . . . presented by students. One [workshop on] how to make claymation movies was taught by a group of Year four students. The students . . . offered encouragement, advice and gave instructions without taking over or doing it for the principals. The men and women sat on the floor in their suits . . . negotiated a plot with pieces of coloured plasticene and recorded over fifty images using a digital camera. The students then taught them how to convert the stills into movie format.
>
> (Bigum 2002: 7–8)

While this event is hardly earth shattering, it reflects the principle of examining every opportunity of having students work on assignments that matter to the outside community (Bigum 2002). This entails working to understand activities of data collection, which are common enough in classrooms, beyond the limits of a 'fridge door' mindset – where 'project work' and 'data collection' have no purpose or audience beyond the classroom (other than as a display on a family's refrigerator door). It also involves moving beyond data collection to processes of assembling, analysing and interpreting data in terms that are relevant to community purposes and needs. This amounts to moving beyond 'doing school' and approximating to real world practices of consultant and contract research and professional knowledge production.

The bottom line, however, is that the community must value the work. Hence, 'schools would have to be at least partially remade in the minds of the local community' (Bigum 2002: 8). Rather than a wholesale change, this could be pursued on a project-by-project basis: building 'a repertoire of research skills and products' responsive to 'local needs and interest' (Bigum 2002: 8). This would in turn require discovering what kinds of research activities 'can be sustained by different age cohorts', the kinds of professional support teachers would need in order to work in this way, and the kinds of strategies needed to support such new forms of school and community partnerships. Universities are already engaged in such relationships and taken seriously. The idea is that schools may be too. The way this idea positions use of new ICTs in schools differs radically from the underlying conception of the Grid, and is almost infinitely more *educational* in its vision. It embodies the principle of efficacious learning described above, and actively resists making monkeys out of learners and ICTs alike. In this kind of context,

> CCTs [computing and communications technologies] have a role in supporting and sustaining new relationships. The collection, analysis and dissemination of information is work that computers can support well. In this way, schools don't do computers for computers' sake. [They] can respond to a new communication order by reconsidering the role they play in the community. [I]t is this role . . . of knowledge production . . . that can be usefully supported by the judicious use of CCTs.
>
> (Bigum 2002: 8)

Such an approach is no more or less, however, than the kind of thing implied in Tony Blair's observation that tomorrow's needs will not be met by yesterday's skills. If we are serious about following policy rhetoric where it leads, one place we will arrive at may be schools that provide knowledge contributing to a community's point of view.

CHAPTER 5

Attention Economics, Information and New Literacies

Introduction

In recent years a growing number of writers have begun talking about an economics of attention. They see this operating in relation to information, and within the context of the burgeoning information revolution associated with digital technologies. This trend is often traced back to an observation made more than 30 years ago by the economist Herbert Simon. According to Simon (1971: 40–1),

> What information consumes is rather obvious. It consumes the attention of its recipients. Hence a wealth of information creates a poverty of attention and a need to allocate attention efficiently among the overabundance of information sources that might consume it.

In this chapter we look at the economics of attention – or what some theorists (e.g. Goldhaber 1997) refer to as an emerging attention economy – in relation to digital technologies and a likely array of new literacies. We will argue that people's efforts to attract, sustain, and build attention under new media conditions can be seen already to have spawned a range of new social practices and new forms of literacy associated with them. Moreover, it seems likely that this tendency will continue, and that the economics of attention will be a potent catalyst for the evolution and development of new literacies in the years ahead. How schools respond to this will, we believe, become a significant issue, and one which, if taken seriously, will require schools to rethink their current mindsets on attention.

Three discourses of attention economics

The recent and growing interest in an economics of attention is not monolithic. Rather, when we survey the literature that deals with attention economics we find significant differences in how the idea is understood and approached by different writers. Elsewhere (Lankshear and Knobel 2002) we have distinguished what we see as three significantly different 'takes' on attention economics. One of these is the approach taken by Richard Lanham (1994), to which we referred briefly in Chapter 3. The others are associated with work by Michael Goldhaber (1997, 1998a, 1998b), the Aspen Institute (Adler 1997), and the (now reconstituted) NCR Knowledge Lab (MacLeod 2000). We will begin our discussion of attention economics with the work of Lanham.

Attention economics, attention structures and the information explosion: Richard Lanham on libraries in the information age

As we saw in Chapter 3, Lanham's concern in 'The economics of attention' (1994) is with the changing world of the library and, particularly, the changing role of librarians in the age of digitized information and communications technologies. According to Lanham, it is important to understand the economics of attention if we are to address questions like: 'How are libraries and librarians to negotiate the changing terrain of information?'; 'What kind of changes are involved?'; and 'Where should one look for clues to handling the changes?' Lanham begins by observing that we currently seem to be moving from 'the goods economy' to 'the information economy' (Lanham 1994: 1). Within the so-called information economy, we are 'drowning' in a particular form of information. This is what Lanham calls information as raw data. In this form, information is not a scarce resource. It is superabundant.

On the other hand, information in other forms, or senses, *is* in short supply. Lanham argues that we use different terms for information depending on how much attention – that is, 'the action that turns raw data into something humans can use' – has been given to it (1994: 1). No attention leaves us with 'raw data'. Some attention yields 'massaged data'. Lots of attention gives us 'useful information'. Maximal attention yields 'wisdom' (Lanham 1994: 1). To simplify his argument, Lanham reduces these types of information to data, information and wisdom. According to Lanham, information and wisdom are in shortest supply.

As we have seen, Lanham identifies attention as being the scarce resource in the information economy. He is concerned with how to facilitate or enable attention to data by developing new human attention structures for attending to the flood of information-as-data we face constantly. He notes that banks have been early starters here, out of necessity, since the banks' traditional role of safeguarding clients' money and lending it out has largely been taken over by other institutions. 'To survive, banks are now creating from the digital stuff of instantaneous global data new attention structures for savers and borrowers, new investment instruments [which banks call] "securitization"' (Lanham 1994: 1). These provide people with new frames for attending to the financial part of their worlds.

To explain further what he means by attention structures, Lanham takes examples from very different walks of life. First, he considers an example from the world of conceptual art. He describes an environmental art exhibit by the artist Christo. This involved erecting many large umbrellas in two very different kinds of location – a rainy valley in Japan and a desert mountain pass in southern California. By this means, says Lanham, Christo created 'temporary attention structures to make us pause and ponder how we engage in large-scale collective human effort' (Lanham 1994: 1). The 'product' was attention structures rather than objects. 'The center of the project . . . became the contrast in how each culture went about its work, both social and geographic' (Lanham 1994: 1). Lanham sees this example in terms of the *macroeconomics* of attention. Lanham sees the problem of information overload associated in particular with new ICTs in terms of the *microeconomics* of attention. How, in short, can human attention sort out an overwhelming flow of information?

From the perspective of the microeconomics of attention, Lanham asks how the overload of information carried by 'the rich signal' – which he sees as being the heart of the digital revolution – can be managed. This signal can be manifested as alphabetic text, as image and as sound. It 'creates its own internal economy of attention' (Lanham 1994: 1). Moving to an opposite pole from his conceptual art example, Lanham illustrates the nature and role of attention structures in relation to the microeconomics of attention by reference to fighter-jet cockpit displays. He suggests, provocatively:

If one is looking for a glimpse of what literacy will look like in the future, the fighter cockpit is a good place to look . . . The most interesting conversation I have had about literacy at the end of the twentieth century was with a fellow who designed avionic displays for fighters. He knew all the basic questions and a good many of the answers.

(Lanham 1994: 1)

In the cockpit digital data arrives at quantum rates in alphabetical and numerical information, in iconic displays, and as audio signals. This posed a design question of how to mix all this data–information into 'a single functioning information structure' that would allow the pilot's mind to make sense of data coming 'thick and fast' (Lanham 1994: 1). It represents a technical instance of the larger questions of how to develop structures – frames and organizers – that facilitate paying attention to data so that we can turn it into something useful. And, perhaps more importantly, prompts us to ask *who* will develop these structures.

We saw in Chapter 3 how Lanham addressed these questions to librarians. He believes that models based on the old dominant metaphor of matter will no longer serve. He suggests that the new dominant metaphor of information directs us to attend to what lies behind or beneath 'stuff' – the world of objects – and to see 'hidden forces and forms . . . which those objects allegorize' (Lanham 1994: 1). In an interesting move, Lanham suggests that our efforts to learn and understand how to handle the new conditions of 'seeing' and thinking about the world, and of style and expression – in short, how to develop appropriate attention structures – may be usefully informed by earlier and long-standing arts and habits. These include the Western tradition of rhetoric and the medieval allegorical habit of life and thought that saw 'the immanence of God as informing all things' (Lanham 1994: 1).

It is difficult at present to see what forms new attention structures might take, and where we should best look for inspiration. Nonetheless, Lanham accepts that gateways will need to be developed to facilitate attention to information, to turn it into something useful for users and to enable users to use it usefully in terms of their wants and goals. One thing, however, is clear, according to Lanham. This will involve much more than the current development of intelligent software agents like search engines, specialized bots, the practice of 'data mining', and the like. This is because a frame issue is involved. Building attention structures is more than a software issue or a 'technical' issue alone. It calls for an architecture that incorporates frames, and for a 'new kind of human architect' who will mediate the economics of attention. This will be far from a technical task and Lanham believes it will comprise the highest order and most powerful, sought after and rewarded literacy.

Advertising and the attention economy: the Aspen Institute and National Cash Registers' Knowledge Lab

A variation on the notion of attention being a scarce resource within contexts of information can be found in the world of advertising. The challenge of gaining attention, as it becomes an increasingly scarce resource in proportion to information sources competing for it, has emerged as a key motif within advertising discourse during recent years. As a domain of human practice advertising has a strong stake in the economics of attention. According to Richard Adler (1997: 5), the 'first challenge for every advertiser is to capture and hold the attention of the intended audience'. Advertisers actually have to create attention to products in which those people being pitched at typically have no inherent interest. Notwithstanding the massive and increasing amount of time citizens in affluent countries spend using or consuming media of one kind or another, advertising faces ever-increasing competition for attention. Furthermore, the viability of those same media that are used for advertising – from TV (whether public broadcast or cable) to the Internet, via newspapers, magazines, and radio – fluctuate with and depend upon levels and constancy of advertising revenue.

In 1996 the Aspen Institute hosted a seminar to assess the current state of and prospect for the field of advertising and to identify perspectives on how individuals choose to allocate their attention. The seminar made particular reference to the context of emerging new media, notably the Internet, and to the World Wide Web (WWW) in particular. These have the potential to challenge established media as advertising channels. During the past decade, as use has continued to grow rapidly, the Internet has been transformed 'from a non-profit medium for academic and personal communication into a dynamic commercial medium'. Most major corporations and many small companies have now established an online presence – the dotcom industry crash of 2000–01 notwithstanding. At present, Internet advertising accounts for only a tiny proportion of total current advertising expenditure. Nonetheless, it is growing rapidly. Marketers and advertisers have mounted a hot search in attempts to create ever new and more effective means for gaining attention.

The Internet, however, presents advertisers with issues and challenges that differ in degree and kind from other media. Adler notes that the Web produces a *massive* 'fragmentation of channels' (Adler 1997: 21), on a scale far greater than anything advertisers have yet faced. As the original situation of a very small core of television networks became dozens and then literally 'hundreds of different cable- and satellite-delivered channels', advertisers had to switch from broadcast to narrowcast strategies. With the advent of the Net, however, 'there are now potentially millions of channels available, with the conceivable end point being a separate, cus-tomized channel for each individual' (Adler 1997: 21–2). The growth of new interactive media creates the possibility for one-to-one marketing. This involves a strategy that focuses less on building advertising market share than on 'investigating a company's *best* customers and building a one-to-one relationship with them' in order to get more purchasing or con-suming per customer by 'treating them as individuals . . . [to] build loyalty' (Adler 1997: 24).

This is a context where there is much to play for and where old kinds of intermediaries and partnerships change and new ones are invented. For example, distribution expenses may account for 50–80 per cent of the end cost of consumer products. Hence, if producers can bypass conventional marketing and distribution intermediaries and sell direct to the consumer via the Internet, this creates potentially huge advantages for consumers in terms of cost and ease. This ups the ante for advertisers. At the same time, Internet users have greater potential than users of other media actively to *control* the information they receive. In Net advertising, the relative bal-ance of power shifts from producers to consumers of advertising. On the WWW customers do not face the choice of sitting through intrusive ads (Adler 1997: 37). The logic that has to operate in Net advertising is less one of how media users can opt out of advertisements to one of how advertisers can get users to opt *in* to marketing information.

In this environment, new kinds of intermediaries and strategies have emerged in the service of advertising. These include search engines, bots, the active creation of interest-based online communities with potential for commercial exploitation, collaborative filtering technology for sharing views and interests online, and so on. For example, marketers quickly saw and acted on the potential of creating and exploiting online communities concerned with specific topics that would attract key groups or niches of customers. Once these audiences are created and identified, marketers can interact with them to 'sell and support products, provide customer service [and] conduct continuous market research' (Adler 1997: 25). In-genious devices and processes – as well as some gross approaches – have been developed to capture audience attention on the Internet. Gross forms include email 'spam' and 'push' strategies, as well as successive generations of eye-catching 'gizmos' (javascript animation, flashing words, etc.). More subtle strategies include cases where companies hire marketers to create 'ad bots' that inhabit chat rooms and similar spaces on the Internet. These respond to trigger words and can engage potential customers in private conversation that has commercial relevance (Adler 1997).

By the end of the 1990s some high-profile research work, backed by serious budgets, was under way to develop approaches to advertising grounded in the economics of attention. The NCR Knowledge Lab was an early leader in the field. The Lab's work began from the idea that consumers are saturated with potential information sources for practically any requirement and simply cannot use all the available options without eating heavily into time. For producers and vendors operating in the emerging network economy, this creates the challenge of how to get the attention of those consumers they want to attract and/or keep, and how to make their product or brand stand out amid increasing competition for customer attention. In an early statement on a now defunct website, the Lab argued that as the network economy continues to grow, attention will become increasingly scarce. As a consequence,

> firms will have to think of themselves as operating both in an Attention Market as well as their core market.
>
> Attention will be hard to earn, but if it is viewed as a reciprocal flow, firms can use information about consumers and customers to stand out in a sea of content to increase profitability: pay attention to them and they pay attention to you. Relationships are likely to encompass attention transactions. As customers realize the value of their attention and their information needed to get it, we show that they may require payment of some kind for both.
>
> The Knowledge Lab is looking into how we can quantify, measure and track flows of attention in the Network Economy.
>
> (http://www.knowledgelab.ncr.com: accessed July 1999)

The Knowledge Lab established consumer research as a key research focus. The attention economy was one of a series of intersecting themes investigated within this focus. The Lab developed and trademarked the concept of 'relationship technologies' and defined attention as 'engagement with information'. The key to successful business in the future, says the Lab, will be the capacity to generate and maintain personal attention to new and existing customers.

According to Rory MacLeod (2000), one of the research leaders in this field at the time, advertising can create *opportunities* to gain attention, but it cannot actually secure, let alone maintain and build, ongoing attention. Some early work by Lab researchers suggested the importance of using personal information to gain initial attention, and to harness this attention to creating successful 'real relationships' with customers with the assistance of 'relationship technologies' (MacLeod 2000: 3). Successful relationships of all kinds 'contain the elements of attraction, communication, "being there" for the other party, and understanding' (MacLeod 2000: 3). The Lab's idea is that in business as well as in other areas of life, relationship technologies will serve to 'enable, support and enhance these key elements of real relationships' (MacLeod 2000: 3).

According to the Lab's research, this can be done by using relationship technologies to create *attention transactions*, in which information flows back and forth between content providers (the business or commercial interest) and content users (potential and actual customers). The idea here is quite straightforward. Attention is 'engagement with information'. Hence, both-way information flows grounded in reciprocal interest are, effectively, attention transactions that create and sustain relationships (MacLeod 2000: 7). The Lab believed in the efficacy of *paying* attention in order to gain and maintain attention. Its early research documents various mechanisms used to try and elicit customer attention (such as paying people to view content, providing free computers which come with content, offering free email via portals which bombard users with advertising and other commercial information, and so on). While it did not dismiss these outright, the Lab stressed the importance of attention transactions based on personal information. This requires customers to appreciate the advantages that can come from providing personal information that permits companies to pay personal attention to them in the course of creating and developing successful relationships (MacLeod 2000). Reciprocally, it presupposes that companies will use this information fruitfully. 'Acquiring personal information about a potential customer is useful only insofar as it can be translated into more personal attention' (MacLeod 2000: 19).

According to MacLeod (2000: 19–20), the research conducted by the Knowledge Lab suggested a number of important implications for the strategic approaches of businesses operating in the network economy. He argues that participating in the attention market is a precondition for successful participation in the network economy. This is because it is necessary to have customers' attention before it is possible to develop relationships with them. Advertising can create initial contacts between companies and network users. But to gain users' attention companies must change initial contacts into attention transactions as the basis for developing relationships. This may require companies purchasing information from consumers at the start of a relationship, and in such cases information costs should be seen as 'investments to be unlocked' rather than 'costs to be avoided' (MacLeod 2000: 19). A pinnacle of an attention-based relationship is where a company can 'move from mass customization to engaging customers in the design of products for themselves' (MacLeod 2000: 20). Those companies who are best able to provide 'intelligent agents or intermediaries' will get 'first call' on consumers' attention. To be successful, companies will have to identify technologies best suited to capturing consumers' attention, 'and "own" the newly emerging personal access points' (MacLeod 2000: 20).

Michael Goldhaber on the 'attention economy'

Goldhaber begins from similar bases to Lanham, but ends up in a very different place. Like Lanham, Goldhaber links the superabundance of information to the economics of attention. And like Lanham (and Barlow) he argues against applying concepts and laws from an earlier time and a particular kind of space to what he sees as the new spaces of the Internet.

According to Goldhaber, the fact that information is in over-saturated supply renders the idea of an information economy incoherent. This is because 'economics are governed by what is scarce' (Goldhaber 1997: 1) or, more accurately, because economies are based on 'what is both most desirable and ultimately most scarce' (Goldhaber 1998b: 1). If people in postindustrial societies increasingly live their lives in the spaces of the Internet, these lives will fall more and more under economic laws organic to this new space. Accordingly, Goldhaber (1997, 1998a) argues that the basis of the coming new economy will be attention and *not* information. Attention, unlike information, is inherently scarce. This, says Goldhaber (1998b: 1), is because 'each of us has only so much of it to give, and [attention] can only come from us – not machines, computers or anywhere else'. But like information, attention moves through the Net. Goldhaber identifies cyberspace as being where the attention economy will come into its own.

Goldhaber's particular conception of an attention economy is premised on the fact that the human capacity to produce material things outstrips net capacity to consume the things that are produced. As he puts it, the 'material needs at the level of creature comfort' of those who are 'in a position to demand them' are 'fairly well satisfied' (Goldhaber 1997: 1). This, we should note, is probably the great *minority* of living human beings. Nonetheless, for this powerful minority, the need for attention becomes increasingly important, and increasingly the focus of their productive activity.

When our material desires are more or less satisfied, says Goldhaber (1998a), such that we do not experience scarcity of material necessities like food and shelter, we are increasingly driven by 'desires of a less strictly material kind'. Goldhaber claims that some of these desires, such as a desire for meaning in our lives, converge toward a desire for attention. He sees the quest for meaning as being linked to questions like,

> Why are we here, and how do we know that we are somehow worthwhile? If a person feels utterly ignored by those around her, she is unlikely to feel that her life has much meaning to them. Since all meaning is ultimately conferred by society, one must have the attention of others if there is to be any chance that one's life is meaningful.
>
> (Goldhaber 1998a: 1)

In an important step in his argument, foreshadowed in Chapter 3 earlier, Goldhaber claims that

> the energies set free by the successes of . . . the money-industrial economy go more and more in the direction of obtaining attention. And that leads to growing competition for what is increasingly scarce, which is of course attention. It sets up an unending scramble, a scramble that also increases the demands on each of us to pay what scarce attention we can.
>
> (1997: 1)

This is the genesis of Goldhaber's conception of the attention economy – which differs substantially from Lanham's view and from that advanced by researchers concerned with advertising within the network economy. For example, Goldhaber's account focuses on individuals pursuing attention for their *own* purposes in terms of finding meaning for their lives under 'post-materialist' conditions. By contrast, Lanham addresses the pursuit of attention structures that will enable *other people* to use information effectively in relation to what they are interested in. For its part, the work of the Aspen Institute and the NCR Knowledge Lab seeks in different ways to help companies mobilize attention in the interests of selling consumer items to *customers* who believe their purposes are served by purchasing them.

Goldhaber thinks that people who live in economically advanced societies are socialized in ways that actually orient them toward pursuit of attention. He observes that during recent decades young people in the West have spent a huge proportion of their waking hours within two key contexts: either in school, or engrossed in media – especially television and audio-recordings. The experiences of these contexts involve paying great amounts of attention. And they involve focusing attention on 'a relative few' (Goldhaber 1998a): TV personalities, stars in different fields (music, sport, films, etc.) whom we attend to via television or audio media or contemporary multimedia, teachers, selected members of our peer group, and so on. Goldhaber notes that

> everyone who is seen on television models one common role, as do all teachers in schools, and that role is to be the object of a good deal of attention. Thus, without planning or intention, there has been a kind of cultural revolution, telling us that getting attention is a fine thing. And for many of us, having the attention of others turns out to feel very good, something we often want more of.
>
> (Goldhaber 1998a: 1)

Goldhaber looks in some detail at what he thinks the attention economy will be like, and at what will be required to participate successfully in it. He sees the attention economy having two 'classes'. He refers to these as 'stars' and 'fans'. He implies that there is also the equivalent of an 'underclass'. Stars have large amounts of attention paid to them. Fans pay their attention to the stars. Because paying attention requires effort, fans supply most of the effort in the attention economy. Unlike most workers in the industrial economy who had/have only one boss, fans will typically devote their attention-paying effort to multiple stars. While stars are the great winners in the attention economy, the losers are not necessarily the fans. Fans may receive sufficient *illusory* attention to meet their attention needs. Rather, says Goldhaber, the losers are those who don't get any attention, who are simply ignored. This entails having 'less of a clear identity and place in the community' (Goldhaber 1998a: 1). The extreme case would be a homeless person who dies in the street but who is ignored for days. Goldhaber suggests several factors that may be associated with being a loser. Losers may be people who do not stand out sufficiently to attract attention, or individuals who do not effectively reward attention paid to them, or else individuals who repel others by demanding too much attention.

To participate effectively in the attention economy requires knowing how to pay and receive attention. This part of Goldhaber's argument involves a distinction between real attention and illusory attention, which explains how fans can both *pay* a disproportionate amount of attention within the economy *and* have their own attention needs met. In order to *get* attention, says Goldhaber (1997), one has to pay attention. He argues that in a full-fledged attention economy the goal is simply to get enough attention or to get as much as possible. Obviously, accumulating more than one's 'share' of attention involves receiving more than one puts out. On the other hand, if one is to get attention one has to pay attention. The conundrum so far as the attention rich are concerned is resolved by the distinction between real and illusory attention. Stars and performers pay 'illusory attention' to fans and audiences, whereas the fans pay them *real* attention. Stars create the illusion that they are paying attention to each fan, to each member of their audience. Attention involves an exchange. People will withhold attention if they have no interest in the exchange. When readers lose interest in a chapter they put the book down. To maintain interest they have to believe that the author is attending to them and their needs or desires. Creating illusory attention may be done by 'pretending to flatter' the audience, 'creating questions in their minds which you then "obligingly" answer', claiming you will 'help them with some real problem they have', making eye contact, gesturing and the like (Goldhaber 1997: 1). Methods of creating illusions of attention may lose worth (effect) if they become too common or too well recognized.

The emerging attention economy is creating large markets for technologies that allow us to pursue attention and, with luck, to get it. These comprise both new and old technologies. As we will see, the Internet is a classic example of a new attention technology. Old technologies, however, like performance stages (theatre, concerts, public speaking) also remain important. The recent invention of digitized wearable display jackets (Kahney 2000) is a new technological trend in the pursuit of attention (see below). This may involve gaining attention directly, for example by advertising oneself. It may, however, involve a form of 'three-way attention transaction' (Goldhaber 1998a). This is where one has attention passed to one by somebody else – as when advertisers use stars to pass attention to clients and their products, or show hosts pass attention to guests (but in turn also receive attention from fans who watch the shows). Thus, a jacket wearer might screen clips of a popular star or a favourite game show and receive 'passed' attention from the featured stars.

Finally, gaining attention is indexical to originality. It is difficult, says Goldhaber, to get new attention 'by repeating exactly what you or someone else has done before' (1997: 1). Consequently, the attention economy is based on 'endless originality, or at least attempts at originality' (Goldhaber 1997: 1). Attention is a function of 'everything that makes you distinctly you and not somebody else' (Goldhaber 1998b: 9th principle).

Digital technologies and the economics of attention

Goldhaber (1997) highlights the distinctive significance of new information and communications technologies – especially, but by no means solely, the WWW. He sees the capacity to send out multimedia or virtual reality signals via the Web as a particularly effective and efficient means for attracting attention and paying illusory attention.

> Say you are primarily a writer of mere words, i.e., text; still, on the Web you [are] able to supplement your writings with your picture, with video images, with recordings of your voice, with interviews or pieces of autobiography. The advantages of doing that is that by offering potential readers a more vivid and rounded sense of who you are, you can both increase their sense of who it is who is offering them illusory attention, and have them have a clearer and more definite feeling than otherwise of what it is like to pay attention to you, rather than to some other writer of similar sounding words. Both these effects can help you hold their attention better.
>
> (Goldhaber 1997: 1)

In this way the Web is an ideal means for 'transmitting and circulating attention' and is getting better for this all the time: a precondition, says Goldhaber, for a full-fledged attention economy to emerge. He contrasts the circumstances of Plato with those of any number of people today. Over the past two millennia, says Goldhaber, millions of people have read and studied (paid attention to) Plato. But apart from 'contributing to his "immortality", the vast majority of that attention did him little personal good' (Goldhaber 1997: 1). It came after he was dead! While very few of today's 'attention getters' could aspire to be attended to for thousands of years, they are able to pursue the benefits of attention from many – maybe millions – of people via the Web throughout their lives (Goldhaber 1997: 1). This, says Goldhaber, is what will constitute living very well (on a sliding scale) in the new economy.

At the level of employing digital technologies, working the attention economy can take on very different forms. Three cases must suffice here. They will serve to make wider points as well.

Early in 2000, a number of online magazines (e.g. Dreamcast 2000; Suck 2000) described one young man's special mission and encouraged readers help him meet his goal. Walter, a 16-year-old Canadian high school student, described his special mission on his website located within the Geocities community (www.geocities.com/Walters_Mission). According to Walter's website, a girl from his school had told him that she would have sex with him if his website received a million hits within a given period. Pictures of Walter were published alongside the articles featuring his mission (Dreamcast 2000). They showed him to have an almost-shaved head, braces on his teeth, a sparse goatee, and what would generally pass for an 'unattractive air'. Walter's mission spawned anti-Walter sites (e.g. the now defunct www.geocities.com/walter_sucks) and at least one sympathetic spoof in the form of an animated sequence (Uglytouch.com 2000).

The articles urged readers to visit Walter's website to help him complete his mission before his time ran out. The response was overwhelming. According to Suck magazine, 'Walter's [website] log ultimately showed referrals from 2630 sites, many displaying banner ads in a show of solidarity, and sympathetic visitors flocked from around the world' (2000: 1). Some of these sources also stated that while Walter's Mission might be a hoax people should visit his website anyway, just in case the endeavour was for real (cf. Dreamcast 2000). On the day we visited Walter's website – well before the deadline set by his female peers – the only page that could be accessed told in huge letters that the mission had been accomplished. It also stated that due to still-heavy traffic to his website Walter had been forced to remove it indefinitely from the Internet.

In the second case, Steven Fitch, a graduate of MIT's Media Lab, developed a leather jacket containing in its back panel a complete Windows computer with a '233-MHz Pentium III processor, a 1 Gigabyte IBM micro hard drive and a broadband wireless Internet connection' (Kahney 2000: 1). The jacket was marketed as 'wearable advertising' and even came with 'a built-in infrared motion detector that can tell how many people have seen it close up by sensing their body heat' (Kahney 2000: 2). According to Fitch, the jacket 'allows people to use video as a form of self-expression' (Fitch quoted in Kahney 2000: 1).

As we've already mentioned, the jacket could be used in diverse ways as a medium for initiating or mediating attention flows and transactions. Some uses might essentially serve the owner's own attention-seeking interests simply by attracting the gaze of passers-by and engaging them in information (however briefly or superficially). Alternatively, the owner might use the display as an initial point of contact with potential customers for her or his own goods and services. Likewise companies, advertisers, and 'stars' might hire 'jacket space' as part of their contact-making and attention-attracting strategies. Many uses of the jacket display might serve multiple attention interests conjointly. For example, if the wearer was running a video for a popular band or a trailer for an upcoming movie (that is, for 'stars'), she would be paying illusory attention to fans of the band or movie star, transferring attention to the star, giving the star an opportunity for paying illusory attention to the fans, and generating attention for herself, all at the same time.

Fitch has formed a company called Hardwear International (www. hardwearcorp.com) to market the video jacket. His main company tagline is 'The revolution will be televised'. Hollywood has already shown keen interest, planning to display trailers for upcoming movies on people's clothing. Fitch is currently also working on a range of video jackets for children, as well as lunchboxes, handbags, and hats that all incorporate his video technology. Fitch says, 'I believe display technology will be incorporated into our lives as a form of personal expression' (Fitch quoted in Kahney 2000: 2).

The third case involves a complex example of e-commerce as cultural practice – or a set of cultural practices – developed by an enterprise called skim.com. The company aims to design and sell images of urban lifestyles and ways of being interconnected and noticed by means of a communications network and uniquely designed products. As skim.com's marketing manager Johne Eisenhut (2000: 1) explains, 'Skimmers are urban creatures.' skim.com mainly markets and sells a range of specially designed urban-style clothes (e.g. jackets, skirts, capes, and wristbands). Thanks to strong online sales, skim.com's urban wear has moved recently from being available on the Internet into over 40 stores in Europe, Scandinavia, the UK and the US. skim.com clothes differ from conventional streetwear and accessories (including other forms of 'high fashion') – each item contains the skim.com domain name emblazoned on it as well as a unique number. This number converts into an email address and messaging service via mobile phones and the skim.com website (e.g. the skim number '001' becomes the skim email, '001@skim.com').

The bilingual website includes, among a range of other things, the 'coverstory', which each month features an arty picture of a 'skimmer' – someone wearing a skim clothing item – and a write-up about them. Accompanying each coverstory is a message board where others can comment on the coverstory itself, pose questions to the featured skimmer and so on. The skim.com site also contains personal web-based email accounts that can be accessed from anywhere (cf. Hotmail and Yahoo). Another section of the website is 'webend'. This is a repository of digital detritus, 'dedicated to making the web a little more endless' and comprising 'works in progress', old online bitmap games, hyperlink libraries, an online sitcom, failed coding experiments, skimmers' reports on things that have happened to them via their skim.com numbers and the like. 'Click for Emotions' is a showcase of short digital movies, and viewers are invited to register an online vote for their favourite movie. According to Eisenhut, 'With the skim.com fashion and our communications idea, we're developing our vision of the zeitgeist' (Eisenhut 2000: 1).

New literacies and the economics of attention

Given the kinds of ideas sketched above it is not difficult to identify a range of literacies that might become increasingly significant within contexts subject to the economics of attention. We will briefly identify and outline several such literacies here in a very preliminary way. The sketches that follow are no more than suggestions about some of the kinds of examples we think could usefully be taken into account by an expanded New Literacy Studies. There are many other social practices and embedded language uses beyond the kinds we mention here that will also be worth exploring further (see, for example, Thorne 2001; Alvermann 2002; Leander and Johnson 2002; Gee forthcoming). The following sketches are invitations to a way of thinking within wider parameters about new and previously unrecognized forms of literacy, and not in any way exhaustive.

'Contact displaying': jackets (and similar gadgets) that work

This is the idea of using highly customizable, mobile, public media that employ Lanham's 'rich signal' – like the video display jacket – as a medium for conceptualizing, designing and assembling texts of different kinds that are intended to catch the eye and establish a basis for gaining attention. Not every jacket, however, will 'work' in an attention economy. Not every jacket owner/wearer will be able to use it successfully as a means to initiate and gain real attention. Moreover, the jacket itself (or any similar device) cannot be the medium for sustained attention unless its wearer can claim a 'space' to which others 'return' in order to see what he or she is up to today. The technological medium could work very well for designers of a wide range of cultural forms. Fast punchy 'ad busts' lend themselves to this medium, as do other forms of culture jamming. Skilled exponents could use the medium to convey a point of view, mobilizing sequences of clips, comment, cartoons, visual metaphors, montages and the like, to do in short bites the kind of work that, say, Phil Agre's *Red Rock Eater News Service* electronic mailing list does on the Internet (see dlis.gseis.ucla.edu/people/pagre/rre.html). Indeed, the jacket could potentially mediate attention structures of the kinds Lanham has in mind with respect to high-density, topical information.

In many cases, successful displays might take the form more of creating initial *opportunities* subsequently to gain and build attention in the manner described by MacLeod – by establishing initial contacts that may create the possibility of developing relationships via attention transactions. This could take diverse forms. An exponent could broadcast arresting or entertaining 'display bytes' that achieve their task of establishing a sense of identity and presence instantaneously – in the moment of a passing by. Alternatively, a display text might simply announce a product or service that can be 'taken down now' (e.g. a URL, phone contact, email address) or memorized for following up later. Part of displaying successfully is likely to be a matter of 'immediate effects' (rhetorical, quirky, stunning), but much will likely be predicated on having something to say that is worth hearing, something to sell that is worth buying, and so on.

'Skimming'

There is much about the modus operandi of skim.com and their customers that speaks to the theme of new literacies in the service of gaining attention. The company's tagline 'skim.com provokes communication' is a carefully contrived attention-grabbing device that uses language in an arresting way – e.g. *provoking* as distinct from *inviting* communication. The message to consumers is 'wear this item with the skim.com number and you will attract attention!' Indeed, the explanation provided for how the number works begins with '(Step) 1: You attract people's attention . . . (Step) 2: . . . they note the number and send you an email . . .' (www.skim.com).

Communicative practices – literacies – are absolutely integral to skim.com's project (a Discourse) of shaping identity formation in its own economic interests and those of similar organizations. The associations established by the emblazoned URL and unique personalized numbers on the clothing items represent (or symbolize) 'urban creatures' in terms of several defining characteristics. First, they are *highly mobile* (a free email account you can access from anywhere), and *'wired'* (a regular and competent Internet user). They are also represented as *communicators* and *social animals* (who share their interests, tastes, and consumer experiences with others – including people utterly unknown to them who may live anywhere on the planet), and as *information seekers* (who will contact other skimmers to access their opinions and experiences).

These same cases also *reconstruct* ways of consuming, marketing, and other forms of commercial engagement in distinctively new ways. Literacies are central to these new ways. skim.com, for example, has developed strategies for building international *communities of consumers* through use of email. Individuals who would never otherwise know or meet each other are encouraged and enabled to identify themselves as members of the same community or discourse. This enlists the human capacities for and interests in (or 'needs' for) friendship and sociability in the service of building a particular fashion-oriented community that is catered to by a specific enterprise. In this way, the *meaning* (existential meaning, symbolic–representational meaning, and personal meaning) of consuming certain kinds of goods and services, or of being a fashion-conscious person, becomes associated with other powerful domains and practices of meaning, such as *friendship*, *membership* and *belonging*, operating on a global scale.

'Meme-ing' and 'culture jamming'

The idea of 'memes', mentioned in Chapter 2, can also be seen as a kind of metalevel literacy that could prove very effective for gaining attention as well as in processes of constructing attention structures along the lines described by Lanham. The logic of the meme, as a hook or a catch that gets behind the early warning systems and immunity guards of our mindsets, ideological stances and existing discursive 'investments', lends itself well to the rapid fire logic of a display medium like the wearable jacket. On the other hand, the highly public context of the jacket lends itself well to the 'replication' requirements of a would-be-successful meme. Memes, of course, might be seen as a kind of attention structure in their own right. In any event, the main purpose of memes is to harness and mobilize attention. Successful 'memers' command a lot of attention, although that is not to say they are seeking it. But to practise successfully in an attention economy, being a skilled 'memer' would be a definite advantage.

The same comment applies to various forms of culture jamming. As we noted in Chapter 2, the logic of culture jamming tactics is precisely a logic of gaining maximum attention with minimum resources or inputs.

'Scenariating'

Building or narrating scenarios along the lines described in Chapter 2 is a good way of coming up with original or fresh ideas of the kind needed to attract and sustain attention. As we noted earlier, scenarios are catchy narratives that describe possible futures and alternative paths toward the future, based on plausible hypotheses and assumptions grounded in the present. We think of 'scenariating' as comprising a kind of literacy because it is a way of reading and writing the world (of the future). It also, of course, involves the literal production of texts.

In relation to the economics of attention, 'scenariating' is a potentially significant new literacy. In part this is because it provides a basis for coming up with innovative, original, and interesting information. In addition, however, scenarios address a topic in which almost everybody has a keen interest: what the future might be like and how to prepare for it. Scenarios can work very well as attention structures, providing frames within which people can work on information in ways that make it useful. There are many reasons for engaging adolescent students in activities of building and narrating scenarios besides their potential value for facilitating participation in an attention economy. The latter, however, would be sufficient reason on its own because of its fruitfulness as a way of balancing originality and freshness with sheer usefulness for human beings in most areas of everyday life.

'Attention transacting'

This is based on MacLeod's idea of both-way information flows grounded in reciprocal interests that create and sustain relationships (2000: 7). 'Attention transacting' need not be grounded in commercial or business motives. It is about knowing how to elicit information from others, encouraging them to provide it (with appropriate assurances), and knowing how to work with that information so that it becomes an instrument for meeting what the other party believes to be their needs or interests. These may be in terms of goods, services, or more interpersonal concerns. To a large extent there is nothing particularly *new* involved here. It is similar to the kind of thing talkback radio hosts, psychoanalysts, therapists, market researchers, and diverse kinds of consultants have had to learn to do in the past using different media. What *is* new is largely the use of new information technologies to obtain, interpret, share, and act on information of a private nature, knowing how to build and honour trust in online settings, knowing how to divulge and interpret information obtained electronically in appropriate ways, and so on. So far as formal education is concerned, of course, this is an entirely new literacy because it projects into modes and domains of life with which schools have not typically been concerned – even in subject areas like business and commercial practice. Interestingly, various 'meta' approaches to language and literacy education, such as 'genre theory', have access to theories and concepts of direct relevance to developing such a new literacy. Conventional curriculum and syllabus foci, however, have rarely encouraged serious movement into the kinds of reading and writing implicit in attention transacting. Many of these will have to be invented 'on the fly' and by trial and error – as with so much that it is important to know during any significant period of transition.

'Attention transferring' (or 'trickle across')

The principle of transferring is apparent each time one uses a search engine to locate information on a well-recognized expert or authority and turns up a student assignment, or reads a journal article that takes the form of an interview with a well-known person conducted (and published) by a much less (or un)known person, or when one happens upon webpages and zines lovingly assembled by fans. Transferring is based on the principle that 'you have to be in to win'. If one has something to say or offer that might otherwise remain unrecognized and unknown, one has nothing to lose by hitching to it or bundling it up with a personality or theme that enjoys a good deal of attention. This literacy may involve nothing more than inserting references or hyperlinks into a text published on the Web. At a more complex level, it may involve negotiating an interview, conducting, editing, and 'thematizing' the interview, and then getting it placed for publication. Attention transferring will also be an important aspect of other literacies like contact displaying. In many ways, of course, there is absolutely nothing *new* in either chronological or ontological terms about the principle or the practice of 'attention transfer'. What *is* new, we would suggest, is the idea of taking it seriously as a form of literacy that goes beyond standard conceptions of fair acknowledgement, acceptable citation, referencing and bibliographic practices, and so on. To some extent it might be thought of as new in 'paradigmatic' terms. For example, the 'new capitalism' moved from a paradigm of (company versus company) competitive capitalism to versions of 'communitarian capitalism' (Gee *et al.* 1996: Ch. 2) that extend to the level of supernational trading blocs like the European Community. In similar ways, 'networking' and 'collaboration' have likewise become integral to a new paradigm of operating in diverse spheres of daily life in order to benefit each by benefiting the other(s). At the level of language use and textual work, attention transferring might be seen as a form of 'proactive linking' intended to improve one's chances of capturing and sustaining attention in the process of directing attention toward someone else.

'Framing' and 'encapsulating': beyond keywords

Lanham (1994: 1) makes an important and interesting point in his comment on the 'hot search for software intelligence agents that will create "gateways" of one sort or another without further human intervention'. This endeavour has developed in conjunction with attempts to define 'information literacy' and identify the kinds of skills – e.g. locating maximally efficient keywords – integral to being informationally literate. There is another side to this literacy, which relates more directly to attention. One example was evident in the discourse of 'tricks' to use when registering one's website to ensure it comes near the top of the list of returned keyword searches. And if aiming for near the top is too grandiose, the goal is at least to find a place as often as possible within the kinds of searches people are likely to do about the things one has to offer.

This is useful so far as it goes. But Lanham is pitching for higher and richer stakes in his focus on attention structures. He is after ways of *framing* information that hook us into organizing our interests within an area in this way rather than that; or in ways of *encapsulating* information that stand out because they are especially attractive or interesting. This involves the kind of analytical and theoretical work that puts someone sufficiently 'on top of' a subject or area to allow them to find angles that attract and compel. Notions like 'a brief history of time', 'Pythagoras's trousers', 'a language instinct' or 'things biting back' are reasonably familiar (if high-end) examples.

The point here is that reading and writing the world (of information) is very different from the kind of approach evident in providing the usual kind of short lists of keywords and the like. The same kind of difference is evident in titles for works: some (like the examples listed above) are frames and 'capsules'; others are more like keywords (accurate, functional, but short on inspiration). The best, of course, are both. Their production encapsulates the kind of literacy we have in mind here.

Attention, schools!

The examples sketched here are sufficient to indicate and illustrate the nature and extent of the challenge facing formal education if we believe schools ought to be paying more attention to attention. Many of the (new) literacies identified here are 'higher order literacies' and 'meta literacies'. Some are good for creating opportunities to gain attention, others for facilitating and structuring attention, and others for getting and maintaining attention. Some are good for a combination of these. Few of them, however, are closely related to most of what passes for literacy in schools today.

This is a major challenge in its own right. There is, however, a prior problem that, like so much else that concerns us here, can be seen in terms of mindsets. This is that attention is currently constituted mainly as a *problem* for schools. For example, 'attention seeking' is closely associated with – often cited as a cause of – behavioural problems. On the other hand, learning difficulties are often attributed to 'short attention spans' and 'attention deficiency'. Schools are caught between trying to reduce *and* to increase attention.

Interestingly, what we might call postmodern worlds of the Web, channel surfing, and 'playing the future' (Rushkoff 1996) and postmaterialist worlds of the attention economy *openly embrace* tendencies that currently constitute problems for schools. It may well be time in formal education to rethink the issue of attention. The interface between digital technologies and new literacies offers a promising place to start.

For many of us this will present a challenge to existing mindsets. Cathie Walker (1998) – self-styled Queen of the Internet, creator of the Centre for the Easily Amused and co-founder of forkinthehead.com – signals something of what this challenge might involve. In 'Short attention spans on the web', she confesses to having once read in a magazine that if you don't grab the attention of average web surfers within 10 seconds they'll be out of your site. She immediately qualifies that claim by admitting that she doesn't remember whether the exact figure was 10 seconds because her own attention span 'isn't that great either' (Walker 1998: 1).

If we can 'hack' that kind of entree, and accept her celebration of the short attention span as a basic assumption for effective website design, the five short paragraphs that follow in Walker's statement provide an engaging perspective on literacy in relation to attention. Her perspective may well have more to offer that will benefit school-age learners than many scholarly works on literacy that are at present highly valued and widely cited within academic communities. At the very least it would provide learners with resources for problematizing 'attention' and for evaluating literacies that pitch for attention.

At the opposite extreme, the sources we have used to explore the economics of attention endorse the importance of having a good grasp of theory and analysis. This is not necessarily an explicit grasp of highbrow theory and analysis. Our key authors uniformly assume that an emphasis on content and lower order skills is not enough for capturing, sustaining, or – particularly – for *structuring* attention. The kinds of competencies associated with successfully engaging the economics of attention are those that come with a capacity to *re-search* aspects of the world as opposed to merely 'looking at them' or 'receiving them as content'. To repeat, this is not to imply a highbrow or academic approach to research. At the same time, such approaches will be useful if certain things are in place – such as an interest in 'angles', an interest in originality, willingness to take risks, concern for point of view and so on. The generic sense of 're-search' we have in mind here is actually inherent in the very kinds of new literacies we have begun to identify. We think it is now time for us to explore, develop, and encourage such literacies as core components of any viable literacy curriculum. While imaginative and expansive use of new ICTs is not a *necessary* facet of such literacies (e.g. they are not presupposed in scenariating, attention transferring, meme-ing, or framing), it will often enhance and enrich their scope and possibilities.

Finally, if we believe that formal education has something to do with helping prepare (young) people for the worlds they will enter, it will be worth exploring further conceptions and implications of the economics of attention, and relating them to our conceptions and practices of literacy education within formal settings. Moving beyond attention, the next chapter will take us into some other kinds of spaces that will figure prominently in tomorrow's world of today's students.

CHAPTER 6

The Ratings Game: From eBay to Plastic

Introduction

Current educational literature is awash with talk of 'new literacies', 'technoliteracies', 'multiliteracies' and the like in response to the deep incursion of new information and communication technologies into everyday routines within modern societies. Much of this talk is general and impressionistic, however. Considerably less documentation of new literacy practices engendered and mediated by the Internet has been forthcoming, let alone of what social issues and responsibilities such new practices may evoke.

This chapter focuses on the emergence of the community ratings feedback systems on eBay and Plastic as cases of a new literacy – a new way of reading and writing aspects of the world that are important to participants in these online activities. It explores the rise of ratings systems as regulating devices within online communities, and how these are taken up (or not taken up) by community members.

In particular, the ratings system used on eBay will be examined from two standpoints that are evolving to a considerable extent in tension with one another. One standpoint is that of its creators – the owners and operators of eBay – and their communitarian 'visionary' purposes for developing it. The other standpoint is that of its users, among whom many seem to be appropriating the community ratings feedback system for personal purposes – some of which appear mean-spirited and intentionally self-serving to say the least.

The ratings system on Plastic – whose tagline reads 'Recycling the Web in real time' – is an online forum devoted to posting and discussing the 'best content from all over the Web for discussion' (Plastic 2002a: 1). Its rating and filtering system is one of the striking things about Plastic. Participants can use this to screen out comments with low ratings, and read only those rated highly. This saves them time they would otherwise have to spend sifting through postings to sort out those that are worth reading from those that aren't.

The use of rating systems as public evaluations of 'worth' (moral, commercial, intellectual, etc.) is not confined to these two sites alone. Rather, as mentioned earlier, it is spreading rapidly across a range of different web-based communities. For example, Amazon.com – the 'Earth's Biggest Selection™ of products' (Amazon.com 2002: 1) – has set in place a 5-star rating system that users can use to evaluate products and Amazon.com Marketplace sellers (where purchases are made directly from companies, rather than Amazon.com), and a numerical system that alerts buyers to the sales ranking of a product within the Amazon.com system.

Our aim in this chapter is to capture something of the dialectic between *strategies* of producers and *uses* of consumers (de Certeau 1984) at play in the emergence of a distinctively contemporary practice of everyday life online.

What *is* eBay?

eBay was among the first person-to-person auction venues to go online. It is currently the most popular and successful Internet trading community in the world (Friedman 2000; Multex.com 2001: 1). As of early 2002, eBay has over 42.4 million registered users and each day users list millions of items for auction in more than 8000 categories – and it is still growing (eBay 2002a: 1; MSN Money 2002: 1). Categories range from premium artworks, through real estate and cars, to clothing, jewellery, toys, comics and trading cards (with one person recently auctioning off his soul . . .). eBay describes itself as the world's personal trading community, [which] has changed the way people buy and sell collectibles and unique items. By providing a safe trading place on the Internet, the eBay community has flourished. Not only does eBay provide an efficient medium for people to buy or sell items directly from or to a large number of people, it's a forum where buyers and sellers develop reputations and, in some cases, it can change people's lives.

(eBay 2002b: 1)

eBay (www.ebay.com) comprises sets of Internet pages that are basically long lists of new and used items that people have posted to the eBay Internet site for sale by auction. Sellers are responsible for writing item descriptions and for generating pictures of the items that are then inserted into an eBay page template and posted on the eBay website under a self-selected category heading (and where it is automatically allocated an item number). Potential buyers – who must be registered with eBay – browse these lists or use the eBay search function to locate items of interest. They can then bid on or 'watch' these items. Watching involves clicking on the 'watch this item' hyperlink, and the item is then hotlinked to one's personal 'eBay' space (i.e. 'my eBay').

Bidding works in two ways, similarly to conventional auctions. Bidders may make the lowest viable bid possible at that particular point in time and wait to see what happens (or place a new minimum bid after being outbid by someone else). Alternatively, they can place a 'proxy' bid – which is the maximum amount they are willing to pay for the item – and eBay acts for them as a proxy bidder: bidding in their place until the item is 'won' or their specified maximum amount has been exceeded by another bidder. Sellers – who are also always registered members of eBay – pay to list their items with eBay. The fee depends on the starting price or reserve set for an item (e.g. a $0.01 to $9.99 starting price costs $0.30 to list, and a reserve price of $0.01 to $24.99 costs $0.50 to list), or on the type of item being listed (real estate comes with a $50.00 listing set fee, as does a vehicle). Items can also be sold for a fixed price (i.e. not auctioned off) under the eBay stores service. These items are subject to a different listing fee scale. Commission on auctioned and other sold items is charged at 5.25 per cent of the first $25.00, and an additional 2.75 per cent after that up to $1000. From $1000 onwards, 1.5 per cent commission is paid on the remaining amount (eBay 2002c: 1). eBay membership is free, as is bidding and browsing.

eBay currently operates in 20 countries and 10 languages. Although it is certainly advantageous to access an eBay site in your home country (language, currency, dates, time, and shipping wise), it is possible to bid from anywhere in the world whenever payment options and shipping agreements permit.

What's *new* about eBay

While some people might claim that eBay is just an old physical space (auctions) in virtual get-up, we think it is spawning some genuinely new social practices and new literacies associated with them.

We will make our case for the newness of some of the social practices and literacies associated with them from two angles. The first simply identifies some new features of reading relevant aspects of the world occasioned by moving the familiar social practice of auctioning into an unfamiliar space, namely the virtual space of the Internet. One or two brief examples must suffice here.

eBay calls for interesting new constellations or 'batteries' of ways of reading and writing in order to achieve one's purposes as an online buyer or seller. For example, the eBay venue operates as a 'transaction medium'. Nobody at eBay sees or handles what is being bought and sold. And there is nobody to tell one where to go to find what one is looking for (or might want to look for if one knew it could be available). Hence, it is not a matter simply of knowing how to read or write the text of item descriptions. Participants need also to know how to navigate through or add to the website. For example, they need to know how to access and read the battery of 'how-to' texts provided on the eBay website (e.g. how to bid, how to post an item for sale, how to leave feedback, how to lodge formal complaints about a buyer or seller, how to access user-to-user help and advice discussion lists). Users also need to know how to read and write 'taxonomically' in the sense of knowing what is likely to be in or should be in each category – of which there are thousands. They need to be able to read between the lines in item descriptions (e.g. a Clarice Cliff-style crocus jug is *not* a Clarice Cliff crocus jug). In many cases it is necessary to be able to read digitized images accurately (e.g. know that colour is often not true-to-life in digital images of objects, understand depth of field and the effects it has on objects, be wary of out-of-focus or soft focus images or lighting effects). Knowing (how) to convert from imperial to metric measures, or even one currency to another, is often required for international dealings; and so on. Fakes and forgeries are much easier to disguise on eBay than in meatspace. Collectors appear to have developed a whole new set of criteria for judging the authenticity of an item. These include evaluating the source of the product (e.g. if the seller is the daughter or son of a famous sportsperson, then it's likely the sports memorabilia he or she is selling is genuine); judging the seller by location (e.g. someone selling art deco ceramics and living in England or ex-English colonies is most likely to be selling authentic pieces in good condition); judging the seller by the other products he or she has listed for auction (cf. Smith and Smith c.2002). They also include a wariness of what some call 'overdocumentation'. This is the presence of too many documents 'verifying' the authenticity of an item (Sherman 2001: 63). Perhaps most importantly, however, the reader of item descriptions and images has to pay careful attention to what is *not* said or shown. For example, sellers who list high-end designer handbags (e.g. Gucci, Hermés, Coach) without mentioning that the bag has a serial number, or who do not list the silver content stamp (.925 or higher) for a purported solid silver item, may be less likely to be selling an authentic item.

Moreover, physical or meatspace literacy practices often *mean* different things within eBay. For example, one regular eBay user we interviewed said she loves coming across item descriptions that include misspelled words. To her it means she is more likely to 'win' a bargain from this person than from someone who spells correctly. Non-standard spelling indicates to her someone who is less likely to be in a professional job or to own a shop and hence, in her eyes, to be less likely to know the real value of the ceramics or other objects they are offering for sale.

The second way of considering what is new about eBay is by reference to Bezos's distinction between first- and second-phase automation introduced in Chapter 3. Indeed, eBay provided Bezos with an exemplar of the kind of thing he wanted to do. We may recall Bezos's distinction here by way of Robert Spector's (2000: 16) account of Bezos's passion for 'second-phase automation':

> Bezos has described second-phase automation as 'the common theme that has run through my life. The first phase of automation is where you use technology to do the same old business processes, but just faster and more efficiently'. A typical first phase of automation in the e-commerce field would be barcode scanners and point-of-sale systems. With the Internet 'you're doing the same process you've always done, but just more efficiently'. He described the second phase of automation as 'when you can fundamentally change the underlying business process and do things in a completely new way. So it's more of a revolution instead of an evolution'.

Bezos's distinction enables us to distinguish further between processes and

practices that have simply become 'digitized' and those practices and processes that exist only because digital technologies do. As we can see by
reference to its community feedback ratings system, eBay is a case of the
latter.

In his analysis of globalization, Thomas Friedman (2000) distinguishes
between two roles available for companies, governments and institutions
in the 'Evernet world' of globalized networks of communication, service
and power. He calls these roles 'shapers' and 'adapters' respectively.
Shapers are agents that shape up activities within a globalized world of
networked coalitions and practices – whether that activity is 'making a
profit, making war or making a government or corporation respect human
rights' (Friedman 2000: 202). Shapers design rules, create interaction
frameworks and set new standards for global practices. Adapters, on the
other hand, follow shapers' leads and adapt to the 'scene' being created.

Friedman identifies eBay as a foremost and highly original shaper. He
sees it as having been a leader in creating a whole new market place and
instigating an entirely new set of interaction protocols for buyers and sellers. eBay, says Friedman, 'came out of nowhere and within three years created a new set of rules and forms of interaction by which consumers would
buy and sell things on the World Wide Web' (Friedman 2000: 202). At the
core of eBay's business process is a simple rating scale and 80-character
feedback system by which buyers can rate and respond to the effectiveness
of sellers over the course of a transaction, and *vice versa*. This ratings
system has been absolutely integral to eBay's success in its enterprise. It has
simultaneously transformed relations between buyers and sellers on the
Internet, and been elevated to prominence in the identity-shaping and
reputation-making behaviour of many individuals in the practice of pursuing a positive ratings profile.

eBay's rating system involves a three-point rating scale – positive, neutral, and negative – that serves as a public judgement of a person's reputation, trustworthiness and reliability. Once an auction transaction has
been completed (the winning bidder has paid for and received the item) the
buyer can leave feedback about the seller and *vice versa* by means of the
item number. Only the buyer and seller are authorized to comment formally on a particular transaction. Feedback consists of the actual rating
(positive, neutral, negative), and a written recommendation.

eBay's website reminds eBayers that 'honest feedback shapes the community' (eBay 2002d: 1). The higher the positive ratings a person has, the
more 'reputable', 'trustworthy', and 'reliable' they are in eBay terms. On
the other hand, accumulating a net feedback rating of −4 (minus four)
means an individual can be excluded from the eBay community. Exclusion

is not automatic, however, since it is up to users to notify eBay that someone has received four or more negative ratings.

As an aside, eBay's success has spawned a diverse range of complementary products and services, many of which entail literacies of one kind or another. For example, *eBay a-go-go*™ has been purpose-designed to be an eBay wireless auction alerting service that operates via one's mobile phone or pager. It alerts users when they have been outbid on, won, or sold an item. There are also various auction 'tracking' and bidding software programs and online services (e.g. eSnipe: www.esnipe.com; Bid Napper: www.bidnapper.com/), online mediation services for auction transactions that go wrong, escrow and e-cash services (e.g. BidPay and Billpoint), a range of how-to-bid-successfully books (e.g. Collier and Woerner 2000; Reno *et al.* 2000), and online beginners' introductions to eBay (e.g. SoYouWanna 2000). Finally, for those who are truly serious about learning how to read and write the world according to eBay, there is eBay University (pages.ebay.com/university).

Why *ratings*?

eBay's overt intention in devising and implementing the feedback ratings system is to build a self-monitoring ethical community of eBay users – or 'eBayers' for short. We would argue that the feedback ratings system might actually be read as an embodied ideological induction into a certain community-based 'cyberspace'. That is, eBay is not only a shaper within the new technologies arena, but it is also an 'educator' in that it 'teaches' people how they *should* act within this new cyberspace, and therefore, how they should act in relation to each other. It is, therefore, a space of induction. It plays a role in shoring up new discursive norms. It socializes people about what counts as an exemplary global space, and helps generate good global citizens by encouraging the 'right' kind of cyber practices that lead to a well-organized and civil World Wide Web.

Indeed, even this side of the eBay experience is held up as an exemplary model for other companies to emulate on the Internet.

> Besides being creative about using the Internet, Kanter says, there are other ingredients of the eBay model that companies should study as they expand their Web initiatives. She emphasizes principles rooted as much in social interaction as in the tenets of business: a sense of community where people can talk to one another as well as with the company they patronize and a corporate culture that reinforces those connections and serves all members.

As an example, Kanter points to eBay's Giving Board, where users can post a problem and receive advice from other eBay members. 'You get a lot of loyalty by treating people as members of a community', she says. 'Analysts can't quite quantify that, but it sure shows up in eBay's profitability.'

(Heun 2001: 1)

eBayers and their ratings

eBayers are very clear about the importance of their ratings. Many go to extraordinary lengths to obtain positive ratings. Some item postings contain a 'customer assurance statement' that resembles an airline 'thanks for flying with us' patter to stand in as a 'bid confidently' statement. For example,

> A Word of Thanks . . . We at Lorelei's Jewelry would like to Thank all of our Customers for their Patronage over the last 4 years. Our number 1 priority is to give you the best Customer Service in the Business. We know that you have choices and appreciate your business. Our Goal is to provide an Exceptional Line of Jewelry at the Absolute Lowest Prices. We are here to answer any Questions that you may have in a Timely Manner Via Telephone or Email. All Winning Bidders are Notified Promptly and Items are Normally Shipped the Day Payment is received. We hope that you will join our long list of Satisfied Customers . . . Over 10,000 Feedbacks and Growing Daily.
>
> (Lorelei's 2000: 1)

The reference to 10,000 feedbacks is the clincher here. It is worn like a badge of honour (although canny eBayers will note that the company does not advertise '10,000 *positive* feedbacks' and will immediately go to the company's ratings page to verify the ratings are positive as implied). Some sellers email successful bidders at the end of a transaction to let them know the seller has left them positive feedback. The email can even contain a hyperlink to automated feedback forms. Customers need only fill in the actual rating and the written feedback line.

Many individual eBayers have constructed elaborate processes that aim at ensuring as many positive feedback statements and ratings as possible:

> I have a spreadsheet that i use to keep track of my items, buying and selling and there is a space for me to check off that i have left feedback for a buyer/seller. When the buyer/seller leaves feedback for me in return, i circle the check mark, letting me know the transaction has come full circle. when i sell something, i include a thank you card with the item number listed, the item name listed, my ebay name and a note

stating that i have left positive feedback for them and would appreciate the same in kind and i still have problems getting them to leave me feedback! So every month, i go down the spreadsheet and e-mail those who have failed to leave feedback asking them why they have not done so and if there were problems i was not aware of. this is very time consuming but it has worked on most of the delinquents. it more or less embarrasses them into leaving feedback.

(eBay Feedback Discussion Board, 2001)

Having even one negative feedback is perceived as bad for business:

[Ratings and feedback] are very important as it's the only real way of knowing how good sellers are. I have never bought off someone with a bad rating and there are quite a few of them out there . . . I have had to give out a few bad ratings to people who have won auctions and have never paid me or contacted me for that matter.

(*arkanoid2020* email interview 12 February 2001)

[Ratings] are extremely important. I don't want to buy from vendors with negative feedback, and I don't expect people to want to buy from me if I have any. Those comments are listed in red, and they show up like a neon sign!!.

(*bea1997* email interview 25 September 2000)

Ratings have actually become a 'currency' for the eBay community, assuming the kind of role local community networks and character references have in physical space. One of our interviewees, *susygirl*, says:

I really take pride in [my ratings]. And for me it is the alter ego – it is susygirl's not mine. And so I get pissed [off] if someone doesn't send me a positive feedback. But I never write and ask them to. Some sellers do that and I usually don't respond to that.

(email interview 1 February 2001)

Others, like *bea1997*, a long-term and very experienced eBayer, have preferred to be 'duped' by buyers than risk negative feedback. *bea1997* explained to us,

Sometimes I lose money from customers who break an item and ask for money back. I just don't want to risk having my good reputation ruined for a few lousy bucks so I just take the blame and send their money back.

(email interview 25 September 2000)

bea1997's experience tallies with others reported elsewhere. For example, Erick Sherman recounts,

Both buyers and sellers get burned from time to time, but usually not badly. Shamus remembers someone who bought a $25 trading card from him on eBay then returned it, but with a corner newly bent. 'He said, "That's what you sent me" ', says Shamus, who didn't argue because the amount was too small and negative feedback would hurt his future sales.

(Sherman 2001: 63)

Others have vigorously fought with eBay to have what the eBayer regards as unjust negative feedback removed (which is almost impossible to have done), and various eBayers have established entire websites devoted to explaining the events behind any negative feedback they have received.

Ratings are considered by most eBayers to be so important that the dedicated discussion board attached to the eBay website (located on a server in the US) for discussing feedback is a popular and much-used service. This 'board' is a web-based service that allows people to post messages (or responses to messages) about their ratings and feedback problems, warnings about 'deadbeat' sellers or buyers, 'sniping' (bidders waiting until the very last moment to place a winning bid), how to go about lodging a complaint about an unfair negative rating, and so on. Despite eBay's emphasis on *community*, however, the rating and feedback system has not made for close-knit and harmonious fellowship.

Reciprocity is a key value enacted on eBay in relation to ratings. As *susygirl* observed, she is 'pissed [off]' if she completes a transaction and the seller doesn't leave feedback for her. Reciprocity in ratings is likewise important to *arkanoid2020*: 'I have also had the problem of people not giving me a rating after a successful transaction, which is a shame because I always make the effort' (email interview 12 February 2001). Other eBayers express their feelings about a lack of reciprocity very strongly. Much of the eBay-based discussion about ratings is taken up with who should leave feedback and a rating first, and why. For example,

I figured out feedback right away. When I receive an item I immediately leave feedback. That's my way of keeping track of things. I then immediately email the seller and thank them for good service (I've been very fortunate in this regard.) and ask them to leave feedback. It seems to me that sellers will only leave feedback if requested to do so and _if_ I leave positive feedback. Sellers should leave feedback when they get my prompt payment in my opinion. Why do I have to gently nudge them and leave my feedback first? They get my money first.

(eBay Feedback Discussion Board 2001)

In bad-case scenarios, the power of leaving feedback is held over the buyer or seller. For example, when a buyer has received an item and for some reason wants to return it to the seller, but the seller does not agree to receive it back, the buyer may threaten to leave negative feedback if the seller does not comply with his or her wishes. eBay members refer to this as 'feedback hostage taking' – where the seller (or buyer) is held hostage to receiving feedback (e.g. 'I'll leave you feedback only when you've left me feedback'). In worst-case scenarios, this is what eBayers refer to as 'feedback extortion', and it is taken very seriously by eBay itself.

The eBay feedback system has actually generated a metalanguage for talking about participant practices. This vocabulary comprises mostly new, mostly pejorative terms that eBayers invent, and use freely and fluently (see Table 6.1).

Not surprisingly, exchanges on the feedback discussion board can become heated, with little evidence of the kind of tolerance one would expect in a community of the kind eBay aims to foster:

> and i agree if you knew the answer why bother asking? i get lots of people asking stupid ? [trans: questions] like what does it measure? when it is already posted on my auctions ... i tell them to go back and read the description. i don't find that to be rude.
>
> (eBay Feedback Discussion Board 2001)

And responses from two different people:

> not rude? must be why you have so many successful transactions ... Why not just answer the question and accept that stupid people make up a big percentage of customers?

> The guy's sarcastic, not rude. Read his very limited, posted feedback for a good laugh.

The reference to the first poster's 'successful transactions' and 'very limited, posted feedback' are snide comments on the poster's beginner status: one positive rating. Such reactions indicate a tendency for eBayers to read ratings both as statements of their public reputations and as indicators of 'wisdom' and knowledge where all things eBay are concerned.

eBay's response to the soap opera-like dimensions of the community feedback and ratings system is to continue holding out for a self-regulating, 'trustworthy' and intelligent community:

> Hello folks,

> Thanks for the discussion. Let me offer you eBay's perspective on Feedback for consideration:

> The real value in Feedback is in the trends that it reveals. While it is an admirable goal to work towards a perfect rating, it is IMPOSSIBLE to always please everyone all the time anywhere in life, right? An occasional isolated negative will not impact the VAST majority of users when they are deciding whether or not to bid or accept a bid. (I would say 'ANY' users, but then someone would post to prove me wrong, hehehe).

> We hope you will use the Feedback forum faithfully, despite the risk of receiving a negative that you feel you don't deserve, because in this way our whole community is served best. The purpose of Feedback is to help keep the site safe. If we use it appropriately, the good guys are always going to have FAR more positive comments than the less-scrupulous users who will quickly earn track records that show their true colors for all to see, as well.

> Daphne will step down from her soapbox now. :)

Table 6.1 Shared metalanguage on eBay's Feedback Discussion Board

Term	Definition
Feedback bombing	Two senses: (1) The process whereby two or more people gang up on someone, purchase products, then leave negative feedback (regardless of the quality of product or service). (2) The process whereby two or more people gang up on someone, purchase products, then leave positive feedback (and this is usually reciprocal – those in on the scam positively bomb each other's auction).
Feedback padding	One person creates two eBay bidding accounts and uses one account to pad out the feedback on his or her other account.
Feedback extortion	eBay defines feedback extortion as 'demanding any action from a fellow user that he or she is not required to do, at the threat of leaving negative feedback'.
Retaliatory negative feedback	When a negative feedback rating is given to one person in an eBay transaction by the other, the first responds with a negative rating, regardless of the quality of service received. This often goes hand in hand with feed-back hostage taking (e.g. 'I was really unhappy with this transaction but can't leave feedback until the other one does because I want to leave a negative feedback, but I am worried that if I leave it first then the person I'm dealing with will give me a negative feedback in response!').
(To be) neutralled	To receive a 'neutral' rating (it is also possible to 'neutral' someone, too; that is, to give them a neutral rating).
(To be) NEGed (also 'neg')	To receive a 'negative' rating (it is also possible to 'NEG' someone, too; that is, to give them a negative rating).
Deadbeat bidder or seller (also referred to as 'deadbeats')	This is the term eBayers use to describe people who do not deliver on their half of the transaction (i.e. who do not pay or do not send the item, or who send the item in poor condition, etc.). eBay's official term for bidders who skip out on a deal is 'Non-Paying Bidders', or NPBs for short.

Daphne
eBay Community Support

(eBay Feedback Discussion Board, 10 March 2000)

Interestingly, eBay has recently instituted a feedback service that alerts participants to items they have yet to leave feedback on. It is also possible to access a list of feedback each user *leaves* others. This adds a second dimension to a user's feedback and rating profile, and often makes for interesting exchanges in the discussion spaces of eBay.

Plastic

eBay users are not the only ones to take the ratings game seriously. eBay's ratings system has impacted powerfully on Internet-based social interactions, with numerous other interactive Internet sites using ratings systems as public reputation markers. Plastic is a good example of this. It is somewhat unusual on the Internet, however, since it evaluates quality of thinking and expression rather than business conduct.

Plastic began in January 2001, with the aim of being a 'new model' of news delivery: 'anarchy vs. hierarchy, and so on and so forth' (Joey 2001: 1), and promising 'the best content from all over the Web for discussion' (Schroedinger's Cat 2002: 1). This new model of news delivery puts 'the audience in charge of the news cycle as much as possible without devolving into the kind of ear-splitting echo chamber that's turned "community" into such a dirty word' (Joey 2001: 1). Historically speaking, Plastic was the offspring of a merger between Suck and Feed – two popular but culturally edgy content provider web services established in 1995 (Greenstein 2000: 1), combining the quirkiness of Suck newsletters with the insightful and wide-ranging discussions of Feed (cf. Anuff and Cox 1997; Johnson 1997). Plastic was launched in partnership with the editors and services of ten news and content providers – Spin, The New Republic, Inside, Movieline, Gamers.com, Modern Humorist, TeeVee, Netslaves, Nerve and Wired News – who helped to choose from among member submissions which news items would be posted on the Plastic website for discussion (Greenstein 2000). In December 2001 Plastic decided to go it alone with the help of 'user-editors' (Plastic members who act as volunteer submissions editors) after the web service was bought by Carl Steadman – known generically as 'Carl' by Plastic users – who remains Chief Editor and self-appointed site janitor.

The Plastic community is highly heterogeneous. Judging by the comments posted and the historical and cultural reference points used, however, the majority of users appear to be male, North American, and mostly 20- and 30-somethings. Or, as one anonymous poster described the typical Plastic user,

1. Age: 18 – 35
2. Education: Liberal Arts College, 3.5 years, no diploma.
3. Career: 2 – 10 years pulling lattes at Starbucks, 18 months at a failed dot-com, now an 'independent Web-design consultant.'
4. Likes: Digerati, biscotti, anime
5. Dislikes: Math, finance, work
6. Gender: One of six available choices
7. Politics: 60% lefty gonzo, 40% libertarian nutcake
8. Pastimes: S&M, B&D, T&A, LS/MFT (no weirdos, please!)

(Anonymous Idiot 2001: 1)

In other words, Plasticians tend to be self-styled members of an erudite, ironic and humorous 'plugged in' crowd, interested in quirky takes on anything newsworthy – particularly anything connected with popular culture – as well as in serious and informed discussion of current events. Estimates place the number of regular Plastic users at around 15,000 (McKinnon 2001: 1). And anything that will provoke discussion is regarded as postworthy (Carl, in an interview with Mathew Honan 2001: 1).

Although Plastic emulates a long-existing technology news and discussion website service devoted to a technogeek audience – Slashdot.com – it is 'new' in the sense that it turns 'push media' like email-posted newspaper headlines and news websites on their head by having members propose content and comment publicly upon it. 'Plastic's original contribution is a forum to discuss the diverse news pieces it promotes. At Plastic, readers' comments are what it's all about' (Barrett 2001: 1).

Items are written up by users and can be posted to eight topic categories: Etcetera, Film & TV, Games, Media, Music, Politics, Tech and Work. Those whose news items are accepted for posting and/or who post comments on the website are awarded ratings on two dimensions. One of these is 'karma', which is used to rate a participant as an active member of the community relative to the number of newsworthy postings – both in terms of submitting stories and posting comments on stories – she or he has made to the site overall. A karma rating of 50 or over generally elevates the poster to (volunteer) submissions editor status.

The other rating system – which is linked directly to karma – is peer moderation that operates on a scale of –1 to +5 for a posting overall. Nonregistered posters are allocated a default initial rating of 0 when they first post a comment, while the rating baseline for registered users is +1. Moderation points are awarded by Plastic's editors and by a changing group of registered Plastic members who have been randomly assigned the role by Plastic's editors; or, as the message alerting members to their new moderator status puts it, 'Congratulations! You've wasted so much time on

Plastic that for the next 4 days we're making you a moderator' (Plastic 2002a: 1). Each moderator gets 10 moderating points to award to posted comments on a Plastic news item, and the possible ratings each moderator can allocate are:

> Whatever 0
> Irrelevant –1
> Incoherent –1
> Obnoxious –1
> Astute +1
> Clever +1
> Informative +1
> Funny +1
> Genius +1
> Over-rated +1
> Under-rated +1

The moderation points awarded to each post are tallied and the final score is automatically updated and posted in the subject line of the message for readers to see. In other words, 'if four or five moderators think a comment is brilliant, it may end up with a +5; useless comments are moderated down to a –1' (Plastic 2002b: 2).

This ranking practice is based on formal recognition by the site that users cannot read everything that is posted on a topic. With a peer ranking system in place, users can set filters to screen out postings that fall outside a ranking range of their choice. For example, setting the filter threshold at +3 means only those comments that have been moderated and score at or above +3 will be displayed. Conversely, setting the filter threshold at –1 means every comment posted will be displayed. Plastic offers this ranking and filtering function as a means of helping users practise selective reading and to help enhance the quality of postings to the site.

Like the ratings system used on eBay, the moderation and karma system on Plastic does not necessarily ensure a harmonious community of users. 'Meta-discussions' involving litanies of complaints about being 'modded down' unfairly – or being a victim of 'downmod' attacks, where a moderator flushes out all your postings and moderates them down regardless of content – are common. One disgruntled user even went so far as to equate downmod attacks with terrorism:

> Well, to get back to the point I was making, there is a type of attack
> for which Plastic.com is almost uniquely susceptible. In this type of

attack, the terrorist chooses a victim. Then, when he [is] given the opportunity to moderate, he strikes. He goes through the victim's list of comments and then, ignoring Plastic's moderation guidelines, he moderates each of the comments downward. He does not care whether his moderation votes make sense, only that it drives down the rating of the comment. The terrorist's goal is to drive the victim's presence on Plastic 'under the Radar,' below the filtering level of most of the Plastic audience. He also wants to put the victim's Karma into a nosedive.

(Gravityzone 2001: 1)

Other users are accused of being 'karma whores' if they appear to be 'sucking up to' or worming their way into the favour of Plastic editors in the hopes of getting more stories accepted than other users, or having their comments modded up. As one poster put it bluntly to another, 'Tyler, kissing Bart's ass won't get you more stories posted' (jbou 2002: 1) in response to Tyler's comment in a heated discussion of the US's threats to invade Iraq again. Tyler made reference to Bart, one of Plastic's editors, and had written in part: 'My, we're feeling self-important today, aren't we jbou? Could you please point to Bart's "warmongering" posts? And why should he have to answer to you, or to anyone else, on command?' (tylerh 2002: 1).

And, despite some posters loudly and repeatedly protesting that they don't care about their overall karma, karma ratings – and the moderation system – are indeed 'a new arithmetic of self-esteem' on Plastic (Shroedinger's Cat 2002: 1). At stake is public recognition of a poster's incisive mind, keen-edged humour, 'innate hipness', and of being 'plugged in' (Plastic 2002a: 1).

Complexities

The point at which we began, with the idea of website communities that are organized around easy-to-use and read ratings systems as being new socializing spaces that shape people into becoming appropriate users of new cyber spaces, now appears much more complex – indeed, contradictory.

On one hand, eBay's community feedback ratings system has been an important factor in its stunning success to date. In part this is because it has helped establish eBay's mission and identity as a helpful broker, with its clients' best interests at heart, and as a responsible cyber force with whom people who want to be part of the project of building a successful tradition of e-commerce seek to be associated. Moreover, as emulators like

Plastic have found, engaging participants in active roles of evaluators – and content producers – encourages further participation, 'hooking' people in by publicly valuing their contributions. In addition, however, it appears that part of the success of ratings systems in web spaces such as eBay and Plastic has to do with the fact that it helps meet a range of personal needs, including identity and esteem needs. Both 'services' actively recruit membership to an affinity group with which one can identify (Gee 2001), and offer individuals and groups a way of attaining a visible and enviable presence. *susygirl* sums up this aspect of eBay nicely: 'For me it is a kind of therapy. I like it too because i become susygirl and not some English professor. I like to hide behind my new identity' (email interview 12 February 2001).

MayorBob, a well-respected member of the Plastic community, explains it this way: 'The nice thing about the karma [rating system] is that, when you're not getting downmod assaulted, you do get a little feedback on whether you are making sense or getting your point across' (MayorBob 2001: 1). In other words, besides providing a means for mediating responsible and satisfying commercial or intellectual exchange, the ratings system also offers a service to personal identity formation and to what is fast becoming a highly valued 'currency' – an exemplary personal ratings profile.

On the other hand, however, the practice of promoting written feedback and ratings in response to eBay transactions has become a space in which many participants engage in purposes that do not merely contradict the 'cyber civic' goal of eBay, but actually involve a range of malicious, preying, nasty, hurt-causing acts toward others (some of whom doubtless contribute to their own pain by investing more than is wise in the discourse and otherwise taking their 'profile' or 'identity' more seriously than the context merits). Some of the data we have presented concerning eBay smells of interpersonal power-tripping, petty acts of malice, and the desire to belittle others (which is endemic in Internet spaces). Similarly, Plastic discussions readily collapse into searing vitriolic exchanges of hate-laced postings and taunting challenges.

It goes without saying, then, that dynamic relationships exist between technologies and the practices in which they are employed. On one hand, the development of new technologies creates conditions in which people can change existing social practices and develop new ones, as well as change and develop new literacies that are integral parts of these new or changing practices. On the other hand, these practices simultaneously 'constitute' the technologies involved as cultural tools, and shape what they *mean* and, indeed, what they *are* within the various contexts in which people use them. In its complexity and contradictoriness, the 'ratings game' is par for the course so far as literacy and technology are concerned. The point here is simple and well-rehearsed, but bears reinforcing in the present context, since there are still many people who think the Internet unleashes all sorts of undesirable forces that are not equally present in the social practices of physical space.

Literacy and technology are never 'singular', never the 'same thing'. 'They' are always 'so many things' when in so many hands. The same alphabetic code can be used for writing notes to one's children or for publishing sophisticated experimental findings in learned journals. It can be used for writing good wishes to friends and for writing extortion notes to intended victims. The same kind of ambiguity and range is open to practically any tool or body of knowledge and information we care to name. The same is true of more specific literacies, including different forms of feedback and rating genres. We need only to think of the uses to which various kinds of referees' reports can be put for the point to be perfectly clear. The particular 'silicon literacy' of producing (or withholding) ratings and feedback shares the formal character of all literacies (different people put it to different uses, understand it differently, etc.). It is susceptible, then, to the same 'play' of moral, civic, and emotional forces – the way people are and how they live out their (in)securities, pleasures and pains, values and aspirations, and so on.

Strategies and uses: reading the social practice of rating others and feeding back

Among the multiple ways we might try to describe and understand some of this complexity, we find the option offered by Michel de Certeau's (1984) concept of consumer 'uses' particularly fruitful.

de Certeau develops a distinction between 'producers' and 'consumers' which is much wider than – but incorporates – our usual distinction drawn from the domain of commodity production. In this larger sense, producers are those with the power – and, hence, a 'place' (a 'proper') – from which to shape discourses and discursive formation in all spheres of human life. Institutions like universities mediate the producer role to the extent that they are sites where social actors with the acknowledged power to do so can maintain and police what counts as 'science'. Consumers are those (scientists themselves) who 'consume' the discourses by participating in them. The same distinction works all the way down to the level at which consumers consume specific artefacts of commodified popular culture, such as television fare as packaged entertainment. The strength of de Certeau's formulation is that it directs attention away from a narrow focus on particular acts of consuming artefacts and toward a wider and deeper understanding of social *practices* – in which individual acts *participate* but by no means *constitute*. Just as the 'operations' of producers are deeper and larger than we often think – they *produce* the discourse that *constitutes* a TV programme as *entertainment* in the first place, not merely the programme – so too are the 'operations' (*practices*) of consumers.

de Certeau develops a set of concepts including 'strategies', 'uses', and 'tactics' as part of a framework for investigating the nature and politics of cultural production within the practice of everyday life. He is keen to redress perceptions of consumers as passive effects or reflexes of the practices of producers, without denying the relations of differential power that play out across social and cultural groupings everywhere. He nonetheless wants to identify, understand, and explain the power by which the 'weak' manoeuvre within the spaces constituted strategically by producers, to make them habitable, and to meet their own purposes as best they can.

Producers, who have established and defined their own place from which to manage relations with an *exteriority* composed of targets or threats, can develop *strategies* to this end. Strategy is an art of the strong (cf. scientific institutions that define and regulate 'knowledge' through the power to provide themselves with their own place). Through strategic practices producers define the spaces to be lived in by all. Consumers, or the 'weak', cannot strategize. Instead, they can manoeuvre within the constraining order of regulatory fields within which they are obliged to operate by 'making use of' the constraining order and by employing 'tactics'. We will focus here only on 'uses'.

de Certeau illustrates 'uses' with examples like that of North African migrants being obliged to live in low-income housing estates in France and to speak the particular dialect of French used in the city they have migrated to, such as the kinds of French spoken in, say, Paris or Roubaix (see de Certeau 1984: 30–2). These people might insinuate into the system imposed on them 'the ways of "dwelling" (in a house or in a language) peculiar to [their] native Kabylia' (de Certeau 1984: 32). This introduces a degree of plurality into the system. It also confirms consumers as *active* to that extent – albeit still *subordinate* – in working to make such spaces 'habitable'.

We want to argue that this dialectic is present in every case of literacy and technology. In the present context, eBay's 'feedback and ratings' practice and the specific practices of literacy it engenders is a case in point. Where Friedman (2000) talks of eBay as a 'shaper' we may equally speak of eBay as a producer. As a constitutive element of shaping the field of commercial exchange in cyberspace – even if it is trying to do so in 'good' and 'civil' ways according to recognized discursive constructions of these; after all, there is nothing inherently 'wicked' about producers and their productions, since we are talking contingencies of power here as distinct from ethics *per se* – the community feedback and ratings system forms part of a constraining order. One can choose whether or not to *be* a 'consumer' within this space, but if one chooses to participate in this space, then its order applies.

What we think we see in the snippets of data presented above are varying 'ways' of consumers 'making use of' the ratings game. They are 'insinuating' into the system produced for them ways of 'dwelling' with which they are familiar, adept, or which they otherwise find satisfying or reinforcing – no matter how unpleasant we may find some of these. The 'silicon literacy' of ratings, then, can best be understood as endlessly complex and multiple. 'It' is flexed into myriad uses. 'It' is susceptible to policing and 'moralizing' on the part of producers and other consumers alike, just as much as and in parallel manners to the literacies of physical spaces like schools – where the 'players' involved are also inclined to invoke notions of fairness, propriety, and 'getting it right'.

In the end, online community feedback and ratings systems are often an illuminating microcosm of literacy and social practice at large. We may, if we choose, use it as a reference point from which to consider the dialectics of production and consumption of the official literacies of school. We might consider where we, personally, are positioned in these, and with what consequences for learners whose 'right' to consume is, precisely, an obligation in the way that the participation rights of eBay members or Plastic users are not.

PART 3

Changing Knowledge

CHAPTER 7

'Digital Epistemologies': Rethinking Knowledge for Classroom Learning

Introduction

In this chapter we argue why we think it is very important right now to develop a concept of what we call 'digital epistemologies', and to start pursuing innovative approaches to curriculum and pedagogy based upon it. We believe it is not simply our *literacies* that have been powerfully impacted by the information technology revolution. More profoundly, the entire epistemological base on which school approaches to knowledge and learning are founded is seriously challenged and, we think, made obsolete by the intense digitization of daily life.

Epistemology

Epistemology deals with concepts, issues and relationships concerned with knowing, believing, opining, justifying, and with truth, standards of reasoning, and so on. According to Peter Angeles (1992: 89), epistemology is the study of the origins, presuppositions, nature, extent, and veracity (truth, reliability, validity) of knowledge. In down to earth terms, and staying close to everyday educational issues, we can think of epistemology in terms of some straightforward questions. These are questions like: 'What kinds of things can we know?', 'What kinds of things are most important to know?', 'How can we come to know things?', 'What kinds of knowledge are possible?' and so on (Angeles 1992: 89; see also Goldberg 2000).

The school curriculum can be seen as reflecting attempts to answer questions about what *areas* and *kinds* of knowledge schools should be concerned with, and within these areas what will *count* as knowledge. A curriculum will typically contain a mix of different kinds or 'modes' of knowledge. These include 'propositional' knowledge (or knowing *that* something is the case), 'procedural' knowledge (or knowing *how* to do something), and 'explanatory' knowledge (or knowing *why* something is the case), and so on. In science, for instance, learners will ideally know not only that a given substance interacts with another substance in a given way, but also how to test this out and why (according to theory) this occurs.

Our argument here is that certain things that to date have operated as assumptions underlying curriculum theory and practice are currently being challenged. This is because of changes in the world associated more or less directly with recent developments in our capacity to *digitize* aspects of the world and our experience of it. We use the term 'digital epistemologies' as a shorthand to refer to issues and processes we think educators should be taking an interest in with respect to matters of knowledge and truth, as a result of the digitization of so many aspects of the world and our experiences of it. In what follows we will include examples that seem to impact dramatically on many of our familiar assumptions. We do not necessarily endorse these examples, or the kinds of 'visions' and purposes associated with them. Rather, we are simply acknowledging their existence and trying to identify some of the things we believe educationists have to deal with *one way or another* in their work.

Standard epistemology: 'justified true belief'

The broad epistemological model that has dominated school education since its inception is the same standard view of knowledge that has dominated Western thought since the time of Plato. This is widely known as the 'justified true belief' model. According to this epistemology, for 'A' (a person, knower) to know that 'P' (a proposition):

- A must *believe* that P;
- P must be *true*;
- A must be *justified* in believing that P.
(See, for example, Gettier 1963; Scheffler 1965)

This general concept has accommodated many variations since Ancient Greek times. For instance, it has accommodated various theories of truth (correspondence, coherence, pragmatist), in theories of reality (realism, idealism) and so on. Beneath all such variations, however, the kernel of *justified true belief* has remained the epistemological standard in the Euro-Western world. And since the inception of schooling it has been applied in a characteristic way to curricular learning.

Throughout the modern–industrial era of print, learning has been based on curriculum *subjects* organized as bodies of content which are in turn based on work done in the disciplines (history, mathematics, natural science, etc.). The primary object of learning has been seen as being the *content* of subjects. This view has been based on the premise that what we need to know about the world in order to function effectively in it is discovered through (natural and social) scientific enquiry. Even the so-called 'practical' or 'manual' subjects (cooking, woodwork, etc.) have usually contained a substantial 'theory' component. Admittedly, this has typically been 'theory' in a very watered down sense of textbook content as distinct from things to be done by hand.

School learning has been based on a further idea as well. This is that by participating in curriculum subjects derived from the disciplines students could learn about more than content alone. They could also come to see *how* this content gets discovered and justified by experts. To use a concept from 1970s Anglo-American educational philosophy, knowledge has both its *literatures* (content) and its *languages* (disciplined procedures). Ideally, learning will initiate learners into both (cf. Hirst 1974). Of course, it is another matter as to how far this has occurred in practice within schools. It is increasingly well recognized these days how difficult it is to enact communities of authentic practice within classroom settings (Heath and McLaughlin 1994) and to actualize conditions for transferring expertise through processes like 'apprenticeship', 'guided participation' and 'participatory appropriation' (Rogoff 1995). The fact remains, however, that for many educational philosophers, the epistemological ideal for education has been to promote the development of *knowers* as well as to transmit *knowledge*.

A further point here concerns the relative emphasis within classroom learning between propositional knowledge (knowing *that*) which is realized as content knowledge, and procedural knowledge (knowing *how*) which involves knowledge of specific techniques. To a large extent, with the exception of mastering a limited range of techniques like writing, 'knowing how' has been subordinated to the pursuit of content. Even more rarely has school-based learning involved the mastery of *practices* other than characteristic *school* Discourses comprising versions of text-mediated practices. Woodwork and cooking classes notoriously prepare very few students to any significant extent for being carpenters, chefs, or 'domestic kitchen executives'.

The challenge of 'digitization': an overview

We will sample a small but typical range of examples of 'digital fallout' so far as changes impacting on conventional educational epistemology are concerned. We will explore these using a framework comprising four dimensions of 'digitally induced change'. (There are other dimensions and further examples that we cannot deal with here.) The four dimensions are as follows.

1 Changes in 'the world (objects, phenomena) to be known', resulting from the impact of digitization.
2 Changes in conceptions of knowledge and processes of 'coming to know', contingent upon deeper incursions of digitization into everyday practices.
3 Changes in the constitution of 'knowers', which reflect the impact of digitization.
4 Changes in the relative significance of, and balance among, different forms and modes of knowing, which are associated with the impact of digitization.

Changes in 'the world to be known' (resulting from the impact of digitization)

As we noted in Chapter 3, authors of texts about cyberspace often distinguish between 'atoms' and 'bits'. These authors (e.g. Negroponte 1995; Gershenfeld 1999) talk of atoms and bits as being different kinds of *stuff*. Atoms belong to the physical world and to the world of *analogues*. Analogue sound or colour, for example, involves the use of physical processes and components to produce a particular sound or hue. Bits, however, are described as 'states of being' like 'on or off, true or false, up or down, in or out, black or white' that can be represented in binary code of 0s and 1s (Negroponte 1995: 14).

The difference in 'stuffness' between atoms and bits raises all kinds of epistemological questions and issues. In the physical world of atoms, it is customary to think in terms of finiteness and, as a consequence, in terms of concepts like scarcity, control, monopoly, zero-sum games and so on. When information is contained as atoms (e.g. in a book), for one person to have borrowed the library copy means another person cannot access it. This 'reality' and 'logic' impacts on our thought and behaviour in all sorts of ways: from the importance of knowing to put books on reserve, to knowing the fastest way to the library after class to get the book before someone else does. When information is contained as bits, all sorts of alternatives arise. These include not having to know the fastest way to the library, or how to navigate the Deweyan catalogue system, and so on. By the same token, there are other considerations to take into account and things to be known and thought about.

To draw on another example from Negroponte, we can ask what are the implications for how we approach and know the world when the stuff of something as common as a photograph changes fundamentally from analogue to digital form? Are colour and image the same thing under these different regimes? If not, how do we experience the difference and respond to it in terms of thought, practice and so on? Consider, for example, Negroponte's (1995: 14–15) account of a digital black and white photograph:

> Imagine an electronic camera laying a fine grid over an image and then recording the level of gray it sees in each cell. If we set the value of black to be 0 and the value of white to be 255, then any gray is somewhere between the two. Conveniently, a string of 8 bits (called a byte) has 256 permutations of 1s and 0s, starting with 00000000 and ending with 11111111. With such fine gradations and with a fine grid, you can perfectly reconstruct the picture for the human eye.

Here again, the epistemological implications of this are massive. What is now involved in photographic knowledge, in judging the quality of images, in knowing how 'true' an image is and so on? What are the implications for evaluative criteria, for participation in fine arts? What constitutes colour? What is our concept of colour once we have to think in terms of bits, resolution, software trade-offs and the like?

Neil Gershenfeld (1999: Ch. 2) provides a series of parallel examples for sound that test conventional physical–analogue mindsets to (and beyond) their very limits. These involve the work of Gershenfeld and colleagues at the Massachusetts Institute of Technology's (MIT) Media Lab to produce a digital Stradivarius cello: a computerized assemblage of hardware and software that pivots around a 'bow' equipped with intricate sensors. In part the aim is to produce an 'instrument' that can produce the quality of sound a player gets from the original Stradivarius instruments – and thereby make it easier for more people to access musical instruments that play with the sound quality of a Stradivarius. The principles involved include digitizing massive amounts of information about how an instrument turns a player's gestures into sounds and converting these into a computerized model. The implication is that

> once a computer can solve in real time the equations describing the motion of a violin [or a cello] the model can replace the violin. Given a fast computer and good sensors, all the accumulated descriptions of the physics of musical instruments become playable instruments themselves.
>
> (Gershenfeld 1999: 40)

The approach involves taking a great instrument (like a Stradivarius) and a great player (like Yo-Yo Ma), putting the sensors on the instrument, recording the player's actions together with the sound, and then applying state of the art data analysis techniques to get the model. This kind of activity can have some unusual results, including one best recounted by Gershenfeld himself.

> Soon after we were first able to model violin bowing with this kind of analysis I was surprised to come into my lab and see [a student] playing his arm. He had put the bow position sensor into the sleeve of his shirt so that he could play a violin without needing to hold a violin.
>
> (Gershenfeld 1999: 42)

Moreover, in collaboration with some of the world's leading musicians, the MIT team is aiming to produce instruments that make it possible to do things these musicians can conceive of doing but which cannot be done in practice because of physical limits in the 'real' world. For example, a cello can play only one or two notes at a time. Moreover, there are constraints to moving rapidly between notes played at opposite ends of a string, and there are limits to the range of sounds that can be made by bowing a string (Gershenfeld 1999: 33). Some of the musicians working with the Media Lab team wanted to explore what possibilities lie beyond the limits within which a cello, say, functions as the instrument we know. Experimentation aims at using digitized software and customized hardware to transcend existing constraints and enable musicians to conceive musical projects beyond these limits.

Such changes are *ontological*. They change the *stuff* of the world: cellos, sounds, and possibilities for musical composition. This poses questions of what becomes of musical knowledge, compositional knowledge, and unsettles conventional concepts and categories in music, in acoustics, in matters of musical technique and theory, and so on.

On a very different note we can consider some of the ideas and arguments advanced by Barry Sanders (1996). These concern the relationship between the emerging predominance of the digital–electronic apparatus and changes in conditions for constituting selfhood, and what he sees as some of the consequences or downstream effects of that relationship.

According to Sanders, humans as we know them (at least in the Europeanized West) are disappearing; giving way to a very different kind of being. He argues that 'the idea of a critical, self-directed human being [that] we take for granted as the working foundation of our humanness develops only in the crucible of reading and writing' (Sanders 1996: xi). Acquiring alphabetic print literacy, which builds on oral language-based interactions with other humans steeped in vernacular relations and concepts, is for Sanders the basis on which humans develop consciousness of themselves (*their* selves) in relation to others. It is also the basis for developing consciousness of their place in the world, their relationships to others, a moral sense and so on. But now, says Sanders, the

> characteristically European, Western mental space that has been shaped for nearly two thousand years by the alphabet is . . . being displaced by a new perceptual space, one that has been shaped by the computer . . . One dominant metaphor – the alphabetic text – has collided head-on with another – the computer screen [and before that, the television screen]. These two metaphors simply cannot occupy the same space.
>
> (Sanders 1996: 124–5)

According to Sanders, to the extent that the computer screen displaces literacy, we lose our conceptions of guilt, conscience and self. We lose the capacity to *know* persons in the ways we have taken for granted until now. Human behaviour changes dramatically when cut loose from the anchor provided by the metaphor of the text (Sanders 1996: 125). Specifically, Sanders advances the view that the kind of socio-pathic behaviour found in remorseless killing and harm-doing to other people typified in street gang violence, drive-by shootings and the like, should be seen in terms of behaviour change contingent on the demise of literacy (Sanders 1996: 29).

To the extent that this kind of argument can be sustained, the 'reality' it portends comprises a very different social world to be known, by very different kinds of knowers who will be operating without many of the key concepts, ideals, and everyday theories and understandings fundamental to 'Western civilization'.

Clearly, then, diverse arguments have been advanced from a range of positions to the effect that the world to be known – to be managed epistemologically – is changing greatly under the impact of digitization. This in itself need not be problematic for the traditionally dominant epistemology in the West: justified true belief. So far as the kind of changes mentioned here are concerned – and the myriad others that could be mentioned – it remains an open question as to how far the established epistemology is equal to the 'knowing tasks' that lie ahead. Even so, it seems clear from the kinds of changes surveyed here that there is new and challenging epistemological work to be done that focuses on characteristically *digital* phenomena. In the sections that follow we will look more specifically at possible implications of an increasingly digital world, and of 'being digital' (Negroponte 1995), for conventional epistemology.

Changes in conceptions of knowledge and processes of 'coming to know' (contingent on digitization of everyday practices)

To date the most influential and widely recognized view of how knowledge itself changes under conditions of intensified digitization has been Jean-Francois Lyotard's (1984) account of knowledge in the postmodern condition. Lyotard's investigation explores the working hypothesis that the *status* of knowledge changes as societies become 'postindustrial' and cultures 'postmodern': that is, as belief in the grand narratives of modernity diminishes, and as the effects of new technologies (especially since the 1940s) intensify and become entrenched.

The two key functions of knowledge – namely research and the transmission of acquired learning in schools and higher education institutions – change under these twin impacts, which are now powerfully intertwined. Specifically, 'knowledge is and will be produced in order to be sold, and it is and will be consumed in order to be valorized in a new production: in both cases, the goal is exchange' (1984: 4). Knowledge 'ceases to become an end in itself'; it loses its use value and becomes, to all intents and purposes, an exchange value alone. With increasing digitization, the changed status of knowledge is characterized by such features as the following:

- Availability of knowledge as an international commodity becomes the basis for national and commercial advantage within the emerging global economy.
- Computerized uses of knowledge become the basis for enhanced state security and international monitoring.
- Anything in the constituted body of knowledge that is not translatable into quantities of information will be abandoned.
- Knowledge is exteriorized with respect to the knower, and the status of the learner and the teacher is transformed into a commodity relationship of 'supplier' and 'user'.

Lyotard sees some important implications and corollaries associated with this changed status of knowledge. In particular, as institutionalized activities of state and corporation, scientific knowledge (research) and education (transmission of acquired learning) are seen to be legitimated through the principle of *performativity*. This is the principle of optimizing the overall performance of social institutions according to the criterion of efficiency or, as Lyotard puts it, 'the endless optimization of the cost/benefit (input/output) ratio' (Lyotard 1993: 25). They are legitimated by their contribution to maximizing the system's performance. This is a logic that becomes self-legitimating. In other words, enhanced measurable and demonstrable performance is seen as its own end.

The implications for the *educational* function of knowledge are far-reaching. Until recently, education was regarded as a universal welfare right under a social democratic model. It has now been reconstituted in instrumental and commodified terms as a leading contributor to and sub-sector of the economy: indeed, one of the main *enterprises* of the post-industrial economy. The focus of educational work and provision is no longer based on questions of educational aims and ideals in the old sense that drew on language games involving values, aspirations, conceptions of and beliefs about humanity, potential, personal worth and autonomy, emancipation and dignity, and the like. Rather, attention has moved from aims, values, and ideals to a new focus on 'means and techniques for obtaining [optimally] efficient outcomes' (Marshall 1998: 8).

Lyotard suggests that within this kind of regime the primary concern of professionally oriented students, the state, and education institutions will be with judging whether the learning or information is of any use (typically in the sense of 'Is it saleable?' or 'Is it efficient?'), *not* with whether it is true. Notions and practices of competence according to criteria like true/false, just/unjust get displaced by the notion of competence according to the criterion of high performativity. In such a milieu the future prospects of individual learners will depend on factors which vary according to access to new technologies. According to Lyotard, under conditions of less than perfect information the learner–student–graduate–expert who has knowledge (can use the terminals effectively in terms of computing language competence and interrogation) and can access information has an advantage. However, the more closely conditions approximate to conditions of perfect information (where data is in principle accessible to any expert), the greater the advantage that accrues to the ability to arrange data 'in a new way'. This involves using imagination to connect together 'series of data that were previously held to be independent' (Lyotard 1984: 52).

The world of performativity is a world in which 'truth' seems to be far less of a concern than in the past. The object is to get things done, efficiently. We may have here a distinctively postmodern 'take' on Marx's famous *11th Thesis on Feuerbach*, according to which 'The philosophers have only interpreted the world, in various ways; the point is to change it' (Marx 1845–47). The driving motive behind the most powerful knowledge production these days is to *create* 'truths' rather than to *discern* them. At most, the latter seem to be in the service of the former. For example, research is widely commissioned by governments to *vindicate* policies and programmes rather than to evaluate them openly. Consultants can make good livings doing 'research' that finds what their clients want to hear; or, at least, that does not find what clients do not want to hear. Massively funded research is undertaken to determine just how far it is possible to push frontiers in digital electronics and biotechnology (which, of course, involves discovering certain kinds of truths), not whether they *should* be pushed to where they can go (which involves other kinds).

To paraphrase Lyotard, access to perfect information being equal, imagination carries the day: imagination – and, to the same extent, truth and knowledge – in the service of what Gee calls 'enactive projects' (Gee *et al.* 1996). Enactive projects are about bringing visions into reality, about making worlds in the image of visions. This has some very interesting and important ramifications for epistemology in a digital world of emerging cybercultures. Two examples can illustrate the point here.

On April Fool's Day 1999 an Australian group foisted a benign scam using the Internet. They solicited shares in a bogus enterprise. The group was startled at the success of their scam, which they had concocted for pedagogical purposes: to show how easy it is to get conned. They returned every cent they received, but confessed to being surprised about just how many people were willing to part with so much of their money so readily. The other example concerns cases such as the stock invested in e-enterprises like Amazon.com, despite open reports of heavy financial losses over successive years, and the stunning share-raising feats achieved by Internet outfits like Netscape and Yahoo.

In light of such examples it makes perfect sense to ask how important *truth* (in the form of something not being a scam, or the likelihood of their making a good profit on their shares) is to the 'punters'. The sense of being a part of building something and making some history might be a much more important consideration in their eyes. Perhaps just being part of the emerging e-commerce scene – even if one is sometimes taken for a sucker – is more of a consideration than the 'truth status' of an enterprise. This becomes relevant when we ask how far, and for whom, it is important to develop awareness on the part of Internet users so far as matters of 'veridicality' (Goldberg 2000) are concerned. Perhaps the passionate drive to keep the Internet as free of authority and control as possible is the corollary of some conventional epistemological constructs having 'gone down the gurgler' – at least, for the meantime – together with some cherished grand narratives of modernity.

There are many questions to ask and issues to address here that will become part of the stock-in-trade of digital epistemologists.

Changes in the constitution of 'knowers' (that reflect the impact of digitization)

Many changes can be seen in the constitution of knowing and believing subjects – the 'bearers' of propositional, procedural, and performance knowledge – and contingent on intensified digitization of daily life. We will consider two typical examples here.

The first has been well recognized within 'fast capitalist' workplaces and Discourses, and areas of enquiry like cognitive science and social cognition for some time now (for an overview, see Gee *et al.* 1996: Ch. 2). However, it has still to be recognized and taken up in any significant degree within formal education. It involves ideas like 'distributed cognition', 'collaborative practice', 'networked intelligence' and 'communities of practice'.

Theories of distributed cognition, for example, have grown in conjunction with the emergence of 'fast capitalism' and networked technologies (Castells 1996; Gee *et al.* 1996). Within work teams, for example, a collective may share between them the knowledge pertaining to particular processes, or for solving problems that arise. Such teams may operate within a particular area of an enterprise, or be dispersed across several areas. A further instance, identified and discussed by Lyotard (1984), is found in the role and significance of multidisciplinary teams in 'imagining new moves or new games' in the quest for extra performativity within, say, research. Increasingly, the model of multidisciplinary teams supersedes that of the expert individual as the efficient means to making new moves (Lyotard 1984). In addition, as Paul Gilster (1997) describes in his account of 'knowledge assembly', it is often impossible in the information-abundant world of the Internet and other searchable data sources for individuals to manage their own information needs, maintain an eye to the credibility of information items and so on. Practices of information gathering and organizing are often highly customized and dispersed. The individual depends on roles being played by various services and technologies, ranging from search engines and 'bots' to customized news feeds. Hence, a particular assemblage of knowledge that is brought together – however momentarily – in the product of 'an individual' may more properly be understood as a *collective* assemblage involving many minds and machines. For instance, the knowing subject will increasingly make use of search engines, many of which employ bots – or artificial intelligence robots (Turkle 1995; Johnson 1997; Brown and Duguid 2000). These are composed of bits and bytes rather than screws and metal (cf. BotSpot 2002). They can move about in cyberspace and interact with other programs performing a range of tasks, including finding information that answers questions framed in natural language. AskJeeves (2002) is a well-known example of this kind of bot-based program (www.askjeeves.com). In addition, of course, we use all manner of search engines that employ Boolean logic to address our keywords, as well as customized newsfeeds and information feeds, editors that are often mediated by other human beings, and ones that operate as unmediated software programs.

Such examples pose problems for the notion that knowing, thinking, believing, being justified, and so on are located within the individual person (the 'cogitating' subject). This, however, is an underlying assumption of the justified true belief model, which construes propositional knowledge of 'P' as an attribute of an individual, 'A'. Ultimately, schools, too, operate on this assumption at the level of their deep structure. For all of the group work and collaborative activity that has entered classrooms in recent times, knowledge is seen in the final analysis as a private possession, and is examined and accredited accordingly.

The second example is a small-scale variation on the previous notion that to date exists mainly at an experimental level. It seems likely, however, to become much more common in the future. It involves people themselves, and not merely machines, being electronically wired together as networks by means of wearable computers. Gershenfeld's younger colleagues in the MIT Media Lab provide graphic illustrations of what is involved here. One, named Steve, wears a visor that covers his eyes and contains small display screens. 'He looks out through a pair of cameras, which are connected to his displays through a fanny pack full of electronics strapped around his waist' (Gershenfeld 1999: 45). Steve can vary his vision. When riding a bicycle in traffic he can mount a camera to the rear to view traffic approaching from behind, and when walking in a crowd he can point a camera to the footpath to see where he is walking.

Among the many extended applications made possible by virtue of the computer he wears is one that allows other people to see the data that goes to his display screens – via a webpage from which others can access his recent images. By these means his wife can look out through Steve's eyes when he is shopping in the supermarket and help him select fruit, which is something he is not good at doing (Gershenfeld 1999).

This raises intriguing questions about what it means to know that a given piece of fruit is (or is not) of good quality, and to know how to select good fruit at a supermarket stand. In this case, multiple forms of knowledge are involved within the performance of selecting good fruit. Some of it, and only some of it, has to do with fruit. Much of it has to do with managing a wearable computer. As wearing computers becomes a more common practice, it seems almost inevitable that more and more knowing will become collaborative, networked, and distributed processes and performances. While we may be unable at present to foretell the implications of this for curriculum with much specificity, it is clear that they will be enormous, and that now is the time to start thinking seriously about possible scenarios.

Changes in the relative significance of, and balance among, different kinds and modes of knowing

Conventional epistemology has privileged *propositional* knowledge, and supported the overwhelming domination of text-based knowing *that* within classrooms. In principle, the book-centred 'modernist space of enclosure' (Lankshear *et al.* 1996) that is the school and, more specifically, the classroom *could* support a more equitable balance between propositional knowledge and other modes and forms of knowledge – notably, *procedural* knowledge, or knowing *how* – than it typically does. Even so, the abstraction and decontextualization of classrooms from mature forms of authentic non-scholastic social practices has seriously limited the range of possibilities until recently.

Now, however, the proliferation of new social practices predicated on nothing more than networked computers and access to expertise makes it possible to admit distinctively new forms of curriculum pursuits into classrooms that can emulate 'mature' versions of social practices in ways that the cooking and woodwork rooms rarely could. This is because the Internet provides access to online communities of practice. Understanding the importance of this, the extent to which it should be pursued in the name of 'education', and what it may involve in practice, will call for rethinking epistemology in terms of the evolving digital age.

This section will briefly address four of the many facets that are likely to become increasingly relevant and important here.

First, it will be important to understand knowledge in relation to building, inhabiting, and negotiating virtual worlds. This will involve aspects of personal and interpersonal knowledge, as when deciding how best to represent oneself using avatars and whatever other means become available. To 'outsiders' this may seem a trivial matter. To 'insiders', however, it is anything but. For some participants, at least for a while, it may be enough simply to choose from avatars made available by virtual worlds (e.g. as is possible in ActiveWorlds or Outerworlds). Others will want to create their own (as in SeeStorm's avatar factory, or Cybertown Palace), deciding whether and how their avatar will reflect who and what they see themselves as being. According to Michael Heim (1999: 1),

> when people enter these [virtual] worlds, they choose their avatar, determining how they will appear to themselves and to others in the world. Even in worlds where avatar parts can be assembled piecemeal into customized identities, the initial design of the parts still strongly affects the look and feel of the avatar. Avatar design not only affects the perception of the self but it also affects possible ways of navigating through the world and the kind of dwellings that are appropriate for the avatar.

Clearly, all manner of issues will arise here for identity knowledge, as well as for knowing where and when one *is* as one moves between virtual and 'real' worlds: as 'one' moves between 'being' atoms and being bits. Categories like 'real' and 'location' mean differently across the different spaces. Virtual reality splinters our working concepts of 'real life'. The significance of the conceptual shakiness of 'real life' versus 'not real life' is exemplified by the fallout that surrounded the Tamagotchi fad of digital handheld pets that 'died' if not cared for properly.

In a future that looks certain to involve a lot more interaction between humans and more or less human-like 'bit-beings', new forms of inter'personal' knowledge will become increasingly important. Early indications of terrain to be traversed here were documented by Sherry Turkle (1995: 16).

> Many bots roam MUDs [multi-user domains]. They log onto the games as though they were characters. Players create these programs for many reasons: bots help with navigation, pass messages, and create a background atmosphere of animation in the MUD. When you enter a virtual café, you are usually not alone. A waiter bot approaches who asks if you want a drink and delivers it with a smile.

Turkle goes on to explain how she has sometimes – as have others – mistaken a real person for a bot because their actions and comments within the MUD seemed 'bot-like' or 'too machine-like' (Turkle 1995: 16). And, conversely, 'sometimes bots are mistaken for people. I have made this mistake too, fooled by a bot that flattered me by remembering my name or our last interaction' (Turkle 1995: 16).

Turkle describes one very accomplished bot, known as Julia, who was programmed to chat with players in MUDs, to engage in teasing repartee and so on (Turkle 1995: 93). She relates a study by Leonard Foner who describes how one person, Lara, reacted to Julia – both when Lara thought Julia was a person and when she knew Julia was a bot:

> [Lara] originally thought Julia's limitations [conversation-wise] might be due to Down's [sic] syndrome. Lara's reaction when she finally learns that Julia is a bot reflects the complexity of current responses to artificial intelligence. Lara is willing to accept and interact with machines that function usually in an intelligent manner. She is willing to spend time in their company and show them cordiality and respect . . . Yet, upon hearing that Julia was a bot, Lara says she felt 'fright, giddiness, excitement, curiosity, and pride'. There was also the thrill of superiority: 'I know this sounds strange, but I felt I could offer more to the conversation than she could. I tested her knowledge on many subjects. It was like I was proving to myself that I was superior to a machine. . . '
>
> (Turkle 1995: 16)

Interestingly, Lara still refers to the Julia program as 'she'.

A second area for development with respect to changes in the relative significance of, and balance among, different kinds and modes of knowing is inchoate in efforts to wrestle in varying ways with conceptions and issues of 'multi-modal truth'. How do we make sense of truths that are expressed not in propositions but through multiple media simultaneously and interactively?

Since the invention of the printing press the printed word has been the main carrier of (what is presented as) truth. Mass schooling has evolved under what could be called a 'regime of print', and print more generally has 'facilitated the literate foundation of culture' (Heim 1999: 1). Of course, various kinds of images or graphics have been used in printed texts to help carry truth (e.g. tables, charts, graphs, photographs, illustrations). However, Internet technology merges pictures and print (not to mention sound, and developers are currently working on smell) much more intricately and easily than ever possible before. As Heim (1999: 1) puts it, the

> word now shares Web space with the image, and text appears inextricably tied to pictures. The pictures are dynamic, animated, and continually updated. The unprecedented speed and ease of digital production mounts photographs, movies, and video on the Web. Cyberspace becomes visualized data, and meaning arrives in spatial as well as in verbal expressions.

Of course, virtual worlds with their images and forms, the music found in a world or part of a world, the text one writes to communicate with others, the gestures and movements one's avatar can be programmed to make are thoroughly multi-modal in a seamless and 'natural' way. For example, while in ActiveWorlds (www.activeworlds.com), if we teleport to Alphaworld, the music, the lush greenery and strong, sunlit colours suggest to us that this world is probably a happy place. Which is unlike Metatropolis with its eerie music, strange lurking figures and barren, night-time landscape, suggesting one had better take care. Likewise, in Alphaworld there are no hidden tunnels and holes to get trapped in as there are in Metatropolis and requiring an exit from the world to escape. These worlds add up to wholes by means of sound, images, text, movement and change requiring the inhabitant or tourist (there *are* tourists in ActiveWorlds!) to be constantly reading these constitutive elements in order to make sense of the world they are in.

A third consideration inviting us to reassess the relative significance and balance among multiple modes of knowing and forms of knowledge is the idea explored in Chapter 5 of an emerging attention economy along the lines developed by Goldhaber (1997, 1998a, 1998b). Goldhaber alerts us to the question of what kinds of knowledge will be advantageous for operating in the attention economy. As noted previously, Goldhaber (1997) argues that gaining attention is indexical to *originality*. It is difficult to get new attention 'by repeating exactly what you or someone else has done before' (Goldhaber 1997: 1). Consequently, success in the attention economy calls for 'endless originality, or at least attempts at originality' (Goldhaber 1997: 1). This resonates with Lyotard's (1984) focus on imagination as the basis for 'making new moves in language games'.

Some challenges facing conventional epistemology

The ideas and examples we have explored in this chapter pose some serious challenges for the conventional epistemology of justified true belief, and for established educational practices based on it. We will look briefly at four kinds of challenge here.

First, the standard epistemology that is employed in education constructs knowledge as something that is carried linguistically and expressed in sentences or propositions and theories. As we have seen, however, the multimedia realm of digital ICTs makes *normal* the radical convergence of text, image, and sound in ways that break down the primacy of propositional linguistic forms of 'truth bearing'. While many images and sounds that are transmitted and received digitally still stand in for propositional information, many do not. They can behave in epistemologically very different ways from talk and text – for example, evoking, attacking us sensually, shifting and evolving constantly, and so on. Meaning and truth arrive in spatial as well as textual expressions (Heim 1999), and the rhetorical and normative modes challenge the scientific–propositional mode on a major scale.

Heim (1999) speaks of 'the new mode of truth' that will be realized in the twenty-first century. He claims that new digital media are displacing older forms of typed and printed word. Under the conditions of the new dominant media, says Heim, questions about how truth is 'made present' through processes that are closer to rituals and iconographies than propositions and text re-emerge in forms similar to those discussed by theologians since medieval times. Heim notes that within communities of believers incarnate truth as the sacred Word is transmitted through a complex of rituals and images integrated with text-words. In the case of the Catholic church, for instance,

> communal art is deemed essential to the transmission of the Word as conceived primarily through spoken and written scriptures. The word on the page is passed along in a vessel of images, fragrances, songs, and kinesthetic pressed flesh. Elements like water, salt, and wine contribute to the communication. Truth is transmitted not only through

spoken and written words but also through a participatory community that re-enacts its truths through ritual.

(Heim 1999: 1)

Many epistemological questions arise here about how truth is made present, similar to those that have concerned theologians for centuries. Is the presence of incarnate truth granted to the community through ritualized enactment of the sacred word *real*, or should it be seen as symbolic or, perhaps, as a kind of virtual presence (Heim 1999)? Heim suggests that this and similar questions take on new significance with the full-flowering of digital media. If truth 'becomes finite and accessible to humans primarily through the word', he asks, 'what implications do the new media hold for the living word as it shifts into spatial imagery?' (Heim 1999: 1). We would ask further, 'What implications would this in turn hold for curriculum and pedagogy?'

Second, the epistemology of justified true belief, and the dominant educational epistemology of subjects or discipline studies based upon it, is individualistic. Knowing, thinking/cognition, believing, being justified, and so on are seen as located within the individual person (knowing subject). This view is seriously disrupted by practices that are mediated by intensive use of digital ICTs. Theories of distributed cognition, for example, have grown in conjunction with the emergence of 'fast capitalism' and networked technologies (Castells 1996, 1997, 1998; Gee *et al.* 1996). Where knowledge is (seen as) the major factor in adding value and creating wealth, and where knowledge workers are increasingly mobile, it is in the interests of corporations to ensure that knowledge is *distributed* rather than concentrated. This protects the corporation against unwanted loss when individuals leave. It is also, of course, symmetrical with the contemporary logic of widely dispersed and flexible production that can make rapid adjustments to changes in markets and trends.

Moreover, as Gilster (1997) illustrates in his account of knowledge assembly, within the information-superabundant world of the Internet and other searchable data sources individuals often find it impossible to manage their own information needs, maintain an eye on the credibility of information items and so on. Practices of information gathering and organizing are often highly customized and dispersed, with 'the individual' depending on roles being played by various services and technologies. Hence, a particular assembly of knowledge that is brought together – however momentarily – in the product of an individual can be seen more accurately as being a *collective* assembly involving *many* minds (and machines).

Third, according to the traditional view, knowing is an act we carry out on something that already exists, and truth pertains to what already is. In various ways, however, the kinds of knowing involved in social practices within diverse spaces in which digital ICTs are employed are very different from this. More than *propositional* knowledge of what already exists, much of the knowing that is involved in the new spaces might better be understood in terms of a *performance* epistemology – that is, of knowing as an ability to perform. Elsewhere (Lankshear *et al.* 2000) we have tried to anticipate a notion of a 'performance epistemology' which, we believe, will become central in an increasingly intensely digitized world. This is an epistemology of rule breaking and innovation: of knowing *how to proceed* in the absence of existing models and exemplars. It links back to our earlier discussion of Lyotard's account of the changed status of knowledge in the postmodern condition. It also, however, goes beyond scientific knowledge to relate to 'gaining attention' and to operating in other (non-scientific) dimensions of symbolic analysis and manipulation.

At one level this can be seen in terms of procedures like making and following hyperlinks when creating and reading Web documents. What kind of knowing, exactly, is involved in knowing how to make successful hyperlinks and to follow hyperlinks 'successfully'? At another level it is reflected in Lyotard's idea that the kind of knowledge most needed by knowledge workers in computerized societies is the procedural knowledge of languages like telematics and informatics, together with knowing how to interrogate information or situations. Moreover, knowing how to make new moves in a game and how to change the very rules of the game is of particular importance to 'higher order work' and other forms of perform-ance – including performances that gain attention – under current and foreseeable conditions. This directly confronts conventional epistemology. As concretized in what Thomas Kuhn (1970) called normal science, the epistemology of justified true belief presupposes *stability* in the rules of the game as the norm. Paradigm shifts are very much the exception. While the sorts of shifts involved in changing game rules cannot all be on the scale of paradigm shifts, they nonetheless subvert the notion of stability being the norm.

Rethinking epistemology in a digital age might involve thinking of it as practices of knowing that reflect a range of strategies for assembling, edit-ing, processing, receiving, sending, and working on information and data to transform diverse resources of 'digitalia' into 'things that work'. In this sense, 'working' will include attracting attention, enchanting the imagin-ation, meeting demands for innovation, and otherwise satisfying the 'com-plex calculus of pleasure' that Lanham sees people bringing to 'the free market of ideas', where they 'make all kinds of purchases' (Lanham 1994: 1). We think here of the kind of epistemology implied by Ludwig Wittgenstein (1953: 105). As Michael Peters observes (see Lankshear *et al.* 2000), this is based on the relation of knowing to the 'mastery of a technique' in the kind of sense captured by Wittgenstein as: 'I now know how to go on' (Wittgenstein 1953: 105). It is the kind of knowledge involved in becoming able to speak a literal language, but *also* the kind of move-making knowledge that is involved in Wittgenstein's (1953) notion of language, which he termed 'language games'.

Such a view of performance epistemology might be usefully applied to a range of emergent practices. These include 'bricolage', understood as assemblage of elements, and 'collage', understood as the practice of transferring materials from one context to another. They also include 'montage', construed as the practice of disseminating borrowings in a new setting (see Ulmer 1987). From this perspective, the best guides to future developments in digital epistemologies are likely to come much more from areas like composition theory, traditional rhetoric and the like, than from the standpoint of knowledge as justified true belief (Lankshear *et al.* 2000).

Fourth, to a large extent we may actually be looking at some kind of post-truth/belief/justification epistemology operating under conditions of intense digitization. Clearly, none of the three logical conditions of justified true belief is necessary for *information* (Lankshear *et al.* 2000). All that is required for information is that data be sent from sender to receivers, or that data be received by receivers who are not even necessarily targeted by senders. Information is used and acted on. Belief *may* follow from using information, although it may not, and belief certainly need not precede the use of information or acting on it (Lankshear *et al.* 2000).

Likewise, the 'new status' knowledge of Lyotard's postmodern condition – knowledge produced to be sold or to be valorized in a new production – does not necessarily require that the conditions of justified true belief be met. This follows from the shift in the status of knowledge from being a use value to becoming an exchange value. For example, in the new game of 'hired gun' research, where deadlines are often the day before yesterday and the 'answer' to the problem may already be presupposed in the larger policies and performativity needs of the funders, the efficacy of the knowledge produced may begin and end with cashing the cheque (in the case of the producer) and in being able to file a report on time (in the case of the consumer). Belief, justification, and truth need not come within a mile of the entire operation (Lankshear *et al.* 2000).

Even Gilster's (1997) well-known account of assembling knowledge from news feeds stops well short of truth – notwithstanding his emphasis on critical thinking and the importance of trying to avoid bias, his distinction between hard and soft journalism, and so on. For Gilster, the objectives are perspective and balance. As he describes it, the knowledge assembly process is much more obviously a matter of a production *performance* than some unveiling of what already exists. We assemble a point of view, a perspective, an angle on an issue or story. This takes the form of a *further* production, not a capturing or mirroring of some original state of affairs.

Some implications for classroom curriculum and pedagogy

We repeat that we are not necessarily endorsing, advocating, or passively accepting the kinds of changes we have identified here and on which we have based our argument that calls into doubt the viability of conventional epistemology. Rather, we are saying that what we have described here looks like what much of the present and recent past is like, and what even more of the foreseeable future will probably be like. Moreover, we are saying that educationists, teachers, and education policy makers have not taken these matters sufficiently seriously to date.

If our accounts in this book of features, patterns, and the growing significance of diverse social practices involving digital ICTs are reasonably accurate and typical, which we think they are, how should we be responding in terms of school curriculum and pedagogy? Do values like commitment to truth, to knowledge as a use value, to the importance of following arguments and evidence where they seem rationally to lead, and to basing our beliefs and actions on what seems most justifiable, still have a place in how we conceive and implement curriculum knowledge? If so, how much of a place do they have? Should we be trying to shore up more curriculum space for them? To what extent and in what ways should schools be looking for different operating conceptions of knowledge from those that inform subject-based learning? And how do we decide what these are and how to implement them in classroom curriculum and pedagogy?

These are huge questions that cannot be answered here. Our aim has been more to raise them than to pretend to answer them. What we can say, however, is this. Social practices that are evolving beyond the school within digitally saturated milieux seem to be privileging modes of knowing that are more performance- and procedure-oriented than propositional, more collaborative than individualistic, and more concerned with making an impact on attention, imagination, curiosity, innovation, and so on, than with fostering truth, engendering rational belief, or demonstrating their justifiability. To that extent, the subject-based curriculum founded on texts and academic teachers as authority is in trouble. So are procedures that assess *individuals* as the personal bearers of knowledge, and that approach pedagogy in terms of trying to get knowledge into individual heads.

This is not to say there is no room left for developing expertise within what we have known as disciplined forms of enquiry. After all, the people best fitted to thriving in the world of postmodern knowledge described by Lyotard will include people who have strong multi- and cross-disciplinary expertise, who can cross-dress conceptually, theoretically and methodologically in order to come up with new rules and new games. What this *does* say, however, is that this kind of expertise and competence is developed in *performance* and not through absorbing content. It is best acquired in contexts where people are enacting meaningful purposes within authentic and collaborative settings, where high-quality performance exists to be emulated.

This is consistent with the idea of the school as a knowledge producer and provider for communities, mentioned briefly at the end of Chapter 4. It is consistent with diverse forms of activity-oriented learning, such as that which Michael Heim has promoted with students involved in designing and building virtual worlds, among many other kinds. It is also consistent with trying to approximate to the quality of learning and approaches to learning that is characteristic of, for example, single-player and online video and computer games, and the communities associated with them, as currently being investigated by James Gee (forthcoming). In his study of online first person shooter games, Gee has identified more than 20 high-order learning principles, none of which occur to any significant extent in typical everyday classroom learning. This again is not to endorse the games *per se*. Rather, it is to put a finger on forms of learning that occur in areas of social practice that command people's interests, and that reflect operating logics and processes common to high-status and high-kudos pursuits, and to ask what can fruitfully be learned from them for education.

The immediate task cannot be to resolve the matters raised here, because resolutions are not immediately available. They have to be pursued and won. The point is to acknowledge that this is no time to be standing still, digging in, and blindly continuing with what we have assumed and believed about knowledge. We need to be open to the issues and be prepared to take some risks, follow some hunches, and look in some unlikely places in our efforts to address them. In the concluding chapter we will describe one very preliminary and small-scale attempt to practise the kind of attitudes and approaches we think are called for right now within formal education.

CHAPTER 8

New Ways of Knowing:
Learning at the Margins

Introduction

In this concluding chapter we revisit the study introduced briefly in Chapter 3. We will relate the nature and outcomes of work undertaken in one of the four sites comprising the study. The case of Yanga Headlands State High School (see also Rowan *et al.* 2000, 2002: 146–59) suggests some of the kinds of productive learning experiences and results that can occur when learning and knowing are reconceptualized for a digital regime. The innovation study itself was based on the full range of concerns that inform this book. Indeed, many of the ideas we have discussed throughout earlier chapters have emerged directly out of ongoing collaborative work with Leonie Rowan, Chris Bigum and Michael Doneman. The Yanga Headlands case offers hopeful possibilities for future curriculum and pedagogical developments in literacy education, with particular emphasis on 'new' literacies.

Genesis of a project

In 1998, Language Australia funded an innovation project designed to generate research-based practical suggestions for how new technologies would be employed to help enhance literacy learning outcomes among disadvantaged students. Within these parameters we were free to develop our own approach. The main goal of the study was to design and implement an intervention that would employ an innovative pedagogical approach to using new technologies within classroom settings with disadvantaged learners. It was hoped that the approach to be employed would promote 'efficacious' learning and challenge traditional markers and experiences of disadvantage operating in the contexts of the study (cf. Rowan *et al.* 2002: 146).

More specifically, the project was intended to address three main concerns we had collectively identified from our previous research and teaching experiences and that have resonated throughout this book.

First, teachers' cultural identities and experiences are often very different from those of their students. This makes it difficult for them to connect learning as closely as possible to students' varied cultural identities and experiences: that is, to teach for diversity and to minimize disadvantage. During recent decades, issues of diversity and disadvantage have largely been associated with ethnicity, social class, and language. These are important and ongoing dimensions. In addition, however, it must now be recognized that issues arise around how to relate teaching to the identities, experiences and perspectives of increasing numbers of 'screenagers' (Rushkoff 1996) and 'insiders/natives' (Barlow in interview with Tunbridge 1995) who have grown up amidst the saturation of daily life by the digital–electronic apparatus (Ulmer 1987). Learners who 'are digital' may be disadvantaged by learning arrangements that marginalize or penalize important forms of knowledge, understanding and practical proficiency they have acquired.

Second, low levels of technical and cultural knowledge on the part of teachers often result in computer-mediated learning activities being ineffective, inefficacious, or mystifying. This may range from time being lost simply for want of knowing how to operate the machines, to students acquiring odd or confused notions of a practice because of the way it is represented within classroom activity.

Third, teachers often make well-intentioned uses of student 'savvy' with new technologies to get around snags at the technical operation level. If the practices within which these operations (and skill appropriations) are embedded are ineffectual or at odds with 'mature' versions of computer-mediated social practices, the result of drawing on student savvy might be to enlist 'insider' ('native') competence in the service of 'new-comer' (or 'immigrant') practices (Lankshear and Bigum 1999).

The 'logic' of a new project

The project idea was to build four purpose-designed 'networks of prac-tice', each of which was based in a school. Network activities would, how-ever, occur as far as possible outside formal school hours and not be part of formal curriculum work. The learning groups would contain at least one teacher from the school and up to four students. Besides the resident teacher, it was hoped to include a teacher currently in training and one or more 'cultural workers'. These would be older youths or adults with insider knowledge of social practices employing new technologies, and who also were broadly open to perspectives and concerns of young people. At least one researcher and research assistant would be assigned to each group. Ideally, the groups would contain a mix of mindsets, offering scope for negotiation and for developing mutual understandings within a relaxed learning environment. The plan was for each cluster to operate as a face-to-face entity for two hours a week over an eight- to ten-week period. It was hoped that between meetings participants would continue planning and implementing their activities.

The intention was to employ a learning strategy of 'scaffolded co-construction'. Working collaboratively and in accordance with their respective strengths, participants would negotiate a task to be completed during the time frame which would result in an authentic product – the kind of thing that would be produced within a mature form of social prac-tice. The task would employ an electronic ICT and require the group col-lectively to design and implement learning activities of an expert-like nature. Ideally, the innovation would foment a 'pedagogical logic' that could work productively with participants whose mindsets, experiential backgrounds, and existing knowledge and competence were different. The researchers were hopeful that this pedagogical 'logic' would be adaptable to a wider range of educational settings. It was important that the activi-ties and processes involving new technologies should contribute to developing an appreciation of the knowledge bases and mindsets of the other participants in the group, and that all participants would acquire new technical skills with the technologies they chose to work with. It was also important that participants would develop cultural and critical under-standings of literacy practices involving these technologies.

An informal 'warm-up' phase was included, during which participants would get a chance to interact socially and get a feel for the 'operating principles' of the learning group while working with new technologies (e.g. playing a computer game, visiting and commenting on websites). After the warm-up activities the groups would move onto the main agenda: negotiate what they were going to do, how they would do it, and then get on with doing it. Diverse kinds of activities were seen as possible indicative options to be negotiated within the networks. These included:

- designing a webpage for a client (such as an educator at a local university or a local industry group). Participants would be involved in page design, construction and publication;
- constructing a community database to be located in a particular school. The group would identify the kinds of information that are interesting, relevant, and important to the community, and then participate in the collection, organization and online publication of this data;
- engaging in a geographic information systems mapping activity, possibly using university facilities – for example, mapping local skateboarding venues;
- establishing a youth-culture or emergent-artists' network, and using online resources and facilities to inform the public about the network, to advertise events, and to facilitate activities.

Within each learning group participants were to work together to decide exactly what it was they were going to do. This decision would take account of the means they had available to them within the group and via other resources (including expertise) they could access. The groups would be free to determine their own patterns of activity (if any) between sessions. It was important that in conceiving, shaping, and implementing their activities participants would draw on their own skills and understanding *and* consciously pursue 'insider' interpretations of problems and productions of outcomes. Identifying and negotiating across different perspectives, values, experiences and the like in search of an expert-like production would be a key element of the learning and doing process.

The researchers were to play multiple roles in this process in the manner of participant observers. They would observe and document the activities in the manner of qualitative research fieldworkers. They would also, however, be available to act as knowledge and information resources if required and so far as they were able, and to monitor the extent to which authentic expert-like forms of practice were being pursued.

The Yanga Headlands site

Yanga Headlands State High School is on Australia's north-east coast in what is officially designated a rural region in the state Education Department's documents. At the time of the study the school had 975 students. Learning sessions were conducted in one of the school's staffrooms. The staffroom comprised two small adjoining rooms that contained two computers. These were all that were available for the first session, until the teacher participant (Lucy) found a laptop that was used in subsequent sessions. Lucy, who was the English coordinator and a deputy principal, made the decision to use these rooms for the sessions because she believed timetabling issues made it too difficult for the group to access any of the computer 'lab' classrooms. This decision upset the school's technology coordinator (who had initially been extremely supportive in setting up the network). The coordinator thought students should not be using computers that were designated for staff, and stated emphatically that students must *never* be allowed access to staff computers. As a deputy principal, however, Lucy managed to secure approval from the principal for continued use of these rooms and the computers.

At the time of the study the school had four computer labs plus sundry networked computers spread throughout the school. All had Internet access. A system of Internet 'licences' operated in the school. Students were required to sign an agreement that they would not abuse their access to the Internet by visiting pornography and other prohibited sites, and by not downloading software. The four boys involved in the network had all lost their Internet licences for one reason or another prior to the project.

The participants

The project at Yanga Headlands ran between 21 April and 15 June 1999. It included Lucy (albeit in a peripheral role due to her time being taken up elsewhere in the school), a fourth year education (honours) student from the nearby university, two of the principal researchers in the research team, a research assistant, and four boys all aged 14 and in Year 9.

Lucy was a particularly dedicated teacher. She had volunteered her own time to work with this group of boys, who – as we mentioned earlier – were regarded by their regular teachers as 'trouble' and had all been identified as 'having problems with literacy'. The boys did not attend the English sessions scheduled for their class each day. Instead, they spent that time with Lucy working on a range of projects. Prior to the study they had most recently been involved in producing a magazine based on their shared passion for motorbikes. Collecting information for their magazine had included interviewing motorbike mechanics and enthusiasts in the region's main city, 40 kilometres away, about the various qualities of different motorbikes (e.g. evaluating the differences between 2-stroke and 4-stroke engines). The boys prepared their interview questions, wrote them out, and Lucy drove them to the city to conduct their interviews.

The postgraduate student, Pedro, knew two of the boys well from coaching them in soccer during their primary school years. His wife had taught one of them in Year 7. Pedro brought his baby daughter, Holly, with him to each project session. Initially this was suggested as a solution to difficulties arranging childcare. But the researchers soon realized that having the baby in the sessions would be valuable because of how she might help 'disrupt' conventional notions of classrooms and authority; and provide a model of a male taking an active role in childcare.

The two researchers from the University, Chris and Leonie, had not had any real contact with the school prior to this project. Neither had Lynn, the research assistant for the project.

The four student participants were Stuart, Kyle, Ben, and Jarrod.

Stuart was chatty, friendly and engaging. He had a smallish build for his age and was given to wearing oversized, slightly tatty shirts and shorts. Occasionally he would be in school uniform, but even then he managed to look far more casual than other students. He had shoulder-length blonde hair shaved close to his scalp high above his ears. This cultivated 'tough look' contrasted with his rather high-pitched voice. He regarded himself as being about Year 6 level in most things at school, and openly stated his dislike of reading and writing. The other boys shared this sentiment. At home, he would strip down his motorbike and reassemble it correctly. He said that he learned to do this by first watching his dad work on his bike, then from being left to his own devices to figure out a problem, tune the engine, or to rebuild it once his father had taken it apart. When asked what he did when he encountered a difficult problem fixing his bike, he replied without hesitation: 'I read the manual when I get stuck.' Stuart did not see himself as being competent with computers. He said 'I didn't go very well with computer [studies at school]', even though he had a computer at home with an Internet connection which he used to look for pictures and information on motorbikes for their magazine.

Kyle had an olive complexion and long dark hair that he usually wore tied back in a ponytail. Like Stuart, Kyle has a 'tough' look to him. It is easy to imagine that (unlike Stuart) he could pack quite a punch if he wanted to. While not particularly tall, he had well-toned arms that were readily visible through the muscle shirts he liked to wear. Kyle had perhaps the most careworn look about him of all the boys. This disappeared, however, when he started to talk about anything that interested or mattered to him. On such topics he became articulate and entertaining. Based on his comments during sessions and that he tape-recorded for the researchers, we formed an impression that Kyle spent much of his time reflecting on people and events.

Ben lived outside Yanga on a farm of about 200 hectares. He was a fresh-faced kid whose general demeanour had a kind of impishness about it. He smiled readily, but was slow to look people in the eye and was constantly putting himself down and making jokes at his own expense. There was nothing of the tough or rough image to Ben. His family operated a dairy farm and Ben used his motorbike to help round the cows up for his parents. He too could strip his motorbike and reassemble it in working order. Ben had access to a computer at home. However, at school he referred to himself as a 'fast forgetter' and worried for several weeks that he would not remember how to do certain things (e.g. add a hyperlink to his webpage) once Pedro and the others had gone. Ben had a good sense of humour, and a range of lines that regularly drew laughs from the others in the network. For example, when Stuart was being somewhat slow in moving about the different *3D Moviemaker* control icons, Ben commented with friendly impatience, 'C'mon Stu. You move like my grandmother. And she's in a home!'

Jarrod was tall with blond hair, and was regarded by Lucy and the three boys (and seemingly by himself) as a 'computer whiz'. In the course of the first meeting, when one of the principal researchers was explaining to the lads the general gist of the project, Stuart commented that, 'The only person who would understand this is Jarrod, 'cause he's the computer whiz!' There was a hint of resentment, however, in the ways that the boys spoke of Jarrod's confidence. This may have explained what appeared to be an intriguing mix of tentativeness and arrogance he displayed in the sessions. While quick to talk about any computer or technologically related subject, Jarrod was slow to offer his opinions on other issues, and seemed at first to find it difficult to relate easily to the other boys. He seemed comfortable using computers from the outset of the project and recounted how he had done a short course on Basic programming language when he lived in the state capital city two years previously. Indeed, Jarrod almost fitted the caricature of 'computer nerds', and he certainly did not cultivate as tough an image as Stuart and Kyle. Nonetheless, Jarrod was adamant that he preferred hands-on subjects at school like woodwork, metalwork, art and physical education, because 'you're learning trades'.

Explaining the project rationale

The researchers explained the formal project and the students' partici-pation in terms of teachers wanting to learn from students how to teach computing effectively to *their* students. In Pedro's words, 'We want to learn from you how to teach you computers.' This went with a request from Lucy that the four boys help her run a Year 9 subject the following semester on 'Tools and Technology'. The boys seemed to accept the rationale given for the project, but initially resisted the idea of acting as aides for Lucy, claiming that they'd be called 'squares' by the other students.

The group worked on their collaborative project – a website devoted to motorbikes and based on their magazine work – for approximately 30 hours. There were 14 sessions with the researchers (approximately 20 hours in total, including a visit to the university). In addition there were eight 'researcher-free' sessions coordinated by Lucy, totalling 10 hours. During these times the boys continued working on the website and on completing their motorbike magazine project with Lucy.

The webpage project was decided during the first meeting of the net-work (21 April 1999). The catalyst was a comment by Lynn, the research assistant, following a lively discussion of motorbike properties.

Lynn: So we could actually have this really cool motorbike maga-zine and maybe even a motorbike website, the way you guys are talking now.

Stuart: I reckon we should. We've got the magazine, might as well do the website.

Jarrod: We could put the magazine on the website.

Lynn: Yeah, you could and make an online magazine. That'd be great. How would you all feel about using computers to do that?

The four students all nod and say 'Yeah'. In the second part of the session, which was designed to be a warm-up session with the boys generating an animated movie using the Microsoft's *3-D Moviemaker* software, all four as a group wanted to double-check that they would indeed be working on a set of webpages for the project proper. Stuart even spontaneously took a quick vote from the boys to ensure that they all did indeed want to work on a webpage about motorbikes.

The question of 'disadvantage'

Notwithstanding the study's formal interest in disadvantage, neither Lucy nor the school principal described the four boys taking part in this project as 'disadvantaged'. Indeed, Lucy was concerned that other students might see them as privileged in light of their 'special classes' and outings associated with it (including a visit to McDonald's). Nonetheless, the boys' assessed literacy levels (and their designation as underachievers in the literacy field by their teachers) locate them within a particular segment of the Australian secondary school population – boys described as having literacy problems (Martino 1995) – that is increasingly being treated in the manner of a disadvantaged group. In this project, the boys and Lucy unquestioningly spoke in terms of the lads' 'inability' to carry out the kinds of literacy-based activities regarded as mainstream for Year 9 English.

In working with this group of boys, the researchers were committed to collaboratively designing a programme that was able to respond to their (the boys') personal needs as well as their literacy skills. This involved identifying the relationship between the kind of masculinity the boys identified with and their literacy achievements in and out of school. Literacy ability seemingly does not mesh well with influential constructions of masculinity (Browne 1995; Gilbert and Gilbert 1998). In Australia at least, an association between boys, high achievement and English is commonly discounted by boys and teachers alike. In working to introduce these Yanga Headlands boys to a range of literacy and technology activities, the researchers were conscious of the need to be aware of and responsive to the investment these particular boys had in 'acting like (real) boys'. The researchers were also committed, however, to working against some of the consequences of 'being' the particular kind of boys the members of this network most commonly portrayed themselves as being (non-academic, not fluently literate, and so on – see Rowan *et al.* 2002).

The sessions responded to the identified (and fairly stereotypically masculine) interests of the boys – like their shared passion for motorbikes and video gaming – but also provided the boys with non-stereotypical opportunities and experiences (like the teacher's request that they act as assistants in later classroom activities). A particular perspective on disadvantage underpinned these goals. This was a perspective that sees disadvantage as something produced within particular social, cultural and historical contexts and comes to be attached to certain physical markers (like gender, or race, or class). Recognizing the *constructed* nature of disadvantage is an important starting point for any innovative study since it admits the possibility of challenging particular categories of disadvantage and their material consequences.

A note on the learning process

The look and feel of the sessions at Yanga Headlands matched the ideal envisaged in the project proposal. With the exception of Lucy – who, in any event was often on call elsewhere – the adults were all on first name basis with the boys. The researchers were gently firm at times, as in Leonie's 'It's not going to happen' (see below). Their general mode, however, was informal, open, attentive, and highly encouraging. The boys worked in pairs, overwhelmingly with good humour and mutual support. The group was small and intimate. To some extent it could be seen as a luxury, in the sense that the typical adult–student ratio was 1:1 or better. By the same token, given contemporary trends toward classrooms welcoming multiple parents and/or teacher aides, and the growth of partnerships between schools, community and other educational institutions, the possibilities for at least approximating to a ratio more like that found in the Yanga group are promising for many schools in more mainstream settings.

The 'unschool-like' character of the sessions was perhaps most apparent around the presence of Pedro's baby daughter at most of the sessions. The researchers were

> . . . surprised at the extent to which these tough, trouble-making boys welcomed Holly into the group. Every session they would stop by her pram first thing and hold her hand, pull funny faces, speak in gentle, baby like voices and generally show that they liked her and were glad she was there.
>
> (Rowan *et al.* 2002: 152)

The researchers also found that giving the boys responsibility for setting up the research video- and audio-recording equipment helped minimize the development of a researcher–subject relationship. From the second or third session the researchers were effectively sidelined from setting up. The boys took over and became dab hands at using the equipment.

The warm-up session began with having the boys work with Microsoft's *3D Moviemaker* so that a common base of computing knowledge could be established. This was followed by exploring *FrontPage*, which was the school's software for constructing webpages. Some of the boys already knew how to use scanners, which was another key application used in the project. Thereafter, it was a matter of all participants becoming more proficient with the different functions and applications as they went along. None of the researchers was familiar with PC applications – all were Mac users. Given the differences between the operating logics of the two platforms, the researchers were often as deeply involved in learning unfamiliar software as the students were. Learning by doing and learning as you go became the norm for all except Chris who, although unfamiliar with PCs, was at least familiar with webpage and website design and construction. Once the software had been introduced in the initial warming-up phase of the first session, subsequent sessions settled into a familiar pattern. After the research and project gear was set up, the days were based around working on tasks related to 'designing, trying out and testing their web pages. The style of work was based upon mutual support and sharing in which young and old, experienced and inexperienced worked together to solve problems that arose from . . . building . . . the four sets of web pages, one for each student' (Rowan *et al.* 2002: 150). In addition, semi-structured conversations and discussions of issues to be recorded for research purposes were built into the regular pattern. While these were primarily conceived and enacted as facets of the research, they became *bona fide* pedagogical situations in their own right, as questions presented scaffolded opportunities for all participants to reflect on their understandings and viewpoints, and to consider things from other perspectives. The following excerpts from recorded session transcripts and researcher notes capture much of the flavour of the sessions.

Excerpt 1

Leonie: Okay, guys. We've only got until ten past 11, which means the sooner we get this done the sooner we can get onto other activities, so we kinda need to get a bit better at getting started.

Jarrod: What's the idea of the Moviemaker?

Leonie: Well the idea of the Moviemaker is to get used to working with each other, and get you guys working with each other, and get you thinking about what it's like to actually learn something and what it's like to try and teach somebody else. So it's like really easy to say . . . .

Jarrod: With the game in my bag [*Carmaggedon*], we could take turns with that.

Leonie: You people have already put time into getting Moviemaker skills, so we thought it would be a better idea if we focused on that. Otherwise we mightn't get to the webpage activity.

Jarrod: *Carmageddon* skills are good.

Leonie: No. It's not going to happen.

Lynn: It's sort of a different type of thing aren't they? If you are going to be like a teacher and you're going to help other students and other teachers, then you need a few different kinds of skills.

Jarrod: Yep.

(Transcript 3 May 1999)

Excerpt 2

Kyle copied the image and wanted to paste it into his web page. He went through the process of locating *FrontPage Express* again (and I commented that it is easier to move between programs if you don't quit out of them). He got it open and pasted in the image and was pretty happy that he'd been able to do it.

He then decided to re-scan the image with the cover off to see if he could get a better result: this time he didn't quit out of the applications, just minimized them and I said 'Yay!' and he laughed . . .

Soon Kyle had re-scanned the images and went through the process of copying them and pasting them into the web page. After each image I asked him to save the page. He started to do this with the 'save as' command again and I said, 'No you just need to save'. We then worked out that it was quicker to just save – I explained that the file already had a name so he didn't need to name it again.

He repeated the process of moving between scanner and *FrontPage Express* and I made a joke about how he wasn't quitting out of it now and he laughed. It was a very good exchange that I enjoyed a lot. At one point, to get his attention, I leaned over and looked at him really closely and he laughed and said, 'I get it, I get it'. With all the time wasted at the beginning Kyle would have had only about 20 minutes on the program and in this time he created a new web page, a heading, and scanned and pasted in three images. I told him that this was terrific, reminding him that he would never have been able to do this a couple of weeks ago.

(Leonie's fieldnotes, 15 June 1999)

Excerpt 3

Leonie: I'm not convinced that it's worked. We might need to go back to your image and save it as something else.

Ben: Cancel.

Leonie: Okay, we need to go back to . . .

Ben: It's there, I know it's there.

Leonie: Yeah, but we can't see it. Okay let's try again. Right, go back to that image.

Ben: What? That uhm . . .

Leonie: The page that we were on.

Ben: With all the motorbikes?

Leonie: Yep. That's the one.

Ben: I'm getting too good at this.

Leonie: Yeah, we are.

Ben: We'll choose that one.

Leonie: Okay now.

Ben: There we go. He's got them little things around it. This one didn't have them. Okay, now I just go to 'cut'.

Leonie: No, we can't cut it, we need to . . . we might need to 'save it as' . . . Jarrod, to save a picture . . . Can you come here for a sec? . . . We want to copy this and then paste it into Ben's page.

Jarrod: Click, copy, done.

Ben: Now what do I do?

Jarrod: Go into your other file and press . . .

Ben: Do I need to change my disk?

Jarrod: Do you want to be in your file?

Ben: Yeah.

Jarrod: Then go into your file, oh yes, oh shit. You won't be able to do that.

Leonie: No it's all right, you can, you can just put it onto a middle bit, so we'll put it on a page like you were doing before. Just go to 'file' and make a new page and go up to a new page here.

Ben: We'll have to select that picture again?

Leonie: No you've already copied it, haven't you?

Ben: Oh yeah. Now what do I do? Go to a new page?

Leonie: Yeah, and we'll paste it there for a moment. How come it didn't do that before? Okay. now you want to 'save as'. Try the undo thing. Oh, paste again.

Ben: I thought I'd lost it.
Leonie: That was pretty excellent. We might be able to swap the
         disks over. What do you reckon?

(Transcript 15 June 1999)

Some general features of the learning processes

A kind of transcendence

The approach to learning that occurred in the Yanga site and the results or
consequences of that approach reflect a form of *transcendence* we think is
important under contemporary conditions within performativity-oriented
education systems. Teachers are often faced with statements of learning
outcomes, competencies, and the like to be demonstrated by learners
within a given time frame. In some cases teachers have to generate their
own statements of learning outcomes for which they are accountable.

Under such conditions it is common for teachers to adopt the learning
outcomes as the focus or 'top line' for their pedagogy: the goals to be pursued. This is not unreasonable, given the official and public scrutiny under
which schooling has fallen during the past two decades. This has been
accompanied by pressures on funding, increasing linguistic, ethnic and
cultural diversity of students, increased class sizes, retrogressive policy
directives of conservative governments, pressures on employment, criticism of the profession based on allegations of falling standards, and so on.
Under such conditions, meeting required learning outcomes starts to look
like both a necessary and a considerable achievement. At the same time,
many teachers still believe there is more than this to education, and experience doubts, frustration and diminished career satisfaction.

The experience at Yanga Headlands suggests a different logic and
different metaphors. The boys learned a lot of new skills and acquired a
lot of new knowledge related to webpage construction specifically and
computing more generally in the course of the project. Much of this can be
seen better in terms of learning consequences than learning *outcomes*. This
is because what the boys acquired in the way of capabilities was far greater
and richer than the kinds of specific skill and knowledge mastery 'items'
that appear on checklists of learning outcomes. Moreover, from the outset
the pedagogical aims were set much higher. It was intended that participants produce some substantial artefact that encapsulated technical,
cultural and critical dimensions of awareness and proficiency. A high proportion of this had little directly to do with computing or webpage construction, but might be seen as nonetheless deeply educational and, indeed,

central to becoming a good citizen, worker, community person and family member. The case of Yanga headlands illustrates a logic of 'transcendence' where, in many ways, the kinds of capabilities that appear as items on a list of required learning outcomes had a status much closer to a *base* line than a top line. It was more as if these capacities emerged as by-products of a much more rounded pedagogical approach and learning experience.

This logic is hardly novel. It is reminiscent, for example, of a whole-language approach to language education, wherein basics are to emerge as consequences of a much wider and richer language experience (Christina Davidson, in personal communication). We call it a logic of transcendence because the pedagogical approach wittingly transcended pursuit of atomized competencies or learning outcomes that have been abstracted from larger social practices and taught in decontextualized or disembodied ways. At Yanga Headlands the participants engaged in diverse and complex processes that coalesced around a broad task. In the context of pursuing this task there was wide-ranging discussion, skill sharing, wanderings into unanticipated areas of conversation, negotiation, and sustained hands-on activity. The boys were continually challenged to think, anticipate, compare and contrast, evaluate, reflect on aspects from very different areas of their lives, and to bring their varied experiences together in ways that promoted significant cultural and critical understandings of computer-based social practices and, indeed, of learning and the institution of school itself. Numerous illustrations of this logic of transcendence will be apparent in the section on learning consequences, where we present typical slices of data from the learning sessions.

A kind of purposefully decentred learning

The kind of learning that occurred in the network context was much less *centred* and *bounded* than that of the subject-based fixed content approach of conventional approaches to curriculum and pedagogy. The traditional epistemology of school has resulted in the idea of learning being organized around bodies of content to be covered in line with a guiding syllabus. Teaching focuses on covering the quota for a particular period following a mapped out programme and keeping within pre-established bounds. It is, precisely, the job of syllabus developers and curriculum planners to map out the learning terrain and put fences around the content.

In the project, however, there was a broad *task* that provided the catalyst for learning to occur. There were also genuine research purposes operating, in the sense that the researchers wanted to collect data and had put mechanisms in place for doing this. These included recording (in both audio and video formats) conversations instigated and loosely structured by the researchers to tap into the boys' ideas, understandings, thought processes, and perspectives. In addition the interests, purposes, and subjectivities of the boys themselves established a degree of structuring of the learning contexts. These included their shared interest in motorbikes and motorcycling, but also included entrenched forms of masculinity which permeated the sessions and with which the researchers were prepared to engage. Within the loose structure established by these conditions, the highly dialogical nature of the pedagogy allowed for threads and trails of learning to take off in different directions. This is the kind of situation that Michael Doneman (1997) has referred to as 'curriculum on the fly', where things that arise in the moment become stimuli and catalysts for new, unplanned and unanticipated learning and knowledge. And while much of this is incidental, it is not random or unhinged. It winds its way out from broad identifiable learning purposes and tasks, to which it remains linked. But it is not preplanned, and it does not *cover* predetermined ground. Rather, it *uncovers* new ground that produces 'coverage' of an entirely different kind from the conventional curriculum coverage, and that can be extremely rich and fruitful. This is the kind of thing that happened, for example, when Pedro seized on what he saw as the boys' 'games-oriented' view of computing (see below). He prompted them to clarify their understanding of games and programs respectively, where they saw particular kinds of software fitting into this categorization, and how they thought the games and programs taxonomy related to websites and webpages.

Learning consequences

Pedagogical contexts look backwards as well as forwards. They project learners into new areas of capability and understanding, while drawing on what they have previously experienced, learned and understood. The project at Yanga Headlands resulted in very significant *new* learnings for the four boys (as well as for the adult participants). At the same time, however – and very importantly – the sessions provided ample opportunities for the boys to demonstrate literacy- and technology-related cultural knowledge that belied their reputations as poor literacy and English students. The sessions drew out demonstrations of knowledge and understanding that included many examples of language awareness that the state English syllabus identified as necessary conditions for effective and powerful language use. Two of these that we will look at in detail below are an understanding of the importance of context in language use and the ability to use the genre of persuasion effectively.

In this section we consider examples of both new forms of proficiency and significant demonstrations of extant knowledge and capability that challenge the dominant conceptions of these boys within the school. These examples indicate the extent to which the four lads, and other learners more or less like them, are constituted by approaches to curriculum and pedagogy that presuppose conventional economies of attention and classroom space that have outlived whatever 'use by' date they may once have had. The following sections consider aspects of *technical* and *cultural* proficiency relevant to engaging effectively in new and conventional forms of literacy. They also look at changes in the ways the boys regarded and talked about themselves, and how they oriented themselves toward being capable. Finally, we look at some of the ways the project prompted new ways of thinking about the economics of attention within a school by reference to ideas developed by Chris Bigum and Leonie Rowan.

In the area of technical capability

During the period covered by the project the boys showed they were developing a sound base of technical (or operational) abilities relevant to new forms of literacy involving electronic ICTs. They learned to create image and HTML files using a range of techniques including scanning and capturing images from the Internet. They could save these to floppy disk or to a directory structure on their hard drives, and could retrieve them in order to work on them further. They could all work between word processing and HTML editing programs to generate text and create attractive titles for webpages, as well as insert images into webpages, and understand that image files had to be in the same folder as the webpage file. They also learned how to generate links between files, and to other webpages they were constructing or that were already on the Internet, by creating hyperlinks on words and images. Stuart also learned how to use the line functions in *Word* to draw a plan of the main room in which they were working (Rowan *et al.* 2000). With respect to conventional forms of literacy 'the boys willingly keyed in information about motorbikes in general. They also produced short descriptive passages about their own motorbikes and their motorbike riding, and brief reviews of motorbike models and engine types. For at least one of the boys this was a "first" since reaching high school' (Rowan *et al.* 2002: 157).

In areas of cultural knowledge relevant to new and
conventional literacy practices

The boys also displayed a diverse and interesting range of cultural and
metalevel understandings of new and conventional literacy practices.
Some of the examples seem elementary, yet are crucial to understanding
and participating in Internet culture. For instance:

Pedro: I noticed you used the word 'website', Ben, instead of 'web-
page'. What's the difference between them? . . .
Ben: A website is where you can go and get stuff, and a webpage is
just a page.
Pedro: Cool
Ben: [Grinning] See, you can't say I didn't learn nothing.

This exchange was a notable point in Ben moving toward a clear understanding that a website refers to a collection of pages and links and down-
loads, whereas 'webpage' simply refers to a screen within that site.

From the very outset some of the boys showed they were aware of the
institution of copyright, concerns about plagiarism, and their topicality
and significance within Internet culture. The issue was triggered initially
by Jarrod, but was subsequently picked up by the researchers as a focus
for discussion.

Lynn: Okay Kyle, what sort of things do you want to see on the
motorbike site?
Kyle: Well, I'd like to see movies of two stroke motocross.
Lynn: Okay.
Jarrod: Where are we gonna get that?
Lynn: Four stroke or two stroke?
Jarrod: Stu, where are we gonna get the movies?
Lynn: We'll worry about that later, we just want to see what things
we're going to get on the webpage. All right Kyle, what else
would you like to see?
Stuart: I'll steal them from another website.
Jarrod: Copyright laws [said in a 'you-can't-do-that' tone].
(Transcript 5 May 1999)

Later, Pedro returns to Jarrod's comment when he asks:

Pedro: Who knows what copyright is?
Ben: You could be watching a movie or listening to a song from a
CD but you can't just copy it.
Jarrod: If you put something together, if you have photos . . .

Pedro: And put them on the website and Stuart came along here and took all those photos and put them on his web site . . . ?

Ben: That's copyright.

Pedro: Yeah, is he – can he do that?

Ben: It's illegal.

Pedro: It's illegal, yes.

Leonie: So what would we have to do?

Ben: You know what I think is wrong with that? You can't tape songs off *Rage* or *Video Hits* and give them to other people.

Pedro: That's right. That's called copyright, too.

Stuart: Yeah. That's what I was listening to when we went on the weekend, when we were going down to 1770 [a coastal town some distance from Yanga Headlands].

Pedro: So how are we gonna be sure that our site doesn't break any copyright laws?

Ben: Put a lock on it.

Stuart: No 'cause on the computer – they were listening and the guy said now everything on the Internet is nearly illegal, like you can go and look into it but you can't download any of it.

Leonie: Yeah, I heard that too.

Stuart: You can load it onto your computer, like only some things. But if you load that off your computer to another person, that's copyright.

Jarrod: Uh-oh, we've got about fifty people in the school who would probably get caught for copyright laws just 'cause of Pokemon!

On another occasion Ben showed an understanding of the practice we referred to in Chapter 5 as attention transferring. In the context of talking about providing information relating to the engine size of a motorcycle and how this could be done on a webpage, Ben suggests making a hyperlink to the site of a motorcycle company that contains the information. He understood how to enhance the pages they were constructing, and how the worlds of motorcycle enthusiasts and motorcycle businesses are related on the Internet. He understood how webpages can work to pass attention on from one site to another. Moreover, although the idea was not followed up in the discussion, his choice of a link to a *company* site, rather than to another enthusiast site like their own, may have indicated an awareness that links from certain kinds of pages could help give 'authority' or 'cachet' to their own site (Rowan *et al.* 2000; cf. Burbules 1997).

Similarly, Jarrod showed familiarity with the attention device of trading on popular domain names in a URL. He gave the example of a pornography site whose URL (www.whitehouse.com) often captures visitors who are actually looking for the US government website (www.whitehouse.gov). Coincidentally, in the course of using a search engine recommended by the researchers (www.northernlight.com), Jarrod inadvertently happened upon another pornography site by including an 's' in the URL where it was not required, and immediately informed the group of this.

Jarrod's webpage building 'tour' conducted for Lucy and described below demonstrates many of the elements of the metalanguage that had developed by the end of the project, and which was shared to a great extent by all group members.

Pedro: What might help, Jarrod, is if you put the webpage up on the computer and then talk [to Lucy] about the webpage.

Jarrod: Okay then.

Lucy: Now, *Front Page Express*.

Jarrod: Or we could go straight into 'running draft'.

Lucy: No, let's go through *Front Page Express*.

Jarrod: Okay, then. That's different from –

Lucy: Yeah, this scan is scanning the document; it's a virus scanner put on a couple of days ago.

Jarrod: Looks different – *Front Page Express*. Now we were doing a page on the . . . Yesterday you and I were doing the page on the English Department and now we're going into 'file' [clicks on menu].

Lucy: We could go in today to the English Page on the Internet, couldn't we?

Jarrod: Yep. Now 'file', 'open', 'browse', and 'go to' – press down and go up, scroll upwards, go into three-quarter floppy and go into nineteen-ninety-nine, and there's your page.

Lucy: Beautiful. Okay, so what are we doing now? How about we have a look at the English one, the English Department one and then maybe we'll make it a bit fancy.

Jarrod: Just 'E' here; just double click on there.

Lucy: What's 'E' stand for?

Jarrod: Internet Explorer. It's a short cut.

(Transcript 15 June 1999)

Finally, from the realm of everyday conventional forms of speaking and writing, Kyle spontaneously offered a very articulate account of the importance of context in communication. Leonie had asked him if he could help her decipher a note left by Lucy explaining where she would be if she was needed during the session. Leonie needed to get Lucy's computer network access password so asked Kyle if he could identify a phone number in the rather cryptic note. Kyle looked at the note and the following conversation took place:

Kyle: Just like my mum, no detail.
Leonie: Yeah, not very helpful.
Kyle: My mum never gives enough detail. She'll say, 'Buy some sugar', and I'll say, 'What kind?' And she'll say, 'Just sugar' and I'll go [to the shop], and there'll be all these kinds of sugar. Not enough detail.

(Transcript 15 June 1999)

This was followed by comments from Kyle indicating the importance of understanding the context in which one was learning or doing something. He identified that he was unable to decide what kind of sugar to buy because he didn't understand what his mother wanted it *for*.

In the area of how the boys spoke about and regarded themselves as learners

Over the eight-week period in which the network met there were some notable shifts in the ways the boys regarded and spoke about themselves in terms of being learners. They moved palpably from describing themselves as students in negative ways to being much more willing to recognize and own their strengths and abilities in situations where these were apparent. Early on, and even well into the sessions, they affirmed the view held by the principal, other teachers and, seemingly, by Lucy herself, that they were not 'good' students. They were often critical of themselves and their abilities, and were quick to point out when they had made mistakes.

Ben: Then I went to that picture [pointing to an icon on the screen], then I went to that Word Art.
Leonie: Excellent. Now you pick another one.
Ben: That one [he clicks on a word art icon, but it doesn't open]. Oh, I'm so stupid.
Leonie: It's not stupid.

(Transcript 18 May 1999)

Commenting on their concerns about recording their audiotape journals, Jarrod and Kyle make the following points:

Jarrod: It's got ours and Miss Marshall [on it]. I hate doing that. You're sitting there talking and you muck it up, so you have to tape over it.

Leonie: But why? How do you muck something up?

Ben: You forget what to say.

Jarrod: You talk into it . . .

Leonie: But that's okay. We don't expect you to be talking as though you've done a big speech.

(Transcript 19 May 1999)

And Kyle says in response to Leonie's praise for his hyperlinking ability:

Leonie: You were getting pretty good.

Kyle: Ohhh, I don't know. Probably not.

Leonie: Why not?

Kyle: I'm not good enough.

(Transcript 3 May 1999)

And Stuart's comments foreshadow the others':

Stuart: I don't really get what we're doing so far 'cause I'm a slow learner, but I'll catch up.

(Transcript 28 April 1999)

Later on, however, the boys came to assume more and more that they *would* be able to do things successfully and were more eager and willing to take on tasks and activities.

Leonie: Do you want to save your page?

Ben: Yep. I got my little thing-a-ma-jig in there, so I can save on that, can't I?

(Transcript 18 May 1999)

And later:

Ben: I wonder if I can do that again. And now I need another picture.

Leonie: Well, we know how to do it now.

Ben: Yep, and I'm going to do it.

(Transcript 9 June 1999)
(See Rowan *et al.* 2000; Rowan *et al.* 2002: 154–5)

Rethinking the economics of attention

As noted previously, the project contributed much to the learning of the research team as well. One notable dimension of this involves the way the data and *in situ* experiences stimulated members of the team to use the economics of attention as a construct for analysing the data. There is not space here to go into this theme in the detail it deserves. We will, however, present some aspects of the analysis that take up the issue of how schools conceive and manage attention from where we left off in Chapter 5.

As argued in the original project report (Rowan *et al.* 2000), schools and teaching have always worked on the assumption that attention is in scarce supply. An economics of attention has always operated in schools. Unlike the deregulated contemporary attention economy that operates in public domains outside school, and that has burgeoned and become highly sophisticated in concert with the growth and development in mass media and communications technologies, the attention economy of school is highly regulated and controlled.

> There are well-established patterns of student behaviour that attract the attention of teachers and there are well-established practices of teachers that attract the attention of colleagues, principals and other administrators. In attention terms then, the school is a *closed* economy.
>
> (Rowan *et al.* 2000: 301)

That is, attention flows within the school are shaped and regulated by rules of giving and receiving attention that are well established, albeit largely *unwritten*. We also find a kind of economy of attention operating in schools that is analogous to what is referred to as the black or informal economy found in highly controlled and regulated material goods economies. This involves what the boys in the study referred to as their 'brat level', where seeking and gaining attention by illegitimate means constitutes resistance to the tight controls of the school attention economy.

As we observed in Chapter 5, modern mass media and communications technologies, reaching their current high point in the explosion of the Internet, provide enormous capacity for individuals, groups and institutions in the world outside school to seek and pay attention across wide gulfs of time and space (Rowan *et al.* 2000: 301). This is largely a de-regulated economy so far as formal rules and controls are concerned. As we argued in Chapter 5 there certainly are *criteria* (e.g. originality) and *standards* that work like the purported invisible hand of the free market to mediate supply and demand of attention in this external attention economy. But almost anything goes so far as competing for and allocating attention against these criteria and standards are concerned (cf. Walter's Mission described in Chapter 5).

As a consequence there is a tension between the attention economy operating outside school and the economics of attention within school. Outside school, students have wide freedom of choice how and where to pursue and allocate attention. Within school, however, the constraints are tight. Moreover, the means and strategies for seeking and allocating attention outside school have no recognized place inside school. Conversely, the nature of attention flows – including who is permitted to be a 'star' – and 'the quaint rules' that define the school attention economy 'appear to have little relevance in the external economy' beyond equipping a small proportion of students to subsequently acquire credentials (after they leave school) that have the potential to attract attention (see Rowan *et al.* 2000: 302).

According to Bigum and Rowan, today's students have grown up in a deregulated attention economy and have been living by its rules.

> They learn how to allocate their attention between and among a wide range of communication technologies, both mass and personal. They are adept at juggling the inputs of various attention seeking technologies. They have learned how to gain attention in this space, in part, by mimicking the expert performance of a broad set of attention seeking and giving patterns that are available to them. Importantly, they know what does and does not attract attention in this deregulated world. They know that much of what they do in school is of a different order, only useful in terms of attracting attention within a closed attention economy. In this respect, the attention economy of schooling is only relevant to those students for whom it provides a basis for attracting attention in the world outside.
>
> (Rowan *et al.* 2000: 302)

Moreover, it is important to note that apart from a small number of tightly delineated spaces, like prefect systems and the sports arena, the attention economy of school largely withholds from students the option to be 'stars'. Schools do not 'position students as "stars": rather they are rewarded most commonly for their ability to act as devoted "fans" – for their attendance, their enthusiasm, their allegiance, their adoption of "star" behaviours and interests etc.' (Rowan *et al.* 2000: 304).

Given the research goal and the personal interests of the researchers in addressing issues of disadvantage at the interface of literacy and new technologies, the research team aimed at providing the boys with the kinds and qualities of attention that would help them to be able to participate on more equal terms with other students in the 'regular' attention economy of the school. Indeed, by trying to help get them on the inside of various technological capabilities that had kudos in the school, the researchers hoped that from time to time and within particular spaces the boys might actually be able to participate on better than equal footing with other students (Rowan *et al.* 2000: 304).

> To this end the researchers developed a series of activities that were designed to give students the attention of the researchers. We sat them down in round table-like discussions and listened to them. We drew on their interests and resources in negotiating a project using computer technology. We developed a rapport with them that was probably outside their experience in schools. In these ways, the researchers 'passed on' their interest in the students to other teachers and students – this served to disrupt at least partially the dominant models for understanding these four boys that circulated within the school.
>
> In addition to this, we worked to provide students with the kinds of skills in webpage construction that they could then use in teaching other students in a standard classroom. This positioned the students as the experts – the people whose attention was required by other students. This inversion of their role from fans to stars has, in our opinion, the greatest potential for allowing the boys themselves, and those who studied with and taught them, to recognise that their position as 'failures' was not a fixed, permanent, and natural position but rather something that could be challenged, disrupted, and rejected.
>
> (Rowan *et al.* 2000: 303–4)

This approach had interesting consequences in terms of harnessing the boys' persuasive abilities and performances to a new way of relating to being perceived as competent and to new ways of participating in the school attention economy.

Transcripts of the network sessions provide excellent examples of the boys using strategies of persuasion that had the potential to be used constructively and to their benefit in the school's attention economy. Early on in the project, however, the boys tended to use persuasion in order to *deflect* certain kinds of attention away from themselves. During the inaugural session, for instance, Lucy prompted discussion around the fact that when the project was over she would like the boys to be able to help teachers with the 'Tools and Technology' curriculum subject. The boys resisted the prospect vehemently. Stuart protested that he would 'get called a square by all my friends'. In a kind of ensuing negotiation the boys persuaded the adults *not* to refer to them as 'experts' or 'teachers'. Eventually the boys agreed to 'editor' and 'coordinator', and everybody agreed, in Lucy's words, to have 'nothing to do with the word "teach"'. An interesting facet of the attention flows in this situation is that at first glance it might appear that Lucy finally persuaded *the boys* to agree with her idea. On the other hand, she *needed* them to agree, otherwise they would not have helped the teachers in Tools and Technology. Hence, it can be seen that unlike their normal classroom situations the boys *were receiving the full attention of a teacher* (Rowan *et al.* 2000: 313).

This situation contrasts markedly with a number of open reflections the boys made about the kind and quality of attention they received in class, and how these differed from what they got in the project setting. Ben provided two examples of what he saw as common experiences.

> Yep. There's like teachers here [in the learning group] that listen to you, not like the ones in class. 'Miss, Miss!', 'Yeah I'll be there in a minute.' Half an hour later [still no help]. Here you just have to call out a name and they come.

and

> Mr Y. . . . just tells me to sit there and do nothing if I don't know how to do it. So I just sit there and get my Walkman out . . .

A discussion at the end of the final project session provided good evidence that the relationships, processes, and strategies that characterized the network's *modus operandi* worked successfully to disrupt the kind of 'deflective attention work' they engaged in at the beginning of the project. In so doing, it helped create space for the boys 'to (re)negotiate their social place in the school' (Rowan *et al.* 2000: 313).

When Lucy, near the end of the final session, again asks the boys about helping in the tools and technology subject, they replied with, 'Sure', and 'Easy'. Encouraged, Lucy asked how they thought the logistics could be handled in terms of available computers, number of tutors, numbers of groups, and so on. During the 'brainstorm' that ensued, the boys effectively moved the discussion away from Lucy being the focus of attention as the one controlling the conversation. Instead, *they* became the focus of attention. This represents a marked change in the boys' confidence and strategies with respect to competing for attention. It also reflects a very different personal orientation on the part of the boys toward being competent – which was now something they could 'own', despite other trappings of their commitment to a version of masculinity remaining securely intact (cf. Rowan *et al*. 2002: 146–69). The shift is captured graphically in the following transcript excerpt.

Lucy: Well, how do you think that would work, folks? How many in the class? There's 25 [students in the class] and we've got four computers. So how would we go about doing this? The other thing that just clicked with me a couple of seconds ago when you mentioned the library, how many computers are in the library that we could use?

Ben: Four.

Jarrod: We could hook up a couple of laptops.

Lucy: Students aren't allowed to use the school laptops.

Jarrod: Oh, okay.

Lucy: So we might be able to have Miss Bear with a couple of students up in my room.

Jarrod: Two of us could go into the library and two of us could go in to the classroom, so we could have eight computers running at once. And we alternate use every week.

Lucy: The only other alternative is if we could hook up the library then Mrs Allen wouldn't have to move out of the classroom, 'cause she'd have to go somewhere. I'll see Mrs Allen and see if we could possibly go for that option so we could have four up here and four down there and –

Kyle: Me and Jarrod could do up here.

Jarrod: Yep.

Lucy: Okay then, Ben and Stuart . . .

Stuart: No, me and Kyle, I'll go with Kyle.

Jarrod: Yeah, I'll go with Ben.

Lucy: Okay.

Jarrod: Have to have one smart person in each group [laughter].

Lucy: I'll see if I can make that library booking and I'll see if we can do that folks. If Mrs Allen doesn't want me to have the classroom, it's going to stuff things up.

Stuart: Oh well, then we just go four students at a time at the library. One single [lesson] and every time we got a double [lesson] we get eight people in a double.

Ben: And who are you going to teach, Longmire, yourself?

Lucy: Stuart, Stuart, Stuart. This may be the stroke of genius I've been waiting for. Run that idea by me again.

Stuart: We can have four students per lesson, for one lesson, and then in a double lesson we can run eight students.

Lynn: Brilliant! Bravo!

Lucy: Why didn't I think of that?

Bigum and Rowan identify an interesting implication here with respect to the state's English syllabus that shaped the English programme at Yanga Headlands. The syllabus was strongly informed by genre theory, and mastery of a designated range of genres was a key aim of language and literacy education at all levels of schooling. Persuasion was among the genres identified in the syllabus as integral to language operating as 'a powerful social instrument' that helps people to 'negotiate their places in social groups' (DEQ 1994: 8). In the exchange between Lucy and the boys transcribed here, the boys *do* approximate to using language in a socially powerful way within the regulated attention economy of the revamped school setting in which the network operated. Interestingly, what we have here are insights into the role of persuasion, *not as texts to be studied or produced in a classroom*, but as 'a practice central to the flows of attention within schools and classrooms' (Rowan *et al.* 2000: 316). This, perhaps, makes as clearly and concretely as it can be made the point about what is at stake between the traditional epistemology of school and the kind of epistemological perspective we have begun to argue for in the final two chapters of this book.

End notes: between rocks and hard places

The position we have argued for in this book is increasingly *not* the kind of position being taken up by state schools in North America, Britain, and Australasia. A definite direction has emerged under the powerful impetus of state guidelines, policies, and funding arrangements. This is toward defining literacy in terms of state mandated standardized tests and proficiency statements and knowledge in terms of the content of a national curriculum. It emphasizes meeting teacher and student technology proficiency standards and performance indicators, and favours incorporating new ICTs into homework activities and the kinds of experiences offered by the Grid and similar initiatives.

For example, on the day we keyed these final paragraphs we learned of a school serving an economically deprived US community that has made computers available in the homes of students. At the same time, the state's learning standards shape most of the decisions the school makes about computing and the new technological applications it will invest in. The school has committed to a testing, diagnostic and monitoring software system for teachers to use for diagnosing, monitoring and then teaching to their students' learning needs: this system incorporates a range of maths and reading assessment programs, subject area practice software, testing packages, and so on. These various software programs have been correlated with a range of standardized tests in the US and are found to be well suited to assessing student performance in relation to the state Department of Education's performance standards and indicators. The scores of students from this school on state mandated standardized tests have increased markedly in the past two or three years. This is quite reasonably regarded as a significant achievement within the community as well as in the school. The school is running hard with the school–business partnership concept (with businesses providing a range of network, hardware, a range of electronic devices, and software items free or heavily discounted), and has adopted the practice of welcoming companies to pilot new hardware, software and learning programs there. The latest development involved the representative of a software company meeting with school and district office personnel. The school, in partnership with the company, had won a large state government fund to develop a dedicated home–school digital network – replete with password access and firewalls to keep non-school people out – along with a web-based learning package. The main purpose of the network, as explained by the representative, is for teachers to be able to set tests in a range of subject areas to be taken online as homework and to be fed down the network to the teacher each evening.

Without wanting to criticize, let alone belittle, the wholehearted efforts made by such schools on behalf of the interests of their students and communities, we have advocated an opposing view here. Our top line is that formal education can be so much more, and make far better, more direct, and more enabling connections between what students learn now and what they will do and be later, and this is what we should be struggling for. Our bottom line is addressed more to teachers and the very real complexities they face on a day-to-day basis. These are teachers who may read books like this and say: 'Oh yeah, right! Like I could really practise new literacies and operate off a new epistemology in my classroom given everything else I'm expected to deliver on!' To such teachers we would extend solidarity. More than this we would say that even if teachers feel too beleaguered and encumbered to incorporate new literacies and new ways of learning and knowing into their teaching, it is nonetheless important for them to know and acknowledge the kinds of things young people are doing and being *outside* school in order to make effective pedagogical connections to them in class. In the final analysis, however, we believe that examples like that provided at Yanga Headlands support the view that not only is our top line viable, but that holding out for it is in the best interests of the education profession and students alike.

References

Adbusters (2002) www.adbusters.org (21 March 2002).

Adler, R. (1997) *The Future of Advertising: New Approaches to the Attention Economy*. Washington, DC: The Aspen Institute.

Alvermann, D. (ed.) (2002) *Adolescents and Literacies in a Digital World*. New York, NY: Peter Lang.

Amazon.com (2002) *About Amazon.com*. www.amazon.com/exec/obidos/subst/misc/company-info.html/ref = gw_bt_aa/102–7116477–9527366 (accessed 25 March 2002).

Anderson, C. A. (1965) Literacy and schooling on the development threshold: some historical cases, in C. A. Anderson and M. J. Bowman (eds) *Education and Economic Development*, pp. 347–62. Chicago, IL: Aldine.

Angeles, P. (1992) *The HarperCollins Dictionary of Philosophy*. New York, NY: HarperPerennial.

Anonymous Idiot (2001) Typical Plastic member profile, *Plastic*. www.plastic.com (accessed 10 February 2002).

Anuff, J. and Cox, A. (1997) *Suck: Worst-Case Scenarios in Media, Culture, Advertising, and the Internet*. San Francisco, CA: Hardwired.

Arber, R. (2001) *Buses of Sunnydown Garage*. www.sunnydownbuses.com (accessed 9 March 2002).

Ashton, C. (2002) Foreword, *Superhighway Safety*. safety.ngfl.gov.uk/schools/document.php3?D=d40 (accessed 2 March 2002).

AskJeeves (2002) www.askjeeves.com (accessed 25 July 2002).

Bail, K. (1997) Deskbottom publishing, *The Australian Magazine*, 3–4 May, 44.

Baker, C. (2002) Power bloggers, *Wired*, May www.wired.com/wired/archive/10. 05/mustread.html?pg=3 (accessed 20 April 2002).

Balson, A. and Balson, S. (1999) About Koala Trouble, *Alex's Scribbles – Koala Trouble*. Online. www.scribbles.com.au (accessed 13 August 2001).

Balson, A. and Balson, S. (2001) *Alex's Scribbles – Koala Trouble*. www.scribbles. com.au/max/about.html (accessed 13 August 2001).

Barrett, A. (2001) Plastic.com invites visitors to shape the site, *PCWorld. com*. Monday, 22 January. www.pcworld.com/news/article/0,aid,39013,00.asp (accessed 10 February 2002).

BECTa (British Educational Communications and Technology Agency) (2001a) *Information Sheet on the National Grid for Learning*. July, www.becta.org. uk/technology/infosheets/pdf/ngfl.pdf (accessed 11 May 2001).

BECTa (British Educational Communications and Technology Agency) (2001b) *Information Sheet on Using E-mail in Classroom Projects at Key Stage 2*, July. www.becta.org.uk/technology/infosheets/pdf/e-mailks2.pdf (accessed 11 May 2001).

BECTa (2001c) *Superhighway Safety*. safety.ngfl.gov.uk (accessed 11 August 2001).

BECTa (British Educational Communications and Technology Agency) (2002a) *NGfL Research and Evaluation Series*. www.becta.org.uk/research/reports/ ngfl_es.html (accessed 21 March 2002).

BECTa (British Educational Communications and Technology Agency) (2002b) *Young People's Use of ICT*. www.becta.org.uk/youngpeopleict/ (accessed 21 March 2002).

Bell, D. (1974) *The Coming of Postindustrial Society: A Venture in Social Forecasting*. New York, NY: Basic Books.

Bennahum, D. (1998) *Extra Life: Coming of Age in Cyberspace*. New York, NY: Basic Books.

BESA (British Educational Suppliers Association) (2001) *Teachers and Computers: Competent and Confident?* (Press release) www.besanet.org.uk/news/ict2000. htm (accessed 11 August 2001).

Bigum, C. (1997) Teachers and computers: in control. being controlled?, *Australian Journal of Education*, 41(3): 247–61.

Bigum, C. (2002) Design sensibilities, schools, and the new computing and communications technologies, in I. Snyder (ed.) *Silicon Literacies*, pp. 130–40. London: Falmer-Routledge.

Bigum, C. and Green, B. (1992) Technologizing literacy: the dark side of the dream, *Discourse: The Australian Journal of Educational Studies*, 12(2): 4–28.

Bigum, C. and Kenway, J. (1998) New information technologies and the ambiguous future of schooling – some possible scenarios, in A. Hargreaves, A. Lieberman, M. Fullan and D. Hopkins (eds), *International Handbook of Educational Change: Part One*, pp. 375–95. Dordrecht, NL: Kluwer Academic Publishers.

Bigum, C., Lankshear, C. and Knobel, K. (in process) Schools as knowledge producers. Research proposal under development. Rockhampton: Faculty of Education and Creative Arts, Central Queensland University.

Blair, T. (1997) *Connecting the Learning Society: The Government's Consultation Paper on the National Grid for Learning.* www.dfee.gov.uk/consultations/docs 42_1.pdf (accessed 26 July 2001).

Blair, T. (1999) Foreword, *National Grid for Learning: Open for Learning, Open for Business.* The Government's National Grid for Learning Challenge. London: DfEE. www.dfee.gov.uk (accessed 3 May 2000).

BotSpot (2002) *BotSpot Categories: Chat Bots.* botspot.com/search/s-chat.htm (accessed 21 March 2002).

Brown, J. and Duguid, P. (2000) *The Social Life of Information.* Boston, MA: Harvard Business School Press.

Browne, R. (1995) Schools and the construction of masculinity, in R. Browne and R. Fletcher (eds) *Boys in Schools: Addressing the Real Issues.* Lane Cove, NSW: Finch Publishing.

Burbules, N. (1997) Misinformation, malinformation, messed-up information, and mostly useless information: how to avoid getting tangled up in the 'Net, in C. Lankshear, C. Bigum, C. Durrant *et al.* (investigators) *Digital Rhetorics: Literacies and Technologies in Education – Current Practices and Future Directions,* Vol. 3, pp. 109–20. Children's Literacy National Projects. Brisbane: QUT/DEETYA.

Castells, M. (1996) *The Rise of the Network Society.* Oxford: Blackwell.

Castells, M. (1997) *The Power of Identity.* Oxford: Blackwell.

Castells, M. (1998) *End of Millennium.* Oxford: Blackwell.

Channel 4Learning (2002a) *4Learning.* www.channel4.com/learning (accessed 9 March 2002).

Channel 4Learning (2002b) What would you call these things? *4Learning: Preschool.* www.channel4.com/learning/microsites/H/Hoobs/activities/108_ activity.shtml (accessed 9 March 2002).

Channel 4Learning (2002c) Activities archive. *4Learning: Preschool.* www. channel4.com/learning/microsites/H/Hoobs/activities/archive.cfm (accessed 9 March 2002).

Channel 4 Learning (2002d) Hoob dictionary. *4Learning: Preschool.* www. channel4.com/learning/microsites/H/Hoobs/dictionary/sub1.shtml (accessed 9 March 2002).

Christie, F. (1987) Genres as choice, in I. Reid (ed.) *The Place of Genre in Learning: Current Debates,* Typereader Publications No. 1, pp. 22–34. Geelong: Deakin University, Centre for Studies in Literacy Education.

Collier, M. and Woerner, R. (2000) *eBay for Dummies,* 2nd edition. New York, NY: Hungry Minds.

Cope, B. and Kalantzis, M. (eds) (1999) *Multiliteracies: Literacy Learning and the Design of Social Futures.* London: Routledge.

Coupland, D. (1991) *Generation X: Tales for an Accelerated Culture.* New York, NY: St Martin's Press.

Coupland, D. (1995) *Microserfs.* New York, NY: HarperCollins.

Coupland, D. (1996) *Polaroids from the Dead.* New York, NY: HarperCollins.

Coupland, D. (2000) *Miss Wyoming.* New York, NY: Pantheon.

Cowan, J., Eidenow, E. and Likely, L. (1998) Destino Colombia: a scenario process for the new millennium, *Deeper News,* 9(1): 7–31.

de Certeau, M. (1984) *The Practice of Everyday Life*. Berkeley, CA: University of California Press.

DEQ (Department of Education, Queensland) (1994) *English in Years 1 to 10. Queensland Syllabus Materials: English Syllabus for Years 1 to 10*. Brisbane: Department of Education.

DfEE (Department for Education and Employment) (1999) *National Grid for Learning: Open for Learning, Open for Business*. www.dfee.gov.uk (accessed 3 May 2000).

DfES (Department for Education and Skills) (c.2001) Making the Internet safe, *Superhighway Safety*. safety.ngfl.gov.uk/?S=2 (accessed 11 August 2001).

Digitarts (2000) digitarts.va.com.au (accessed 21 March 2002).

Doneman, M. (1997) Multimediating, in C. Lankshear, C. Bigum, C. Durrant *et al.* (investigators) *Digital Rhetorics: Literacies and Technologies in Education – Current Practices and Future Directions*, Vol. 3. Children's Literacy National Projects, pp. 131–48. Brisbane: QUT/DEETYA.

Dreamcast (2000) Walter needs us! 27 June. dreamcast.ign.com/news/21457.html (accessed 4 November 2000).

Duncombe, S. (1997) *Notes From Underground: Zines and the Politics of Alternative Culture*. London: Verso.

eBay (2002a) *About eBay: Company Overview*. pages.ebay.com/community/aboutebay/overview/index.html (accessed 10 February 2002).

eBay (2002b) *About eBay: The eBay Community*. pages.ebay.com/community/aboutebay/community/profiles.html (accessed 10 February 2002).

eBay (2002c) *Seller Guide: Fees*. pages.ebay.com/help/sellerguide/selling-fees.html (accessed 10 February 2002).

eBay (2002d) *Frequently Asked Questions about Feedback*. pages.ebay.com/help/basics/f-feedback.html (accessed 10 February 2002).

eBay Feedback Discussion Board (2001) forums.ebay.com/dwc?14@1017295028187@.ee7b9c6 (accessed 25 July 2002).

Eisenhut, J. (2000) Coverstory. *skim.com*. Zurich, 3 July. www.skim.com (accessed 12 July 2000).

Eureka! and Publitek New Media Limited (2001a) *Let's Discover*. www.letsdiscover.org.uk (accessed 9 March 2002).

Eureka! and Publitek New Media Limited (2001b) Website aims. *Let's Discover*. www.letsdiscover.org.uk (accessed 9 March 2002).

Forbes, R. (1958) Power to 1850, in C. Singer (ed.) *A History of Technology, Vol. 4: The Industrial Revolution 1750–1850*, 148–67. Oxford: Oxford University Press.

Freire, P. (1972) *Pedagogy of the Oppressed*. Harmondsworth: Penguin.

Freire, P. (1973) *Cultural Action for Freedom*. Harmondsworth: Penguin.

Freire, P. and Macedo, D. (1987) *Literacy: Reading the Word and the World*. South Hadley, MA: Bergin and Garvey.

Friedman, T. (2000) *The Lexus and the Olive Tree*. New York, NY: Anchor Books.

GBN (Global Business Network) (2002) www.gbn.org (accessed 25 July 2002).

Gee, J. P. (1990) *Social Linguistics and Literacies: Ideology in Discourses*. London: Falmer.

Gee, J. P. (1991) What is literacy?, in C. Mitchell and K. Weiler (eds) *Rewriting Literacy: Culture and the Discourse of the Other*. New York, NY: Bergin and Garvey.

Gee, J. P. (1996) *Social Linguistics and Literacies: Ideology in Discourses*, 2nd edition. London: Falmer.

Gee, J. P. (2000) Teenagers in new times: a new literacy studies perspective, *Journal of Adolescent and Adult Literacy*, 43(5): 412–23.

Gee, J. P. (2001) Reading as a situated practice: a sociocognitive perspective, *Journal of Adolescent and Adult Literacy*, 44(8): 714–25.

Gee, J. P. (forthcoming) *Literacy and Learning in Video and Computer Games*. New York, NY: Palgrave.

Gee, J. P., Hull, G. and Lankshear, C. (1996) *The New Work Order: Behind the Language of the New Capitalism*. Sydney: Allen & Unwin.

Gelernter, D. (1998) *Machine Beauty: Elegance and the Heart of Technology*. New York, NY: Basic Books.

Gershenfeld, N. (1999) *When Things Start to Think*. New York, NY: Henry Holt and Company.

Gettier, E. (1963) Is justified true belief knowledge?, *Analysis*, 23: 121–3.

Gilbert, R. and Gilbert, P. (1998) *Masculinity Goes to School*. St Leonards, NSW: Allen and Unwin.

Gilster, P. (1997) *Digital Literacy*. New York, NY: John Wiley and Sons.

Goldberg, K. (2000) The robot in the garden: telerobotics and telepistemology on the Internet. www.ieor.berkeley.edu/~goldberg/art/tele/index.html (accessed 21 March 2002).

Goldhaber, M. (1997) The attention economy and the net, *First Monday*. firstmonday.dk/issues/issue2_4/goldhaber (accessed 2 July 2000)

Goldhaber, M. (1998a) The attention economy will change everything, *Telepolis* (Archive 1998). www.heise.de/tp/english/inhalt/te/1419/1.html (accessed 30 July 2000).

Goldhaber, M. (1998b) M. H. Goldhaber's principles of the new economy. www.well.com/user/mgoldh/principles.html (accessed 2 July 2000).

Goodson, I., Knobel, M., Lankshear, C. and Mangan, M. (2003) *Social Spaces/Cyber Spaces: Culture Clash in Computerized Classrooms*. New York, NY: Palgrave Press.

Graff, H. (1979) *The Literacy Myth: Literacy and Social Structure in the Nineteenth Century City*. New York, NY: Academic Press.

Gravityzone (2001) 'Terrorist' strikes Plastic.com – editors helpless, *Plastic*. www.plastic.com (accessed 13 February 2002).

Green, B. (1988) Subject-specific literacy and school learning: a focus on writing, *Australian Journal of Education*, 30(2): 156–69.

Green, B. (1997) Literacy, information and the learning society. Keynote address to the Joint Conference of the Australian Association for the Teaching of English, the Australian Literacy Educators' Association, and the Australian School Library Association, Darwin High School, Northern Territory, Australia, 8–11 July.

Green, B. and Bigum, C. (1993) Aliens in the classroom, *Australian Journal of Education*, 37(2): 119–41.

Greenstein, J. (2000) *Feed* and *Suck* link up, *The Industry Standard*. www.thestandard.com/article/display/0,1151,16708,00.html (accessed 10 February 2002).

GridClub (2001a) *Grown Ups*. www.gridclub.com/grown_ups/index.shtml (accessed 11 August 2001).

GridClub (2001b) *Have a Go*. www.gridclub.com/have_a_go/index.shtml (accessed 11 August 2001).

GridClub (2001c) *Join the Clubs*. www.gridclub.com/join_the_clubs/index.shtml (accessed 11 August 2001).

GridClub (2001d) *Tell Tales*. www.gridclub.com/have_a_go/english/english.shtml (accessed 11 August 2001).

GridClub (2002) www.gridclub.com (accessed 25 July 2002).

GridWatch (2001) www.ngfl.gov.uk/about_ngfl.jsp?sec=20&cat=99&clear=y (accessed 12 August 2001).

Heath, S. B. (1983) *Ways with Words: Language, Life and Work in Communities and Classrooms*. Cambridge: Cambridge University Press.

Heath, S. B. and McLaughlin, M. (1994) Learning for anything everyday, *Journal of Curriculum Studies*, 26(5): 471–89.

Heim, M. (1999) *Transmogrifications*. www.mheim.com/html/transmog/transmog.htm (accessed 21 March 2002).

Heller, N. (2001) UK government stays the course with NGfL, *Heller Report on Educational Technology Markets*, 12(4): 6.

Heun, C. (2001) What the rest of us can learn from eBay, *Information Week*, 12 March. www.informationweek.com/828/rbebusiness_side.htm (accessed 15 March 2001).

Hirsch, E. D. Jr (1987) *Cultural Literacy: What Every American Needs to Know*. Boston, MA: Houghton Mifflin.

Hirst, P. (1974) *Knowledge and the Curriculum*. London: Routledge and Kegan Paul.

Hoggart, R. (1957) *The Uses of Literacy: Aspects of Working Class Life*. London: Chatto.

Holder, K. (2001) *Internet Safety Guidelines*. Presentation to the Technology Safety Seminar. www.becta.org.uk/technology/safetyseminars/220301/holder.pdf (accessed 28 March 2002).

Homework High (2001) www.homeworkhigh.com (accessed 28 March 2002).

Honan, M. (2001) 'Plastic is all I do'. Part 2: Plastic's Return, *Online Journalism Review*. www.ojr.org/ojr/workplace/1017862577.php (accessed 10 February 2002).

Howard, S. (ed.) (1998) *Wired Up: Young People and the Electronic Media*. London: UCL Press.

Hull, G., Jury, M. and Katz, M. (forthcoming) *Working the Frontlines of Economic Change: Learning, Doing and Becoming in the Silicon Valley*. Berkeley, CA: Graduate School of Education.

jbou (2002) 'I was wrong about Bart . . .', *Plastic*. www.plastic.com (accessed 13 February 2002).

Joey (2001) Anatomy of a Plastic story, *Plastic*. www.plastic.com (accessed 10 February 2002).

Johnson, S. (1997) *Interface Culture: How New Technology Transforms the Way We Create and Communicate*. San Francisco, CA: HarperEdge.

Kahney, L. (2000) Video clothes: 'brand' new idea, *Wired Online*, 7 June. www.wirednews.com/news/print/0,1294,36698,00.html (accessed 7 July 2000).

Kalantzis, M. and Cope, B. (1996) *Multiliteracies: Rethinking What We Mean by Literacy and What We Teach as Literacy – The Context of Global Cultural Diversity and New Communications Technologies*, Occasional paper no. 21. Haymarket, NSW: Centre for Workplace Communication and Culture.

Knobel, M. (1999) *Everyday Literacies: Students, Discourses and Social Practice*. New York, NY: Peter Lang.

Kuhn, T. (1970) *The Structure of Scientific Revolutions,* 2nd edition. Chicago, IL: University of Chicago Press.

Kurtz, H. (2002) Who cares what you think? Blog, and find out, *Washington Post*, 22 April. C01. www.washingtonpost.com/wp-dyn/articles/A25512-2002 Apr21.html (accessed 22 April 2002).

Lanham, R. (1994) The economics of attention. Proceedings of 124th Annual Meeting, Association of Research Libraries. sunsite.berkeley.edu/ARL/Proceedings/124/ps2econ.html (accessed 2 July 2000).

Lankshear, C. (1997) *Changing Literacies*. Buckingham: Open University Press.

Lankshear, C. (1998) Frameworks and workframes: evaluating literacy policy, *Unicorn*, 24(2): 43–58.

Lankshear, C. (1999) Literacy studies in education, in M. Peters (ed.) *After the Disciplines: The Emergence of Culture Studies*, pp. 199–227. Westport, CT: Bergin and Garvey.

Lankshear, C. and Bigum, C. (1999) Literacies and new technologies in school settings, *Pedagogy, Culture and Society*, 7(3): 445–65.

Lankshear, C., Bigum, C., Durrant, C. *et al.* (1997) *Digital Rhetorics: Literacies and Technologies in Classrooms – Current Practices and Future Directions*. Canberra: Department of Employment, Education, Training and Youth Affairs.

Lankshear, C. and Knobel, M. (2001) Mapping postmodern literacies, *Journal of Literacy and Technology*, 1(1). www.literacyandtechnology.org (accessed 25 July 2002).

Lankshear, C. and Knobel, M. (2002) Do we have your attention? New literacies, digital technologies and the education of adolescents, in D. Alvermann (ed.) *Adolescents and Literacies in a Digital World*. New York, NY: Peter Lang.

Lankshear, C., Peters, M. and Knobel, M. (1996) Critical pedagogy and cyberspace, in H. Giroux, C. Lankshear, P. McLaren and M. Peters, *Counternarratives*, pp. 149–85. New York, NY: Routledge.

Lankshear, C., Peters, M. and Knobel, M. (2000) Information, knowledge and learning: some issues facing epistemology and education in a digital age, *Journal of Philosophy of Education*, 34(1): 17–40.

Lankshear, C. and Snyder, I., with Green, B. (2000) *Teachers and Technoliteracy: Managing Literacy, Technology and Learning in Schools*. St Leonards, NSW: Allen and Unwin.

Lasn, K. (1999) *Culture Jam: How to Reverse America's Suicidal Consumer Binge – And Why We Must*. New York, NY: Quill.

Leander, K. and Johnson, K. (2002) Tracing the everyday 'site-ings' of adolescents on the internet: a strategic adaptation of ethnography. Paper presented to the 2002 Annual Meeting of the American Educational Research Association, New Orleans, 3 April.

Lorelei's (2000) *Customer Care Assurance*. cgi.ebay.com/aw-cgi/eBayISAPI.dll? ViewItem&item=412824070 (accessed 11 May 2000).

Lyon, D. (1988) *The Information Society: Issues and Illusions*. Cambridge: Polity Press.

Lyotard, J.-F. (1984) *The Postmodern Condition: A Report on Knowledge*, translated by Geoff Bennington and Brian Massumi. Minneapolis, MN: University of Minnesota Press.

Lyotard, J.-F. (1993) A svelte appendix to the postmodern question, in *Political Writings*, translated by Bill Readings and Kevin Paul Geison. Minneapolis, MN: University of Minnesota Press.

MacLeod, R. (2000) Attention marketing in the network economy. Paper presented to The Impact of Networking: Marketing Relationships in the New Economy Conference, Vienna, 17–20 September.

McKinnon, M. (2001) One plastic day, *Shift Magazine*, 9(4): 1–3. www.shift.com/toc/9.4 (accessed 10 February 2002).

Marshall, J. (1998) Performativity: Lyotard, Foucault and Austin. Paper presented to the American Educational Research Association's Annual Meeting, San Diego, 11–17 April.

Martin, J. (1993) Genre and literacy: modeling context in educational linguistics, *Annual Review of Applied Linguistics*, 13: 141–72.

Martin, J. and Rothery, J. (1993) Grammar: Making meaning in writing, in B. Cope and M. Kalantzis (eds) *The Powers of Literacy: A Genre Approach to Teaching Writing*, pp. 137–53. London: Falmer.

Martino, W. (1995) Gendered learning practices: exploring the costs of hegemonic masculinity for girls and boys in schools, in Ministerial Council for Education, Training and Youth Affairs, *Proceedings of the Promoting Gender Equity Conference*. Canberra: ACT Department of Education and Training.

Marx, K. (1845–47) *11th Thesis on Feuerbach*. hegel.marxists.org (accessed 25 July 2002)

MayorBob (2001) 'This kind of karma attack has happened . . .', *Plastic*. www.plastic.com (accessed 13 February 2002).

Mills, C. Wright (1959) *The Sociological Imagination*. London: Oxford University Press.

Mokyr, J. (1990) *The Lever of Riches: Technological Creativity and Economic Progress*. New York, NY: Oxford University Press.

MSN Money (2002) *eBay Inc.: Company Report*. moneycentral.msn.com/investor/research/profile.asp?symbol=EBAY (accessed 10 February 2002).

Multex.com (2001) *Market Guide: Business Description*, eBay Inc. 2yahoo. marketguide.com/mgi/busidesc.asp?rt=busidesc&rn=A1C7E (accessed 27 February 2001).

Negroponte, N. (1995) *Being Digital*. New York, NY: Vintage Books.

NGfL (National Grid for Learning) (2002a) *National Grid for Learning*. www.ngfl.gov.uk (accessed 21 March 2002).

NGfL (National Grid for Learning) (2002b) Where are you? *National Grid for Learning.* www.ngfl.gov.uk/where.jsp?sectionId=3&categoryId=100&clear=y (accessed 21 March 2002).

NGfL (National Grid for Learning) (2002c) Who are you? Children: under 11s. *National Grid for Learning.* www.ngfl.gov.uk/who.jsp?sectionId=4& categoryId=322&clear=y (accessed 4 March 2002).

Outerworlds (2002) www.outerworlds.com (accessed 25 July 2002).

Oz New Media (2001) *Ozzie Takes a Ride.* Act 1. www.gridclub.com/have_a_ go/english/owl3book1/book01/yr3/book01/parent.htm (accessed 11 August 2001).

Papert, S. (1993) *The Children's Machine: Rethinking School in the Age of the Computer.* New York, NY: Basic Books.

Plastic (2002a) www.plastic.com (accessed 21 March 2002).

Plastic (2002b) *Guide to Moderating Comments at Plastic.* www.plastic.com/ moderation.shtml (accessed 13 February 2002).

Qualifications and Curriculum Authority (2000) *Curriculum Guidance for the Foundation Stage.* London: Qualifications and Curriculum Authority. www.qca.org. uk/ca/foundation/guidance/curr_guidance.asp (accessed 23 April 2002).

Raettig, C. (2001) Analysis and thoughts regarding kpmg (warning: maximum verbosity!), *Chris Raettig – Personal Website* chris.raettig.org/email/jn100040. html (accessed 15 January 2002).

Reich, R. (1992) *The Work of Nations.* New York, NY: Vintage Books.

Reno, D., Reno, B. and Butler, M. (eds) (2000) *The Unofficial Guide to eBay and Online Auctions.* New York, NY: Hungry Minds.

Rogoff, B. (1995) Observing sociocultural activity on three planes: participatory appropriation, guided participation, apprenticeship, in J. Wertsch, P. del Rio and A. Alvarez (eds) *Sociocultural Studies of Mind*, pp. 139–64. New York, NY: Cambridge University Press.

Rowan, L. and Bigum, C. (1997) The future of technology and literacy teaching in primary learning situations and contexts, in C. Lankshear, C. Bigum, C. Durrant *et al.* (investigators) *Digital Rhetorics: Literacies and Technologies in Education – Current Practices and Future Directions*, Vol. 3, pp. 73–94. Children's Literacy National Projects. Brisbane: QUT/DEETYA.

Rowan, L., Knobel, M., Bigum, C. and Lankshear, C. (2002) *Boys, Literacies and Schooling: The Dangerous Territories of Gender Based Literacy Reform.* Buckingham: Open University Press.

Rowan, L., Knobel, M., Lankshear, C., Bigum, C. and Doneman, M. (2000) *Confronting Disadvantage in Literacy Education: New Technologies, Classroom Pedagogy and Networks of Practice.* Rockhampton: Central Queensland University.

Rushkoff, D. (1994) *Cyberia: Life in the Trenches of Hyperspace.* San Francisco, CA: HarperSanFrancisco.

Rushkoff, D. (1996) *Playing the Future: How Kids' Culture Can Teach Us How to Thrive in an Age of Chaos.* New York, NY: HarperCollins.

Ruth, J. F., Furlong, A., Facer, K. and Sutherland, R. (2000) The National Grid for Learning: a curriculum without walls?, *Cambridge Journal of Education*, 30(1): 91–110.

Sanders, B. (1996) *A is for Ox*. New York, NY: Vintage Books.

Scheffler, I. (1965) *Conditions of Knowledge*. Chicago, IL: Scott, Foresman.

Schrage, M. (1998) *Technology, Silver Bullets and Big Lies: Musings on the Information Age with author Michael Schrage*. www.educause. edu/pub/er/review/ reviewArticles/33132.html (accessed 26th January 2000)

Schroedinger's Cat (2002) First plastiversary – happy birthday, Plastic! *Plastic*. www.plastic.com (accessed 15 January 2002).

Schwartz, P. (no date) *Origins: The Map Rap*. www.gbn.org/public/gbnstory/ origins/maprap.htm (accessed 17 August 2000).

Schwartz, P. (1991) *The Art of the Long View*. New York, NY: Doubleday.

Scollon, R. and Scollon, S. (1981) *Narrative, Literacy, and Face in Interethnic Communication*. Norwood, NJ: Ablex.

Scribner, S. and Cole, M. (1981) *The Psychology of Literacy*. Cambridge, MA: Harvard University Press.

Selwyn, N. (1999) 'Gilding the grid': the marketing of the National Grid for Learning, *British Journal of Sociology of Education*, 20(1): 55–68.

Selwyn, N. (2000a) The discursive construction of the National Grid for Learning, *Oxford Review of Education*, 26(1): 63–79.

Selwyn, N. (2000b) The National Grid for Learning: panacea or Panopticon?, *British Journal of Sociology of Education*, 21(2): 243–55.

Selwyn, N., Gorard, S. and Williams, S. (2001) The role of the 'technical fix' in UK lifelong education policy, *International Journal of Lifelong Education*, 20(4): 255–71.

Shapiro, R. and Rohde, G. (2000) Executive summary, *Falling Through the Net: Toward Digital Inclusion*. Washington, DC: US Department of Commerce, Economic Statistics Administration, and the National Telecommunications and Information Administration.

Sherman, E. (2001) The world's largest yard sale: online auctions. The sale of collectibles is migrating to the Web. It's the place where niche buyers meet niche sellers, *Newsweek*, March 19: 62–4.

Sholle, D. and Denski, S. (1993) Reading and writing the media: critical media literacy and postmodernism, in C. Lankshear and P. McLaren (eds) *Critical Literacy: Politics, Praxis and the Postmodern*, pp. 297–323. Albany, NY: SUNY Press.

Simon, H. (1971) Designing organizations for an information-rich world, in M. Greenberger (ed.) *Computers, Communications and the Public Interest*, pp. 40–1. Baltimore, MD: Johns Hopkins University Press.

skim.com (2002) www.skim.com (accessed 21 March 2002).

Smith, C. and Smith, N. (c.2002) *Buyer Beware!* home.earthlink.net/~cardking/ buyer.htm (accessed 10 February 2002).

Snyder, I. (2002) *Silicon Literacies: Communication, Innovation and Education in the Electronic Age*. London: Falmer-Routledge.

SoYouWanna (2000) SoYouWanna Use eBay (and Not Get Ripped Off)? www.soyouwanna.com/site/syws/ebay/ebay.html (accessed 12 March 2001).

Spector, R. (2000) *Amazon.com: Get Big Fast*. San Francisco, CA: HarperBusiness.

Stone, A. (1996) *The War of Desire and Technology at the Close of the Mechanical Age*. Cambridge, MA: MIT Press.

Street, B. (1984) *Literacy in Theory and Practice*. Cambridge: Cambridge University Press.

Street, B. (ed.) (1993) *Cross-cultural Approaches to Literacy*. Cambridge: Cambridge University Press.

Suck (2000) *Walter's Mission*. www.suck.com/daily/2000/07/06/ (accessed 4 November 2000).

Sullivan, A. (2002) The blogging revolution, *Wired*, May. www.wired.com/wired/archive/10.05/mustread.html?pg=2 (accessed 20 April 2002).

Thorne, S. (2001) Prescriptivist epistemologies and the lived communicative activity of online stock traders. Symposium paper presented to the American Educational Research Association Annual Meeting, Seattle, WA, 10–14 April.

Touraine, A. (1974) *The Postindustrial Society*. London: Wildwood House.

Tunbridge, N. (1995) The cyberspace cowboy. *Australian Personal Computer*, December: 2–4.

Turkle, S. (1995) *Life on the Screen: Identity in the Age of the Internet*. London: Phoenix.

tylerh (2002) 'My, we're feeling self-important today. . .' *Plastic*. www.plastic.com (accessed 13 February 2002).

Uglytouch.com (2000) *Toons*. www.uglytouch.com/toons/toons.html (accessed 4 November 2000).

Ulmer, G. (1987) The object of post-criticism, in H. Foster (ed.) *Postmodern Culture*, pp. 57–82. London: Pluto Press.

Vale, V. (ed.) (1996) *Zines!* Vol. 1. San Francisco, CA: V/Search.

Vale, V. (ed.) (1997) *Zines!* Vol. 2. San Francisco, CA: V/Search.

van der Heijden, K. (1996) *Scenarios: The Art of Strategic Conversation*. Chichester: Wiley.

Wack, P. (1985a) The gentle art of reperceiving, *Harvard Business Review*, September–October: 73–89.

Wack, P. (1985b) Scenarios: shooting the rapids, *Harvard Business Review*, November–December: 139–50.

Walker, C. (1998) *Short Attention Spans on the Web*. Reprinted with permission at wondermill.com/sitelaunch/attention.htm (accessed 2 July 2000).

Webb, R. (1955) *The British Working Class Reader*. London: Allen & Unwin.

Weizenbaum, J. ([1976] 1984) *Computer Power and Human Reason: From Judgement to Calculation*. Harmondsworth: Penguin.

Wertheim, M. (1999) *The Pearly Gates of Cyberspace: A History of Space from Dante to the Internet*. New York, NY: W. W. Norton.

Wexler, P. (1988) Curriculum in the closed society, in H. Giroux and P. McLaren (eds) *Critical Pedagogy, the State and Cultural Struggle*, pp. 92–104. Albany, NY: SUNY Press.

Williams, E. (2002) *Blogger: Push Button Publishing for the People*. www.blogger.com/ (accessed 23 April 2002).

Wittgenstein, L. (1953) *Philosophical Investigations*. Oxford: Blackwell.

Name index

Subject index

BOYS, LITERACIES AND SCHOOLING
THE DANGEROUS TERRITORIES OF GENDER-BASED LITERACY REFORM

Leonie Rowan, Michele Knobel, Chris Bigum, Colin Lankshear

Current debates about boys and schooling in many Western nations are increasingly characterized by a sense of crisis as government reports, academic research and the day to day experiences of teachers combine to indicate that:

- boys are consistently underperforming in literacy
- boys are continuing to opt out of English and humanities
- boys represent the majority of behaviour problems and counselling referrals
- boys receive a disproportionate amount of special education support.

This book responds to the complexity of the current debates associated with boys, gender reform, literacy and schooling by offering a clear map of the current context, highlighting the strengths and weaknesses of the various competing solutions put forward, and outlining a range of practical classroom interventions designed for dealing with the boys/literacy crisis. The authors consider the ways in which particular views of masculinity, gender reform, literacy, technology and popular culture can either open up or close down new conceptualizations of what it means to be a boy and what it means to be literate.

Contents

Introduction – Dangerous places: debates about boys, girls, schooling and gender-based literacy reform – What about the boys? The rhetoric and realities of the new gender crisis – How, who, where, when, why and what way? Mindsets on gender reform in schools – Some really useful theoretical company for transforming and transformative literacy education – Mindsets matter: an overview of major literacy worldviews – Making it not so: transformative literacy practices for girls and boys – Exorcizing digital demons: information technology, new literacies and the de/reconstruction of gendered subjectivities – From Pacman to Pokemon: cross-generational perspectives on gender and reform in a 'post-feminist' age – Conclusion – Bibliography – Index.

256pp   0 335 20756 1 (Paperback)   0 335 20757 X (Hardback)

EDUCATION, ENTERTAINMENT AND LEARNING IN THE HOME

David Buckingham and Margaret Scanlon

In recent years, the government has placed a growing emphasis on the need for parents to support their children's learning. Meanwhile, commercial corporations are increasingly targeting the educational aspirations of parents and children. New forms of educational media have emerged, which purport to 'make learning fun' by using devices drawn from popular culture. In the process, the boundaries between homes and schools, and between education and entertainment, are becoming more and more blurred.

This book is based on an extensive research project investigating the developing market in educational materials designed for use in the home. It considers the characteristics of 'edutainment' in children's information books, pre-school magazines and CD-Roms. It discusses the economic forces at work in the production and marketing of these media, and the rhetoric of the sales pitches. Also, it considers how parents and children use them in the home.

As learning itself increasingly becomes a commodity, this book addresses an issue of growing importance for parents, teachers and all those concerned with children's education.

Contents

c.192pp   0 335 21007 4 (Paperback)   0 335 21008 2 (Hardback)